USS *Olympia*

USS Olympia

HERALD OF EMPIRE

Benjamin Franklin Cooling

NAVAL INSTITUTE PRESS
Annapolis, Maryland

Naval Institute Press
291 Wood Road
Annapolis, MD 21402

First printing in paperback, 2007

ISBN-10: 1-59114-126-5
ISBN-13: 978-1-59114-126-6

The Library of Congress has cataloged the hardcover edition
as follows:
Cooling, B. Franklin
    USS Olympia : herald of empire/ Benjamin Franklin Cooling.
        p.   cm.
    Includes bibliographical references and index.
    ISBN 1-55750-148-3 (alk. paper)
    1. Olympia (Cruiser)—History. I. Title

VA65.O6 C66 2000
359.3'253'0973—dc21

                                                    00-042391

Printed in the United States of America on acid-free paper ∞

14 13 12 11 10 09 08 07   9 8 7 6 5 4 3 2
First printing

To the men and women—civilians and military—
who have worked tirelessly through the years
to save, preserve, and interpret the
USS *Olympia* as part of the national heritage.

Contents

Preface

Not the first, arguably not even the foremost, but most certainly the last ship of America's late-nineteenth-century New Steel Navy, the USS *Olympia* symbolizes to this day the spread-eagle diplomacy that so marked the turn to the twentieth century. Even the rakish cut of her swept-back bow and the relatively sleek lines of her superstructure conjure images of speed and confidence, qualities that once defined the American quest for territorial expansion. During the opening decades of the twentieth century, expansionism and imperialism—with their concomitant acquisition of new trade and colonies, their espousal of a "white man's burden" under Social Darwinism, and their projection of a zestful messianic and missionary spirit—infected the United States, along with Europe and Japan, with a sense of purpose quite alien to our current age.

Attending that spirit was a robust navalism, launched upon the industrial world through the philosophies of Alfred Thayer Mahan, through treasury surpluses in home coffers, and through competition for power among nations. For many contemporary doyens, the question was simple: would the flag follow trade or would trade follow the flag? Questions about policing the world for some new world order were foreign to that bygone age.

Rather, aggressive, nationalistic leaders and their followers wanted to stake claim to a place in the sun, to civilize "backward" peoples, and to beat manly chests toward ensuring a vigorous defense of homelands, colonies, and ways of life. According to conventional wisdom, the question was whether to expand trade or die. The USS *Olympia* was an integral part of all that and more during the course of her thirty-year span of service.

On the crest of that riptide of passion, ships of the new steel navies rode around the globe. One such ship was the *Olympia,* and standing now aboard her deck—for she has been preserved as a national shrine on the Philadelphia waterfront—one feels pulsing the very lifeblood of empire that she helped engender. For this is the bridge where Flag Officer George Dewey uttered the immortal phrase that opened the battle of Manila Bay on 1 May 1898, "You may fire when you are ready, Gridley." That was the phrase that vaulted the United States into the imperial world and from here one can still gain a sense of awe at the magnitude of that feat. A generation inspired by the same spirit of Manifest Destiny that had conquered a continent was now about to project its nation onto the world stage—and with a vengeance. Not that a steel warship necessarily epitomized progress to peaceloving, "progressive" Americans at the time. Rather, like Manifest Destiny, war children came to be symbiotically linked with war tools in the history of what one pundit later referred to as "the American Century."

Olympia was designed as a protected cruiser or commerce raider—a traditional ship for a traditional navy at the time of her launching. Her role in the American navy would, however, prove anything but traditional. She was the first vessel in the navy to have a refrigeration system, the first to have electric priming for her principal gun batteries, and among the first to have electrical generators, lighting, and ventilation systems. Later, she would help pioneer naval use of wireless communication. Flagship of a squadron designed for peacetime diplomatic presence and trade protection in the Far East, she became the herald of empire. Baptized in the war with Spain, *Olympia*'s officers and crew quickly became instruments of force projection, as the United States served notice that it would retain the Philippines as its own at that conflict's end. Soon rendered obsolete by world naval developments in the Age of the Battleship, cruiser *Olympia* nonetheless became part of a larger American naval expansion. Integrated squadrons and battle fleets supplanted station squadrons, as the first decades of the twentieth century demanded a different protection of national interests and preparation for possible high seas naval battles against imperial rivals. Her original purpose as squadron flagship—command ship, if you will—ensured *Olympia*'s continued relevance even as memories of Manila Bay faded. Relegation to lesser duties, and even repainting from glorious buff and white to drab militaristic gray, could never completely eclipse the glamour of what Americans styled their "great white fleet of empire."

Olympia's venerable past, however, destined her for one final moment of service and glory. In 1920, she returned the Unknown Soldier from France to that hero's honored resting place in Arlington National Cemetery. The herald of empire now reflected America's desire to retreat from the world stage, and her own retirement soon followed. Her subsequent years as a rusting reserve hulk at the Philadelphia Navy Yard presaged her rebirth as a historic shrine in that city. After 1957, she truly became the sole survivor of the U.S. naval shipbuilding program of the 1880s and 1890s.

Indeed, it was in Philadelphia that I first discovered her and then worked aboard her as curator/historian from 1965 to 1975. This period was memorable for its low budgets and discouraging working conditions, as well as its chronic deck leaks and lack of programmatic focus. Such conditions were, however, offset by members of the private Cruiser Olympia Association, members whose dedication and enthusiasm did so much to preserve the old vessel. Happily, she has become flagship of the Independence Seaport Museum and Penn's Landing configuration, where she provides new opportunities for educating visitors about the nation's maritime heritage. She can now occupy her rightful place among the world's historic ships.

To chronicle *Olympia*'s life and times is like renewing an old friendship. Humanizing her so that others may revere her beauty, longevity, and stalwart service is challenging for any author. This book represents the fourth in the author's exploration of the story of the American steel navy. The first, *Benjamin Franklin Tracy: Lawyer, Soldier* (1973), began the quest by studying a key political figure, one who was instrumental in transitioning the United States Navy from a cruising force to a battle fleet. The second, *Gray Steel and Bluewater Navy: The Formative Years of America's*

Military-Industrial Complex, 1881–1917 (1979), examined early military-industrial arrangements for strategic outreach and imperialism. An updated edition, edited by the author, of Robley D. Evans's classic, *A Sailor's Log* (1994), added the perspective of a contemporary, preeminent naval figure. USS *Olympia: Herald of Empire* is a life-and-times ship's history that concludes my voyage of discovery.

Acknowledgments

There are undoubtedly institutions and private individuals with materials relating to the USS *Olympia* that are as yet unknown. Publication of this groundbreaking story of the ship and the men who served aboard will hopefully cause them to surface for future reinterpretation. But, this volume could not have been possible without the help of key individuals, and I thank them profusely for their contribution. Michael Angelo, librarian, Donald Birkholz Jr., sometime restoration director (who took time to review my manuscript), and Paul DeOrsay, vice president for operations of the Independence Seaport Museum stand out for their support. The research files gathered for this book will transfer to their care in order to further the preservation and interpretive programs on behalf of the ship.

Other institutional helpmates on this project have included Irene A. Stachura, reference librarian of the San Francisco Maritime National Historical Park; Arthur Roth, manager of public relations of the Bethlehem Steel Corporation; Ann Witty, formerly of the Columbia River Maritime Museum in Astoria, Oregon; Karen E. Kearns, curator of Western Historical Manuscripts at The Huntington Library; Susan Seyl, Photographs Library of the Oregon Historical Society; Alice S. Creighton, head of the Special Collections and Archives, Nimitz Library, United States Naval

Academy, and her associates Beverly Leyall and Mary Catalfano; Kathleen M. O'Connor, archivist at the Pacific Sierra branch of the National Archives; and David Keough, archivist at the United States Army Military History Institute. Jack A. Green, of the Curator Branch, and Bernard Calvacante's staff of the Operational Archives at the Naval Historical Center in Washington, D.C., provided the customarily responsive service that one has come to expect from that facility. Lyn Gardner, assistant to the librarian at The Mariners Museum in Newport News, was consistently responsive to my quest for illustrative materials.

Individuals such as Donald J. Loughlin of Bellingham, Washington, Dan Cashin of Havertown, Pennsylvania, and Robert Stewart of West Suffield, Connecticut, lent their special technical expertise. My longtime friend who has followed this project for many years, Louis S. Wall—community planner with the Naval Facilities Engineering Command in San Bruno, California—spent much of his personal time tracking down leads for me in the San Francisco area. Of course, at the Naval Institute Press, Dr. Paul Wilderson, executive editor, patiently waited and provided support and encouragement. Most certainly, my wife Mary Anne—fellow sometime-Philadelphian—warrants thanks for enduring yet another writing project with her husband.

USS *Olympia*

1

A New Navy for an Expansive Nation

In the predawn darkness of 1 May 1898, Commo. George Dewey paced the bridge of his flagship, the protected cruiser USS *Olympia*. He peered toward the shoreline of Manila Bay where even now sharp flashes from Spanish guns had begun to break the peace of that early spring morning. The "whoosh" of enemy shells passing over his little flotilla told the American officer that Spanish gunnery was most uncertain. But it was unnerving nonetheless, especially since the voyage from Hong Kong had been marked only by intermittent rain showers and little else of note. Even passage into the bay had been remarkably easy. Now it was up to Dewey to accomplish his mission, received by Navy Department order six days earlier. The directive had simply announced the commencement of war, and told Dewey to proceed at once against the Spanish fleet in the Far East and capture or destroy it by "utmost endeavors." That objective now lay before him as his six-ship squadron steamed steadily ahead at eight knots to engage the enemy in the heart of Spain's Philippine colony.[1]

Rear Adm. Patricio Montojo y Pasaron's antique but still potentially troublesome "grab-bag" or "flock" of ships, as one author has styled the

I

Spanish fleet, lay close to shore. The admiral sought protection under the friendly support of equally outdated and under-ranged shore batteries. Battle was inevitable. The honor of Spain, not to mention the impertinence of the United States, demanded it. And so the battle was joined when, at approximately 5:40 A.M. that morning, Dewey—ever the dapper sixty-year-old professional sailor dressed in tropical whites—turned somewhat casually to the *Olympia*'s captain and calmly announced, "You may fire when you are ready, Gridley." Immediately, Charles Vernon Gridley's voice barked over the speaking tube to the forward gun turret of 8-inchers and the action began. Each American ship in turn keyed on *Olympia*'s opening salvoes.

The fight was unequal from the beginning. Not that either combatant's accuracy was anything to brag about: the Spaniards fired erratically and Dewey's people aimed with the greater deliberation born of repeated gun drills and discipline. The difference lay in the fact that the American shells found their mark more frequently and with greater devastation. It was little less than a slaughter. Still, there were anxious moments. About 7:30 A.M., Dewey broke off the action when he heard that his flagship was low on 5-inch ammunition. This lull permitted a leisurely breakfast for the American crews while they watched the Spanish fleet burn in the distance. Then, returning to the fray about 11:16, Dewey's flotilla flattened the remaining shore battery and naval gunfire. By early afternoon, Montojo's squadron—scuttled, burning, or sunk—rested on the shoal-water bottom.

Dewey's virtually unscathed armada anchored off the city of Manila. White flags of surrender could be seen everywhere as Dewey sent word to Spanish officials that any more resistance would occasion naval bombardment of the city. Meanwhile, *Olympia*'s band obligingly serenaded the dejected citizenry with soothing Spanish tunes until well after sunset. All told, in the space of a few hours, the American fleet had destroyed Spanish naval power in the Far East. Master of Manila and its immediate environs, Dewey still did not control the Philippines. But, with the war little more than a week old, Uncle Sam had achieved a smashing victory. The dastardly destruction of the battleship *Maine* in Havana in February, which had helped precipitate the war, had now been avenged. Ironically, seven thousand miles away in the United States, nobody yet knew of these startling developments.

Refused permission to cable the results of the battle to Hong Kong, Dewey directed his Jack Tars to sever this link with the outside world. He would send the news via fast dispatch boat instead. But the Spanish authorities had another cable and the news got out. The other major powers reacted with profound surprise. Washington was elated; Pres. William McKinley immediately sent Dewey's name to Capitol Hill for promotion. Americans reveled in the victory while Dewey and the *Olympia* became household words. Soon, an American expeditionary force would be en route to complete what Dewey and his ships had begun. Spanish surrender of the Philippines followed as a matter of course, and a reluctantly colonialist America assumed the mantle of empire as Filipino nationalists reacted belligerently, not wishing to merely trade one master for another. But by this time, Dewey and his flagship would be on their way home.

Indeed, Dewey's and the *Olympia*'s triumphal return from the Far East over a year later signaled America's emergence as a world power. Homecoming itself was a gala fête not seen since the final Grand Army reviews in Washington at the end of the Civil War a generation before. Parades and celebrations in New York and other major cities awaited *Olympia*'s officers and crew. Banquets and toasts to Dewey and his astonishing victory were mere prelude to a brief but crisp "Dewey for President" groundswell. The *Olympia* herself received a new peacetime paint scheme, embellished by gilt bow and stern trappings honoring her ascendancy as the most famous American warship of the moment. Milk glass models of the ship, carnival glass water pitchers, and countless patriotic pictures, paperweights, and other trinkets of celebration soon inextricably linked George Dewey and his flagship in the public's mind. The pair joined a pantheon of American naval heroes that included John Paul Jones and the *Bon Homme Richard*, Edward Preble and the *Constitution*, and David Farragut and the *Hartford*.

Over time, the 1898 spirit of the popular song of the day, "There'll be a Hot Time in the Old Town Tonight," faded before the more maudlin tunes of the First World War. Dewey would go to his grave as Admiral of the Navy, not President of the United States. The proud *Olympia* would be relegated to the navy's rear echelons preparatory to scrapping. Even the American people would tire of world involvement and wonder at the merit of trying to manage the Philippines as part of what historian Frederick Drake has styled its "empire of the seas." All of this within the generation following Manila Bay. Yet, for a brief electrifying moment in 1898 and 1899, a well-decorated new admiral and his flagship strode the world stage to acclaim and recognition. Just how this came to pass merits closer examination.[2]

THE SPIRIT OF THE TIMES

The *Olympia* and George Dewey were both part of a great American theme. That theme was territorial expansion accompanied by fighting spirit. This nation had always had enormous confidence that it would offer something truly unique to the rest of the world, that its institutions were superior, its progress greater, and its civilization somehow loftier than others. Manifest destiny and a place in the sun were ingrained in the American psyche, seemingly from the beginning. When tested by others, Americans rise to the challenge in bare knuckled fashion.

The turbulence of civil war and national unification had interrupted America's progress. The stirring of traditional manifest destiny returned but slowly in the 1870s and 1880s. An earlier, mid-century expression of that spirit disappeared along with much of antebellum society. Still, the postwar decades of recuperation signified change in other ways. Here would be the emergence of a modern nation state, a shift from farm to factory and from rural to urban living, with a wave of new emigrants to provide human resources for new direction. Looking inward, most Americans allowed issues of foreign affairs to drift beyond their gaze. The American navy of the periods called Reconstruction and the Gilded Age mirrored this development, and George Dewey at least had witnessed an indifference if not neglect of the national sea arm.[3]

Then things began to change. Necessary concentration on internal matters and somewhat sterile diplomacy of the postwar decades may have hidden "subterranean forces of change." Americans may well have asked, "so who is going to fight us?" But their trade representatives at expositions in Paris (1867), Vienna (1873), and even Sydney and Melbourne (1879 and 1880) manifested a steady interest in world affairs. Revival of the foreign service—pushed by civil service reformers—and participation in international conferences of the Red Cross (1864, 1882) combined with formation of an international postal union (1874, 1878), marine affairs (1882, 1889), and monetary issues (1881) to contradict the image of an uninvolved America. Much of that image stood in direct contrast to an obviously eroded navy and insignificant army.[4]

Certainly the United States was never commercially isolated from the rest of the world. But fast-approaching saturation of domestic markets by the mid-1880s raised the issue of foreign commerce to prominence once more. Free trade had always been the American standard, but tariff matters rapidly supplanted the Southern question as the Civil War receded from importance. It may have been that the economic factor was but one element of a confusing mélange or surge of philosophical idealism, domestic frustration, political expedience, and quest for national prestige that led to late-nineteenth-century American overseas expansion. But, by this time, a new imperialism coursed through the veins of all the industrializing world.

Any illusion of America's commercial isolation lay buried beneath businesses search for new markets. Exports began to exceed imports in value after 1874. Whether trade followed the flag or vice versa, in reality the inherently adventurous and speculative American businessman pushed his government to reevaluate its foreign policies. Viewed more widely, his foreign counterparts did likewise. And so, ministries from London and Paris to Tokyo, Berlin, and Washington now expended long hours as commercial mixed with strategic issues of national power and policy. The "acquisitive imperialism"—of loans, leases, spheres of influence, protectorates, and finally colonies—formed part of the new vocabulary. Western industry and technology combined with military technique to overwhelm Islamic, African, and Asian opponents to such imperialism. Christian missionaries added to the upheaval. Designed to accrue wealth and power for the home state, imperialism naturally intruded upon visionaries everywhere.

Yet, the United States was relatively slow to respond in kind. One visionary, William Henry Seward (secretary of state during the Civil War and early Reconstruction), had proclaimed that "the empire of the seas alone is real empire." Confident that "technological and commercial expansion" would supplant "landed conquest," as diplomatic historian Walter LaFeber observes, Seward added new interpretation to America's manifest destiny. Asia was Seward's beacon, much as it had been for clipper ships and for Matthew Perry's expedition to open Japan before the Civil War. But most of Seward's contemporaries in the 1860s were not ready to share his concept that the "highway" beckoned America to the Far East.

While securing Alaska, he failed to similarly gain Hawaii. It would be a naval officer who plucked little Brooks Island (renamed Midway soon after the turn of the next century) as a preliminary step.[5]

Still, Seward was in the forefront regarding the lure of Asia. Here lay the real prize—conquest of Asian markets—he claimed, advancing twin principles that would continue to undergird and haunt American policy for decades. The idea of an open door for all traders via cooperation and the use of collective force against recalcitrant Asians—all the while seeking to preserve the semblance of stability and indigenous sovereignty of those Asians—carried inherent contradictions. Neither Seward nor the trading community saw those perils and, despite domestic isolationism, they set in motion the postwar patterns of thought about the rich Far East that ripened and blossomed to full flower as Dewey and the *Olympia* gained Manila Bay.

Indeed, Dewey had long been among the Old Navy enthusiasts for the Pacific arena of action. Cruising with the Asiatic squadron when trouble with Spain over the *Virginius* affair beckoned in 1873, Dewey told his messmates that, contrary to their pessimism about getting a share of the fight, their vessel would lead the charge in capturing Manila. This had not come to pass, as the crisis subsided. Personally, Dewey admitted to feeling isolated in the region, but this hardly dimmed his faith that here lay the future for American conquest and success. Notwithstanding interests in the Caribbean and Latin America, America's westward advance (begun nearly three centuries earlier from the Atlantic seaboard) continued to ripen. Both Hawaii and Samoa beckoned to missionaries, sugar moguls, naval officers, Pacific coast chambers of commerce, and politicians—all stirring the pot. With respect to Asia, LaFeber's deftly turned phrase, "goods, god, and gunboats," obtained not just for the Asian mainland but for the Pacific region as a whole. Just where America would get her gunboats remained to be seen.[6]

A NEW NAVY FOR EXPANSION

As the race for trade and empire embroiled the United States with other powers, many questions arose, not merely about protection for commerce or establishment of hegemony in certain areas. Rather, the fundamental issue of national defense and the historic role of seapower engaged policymakers. The theme of national security and power projection governed the plans and policies of European nations by the 1880s, and the United States reacted in no small measure to their lead. American officials particularly began to realize that their obsolescent Civil War fleet would be no match for technologically modernizing British or French squadrons. Serious interference with American commercial and territorial expansion could come from those and other navies. Not only would American cities from New York to San Francisco be threatened by enemy action, not only could American flag carriers be interdicted in the classic *guerre de course* warfare of the age, but the possibility of European intervention might affect American interests from South American to Pacific waters, even escalate to battle fleet confrontation in *la guerre d'escadre*.[7]

Moreover, by this time domestic conditions permitted consideration of expensive programs like naval rearmament—all in the name of defending American freedom of action. There were skeptics, and the proper policy to pursue was by no means clear or universally agreed upon. But Congress appropriated $1.3 million on 3 March 1883 for construction of four new vessels— styled the "ABCDs" after the first letters of their names, *Atlanta, Boston, Chicago,* and *Dolphin.* These ships were to be fabricated from steel, not wood or iron. Coupled with internal infrastructure reform and the search for industrial partnerships, this signaled the beginning of a naval renaissance. That the initial step was small and such a policy quite transitional was hardly surprising. The main point was that the step had been taken at all.[8]

Indeed, the decade of the 1880s was pivotal. It was then that the *Olympia* was born. As Mark Shulman has shown, the atmosphere was highly charged. At play were the ideas of naval professionals (theorists, advisory board members, traditionalists, and reformers), politicians (isolationists, modernists, and committee members), even public opinion shapers (press, journalists, and anti-war idealists). Strategically, they were concerned with new policies for a changing America. Tactically, at least as far as the navy was concerned, they focused on a new type of instrument for a new national policy. Simply put, was it to be a traditional defensive-offensive (coastal defense/commerce destroying) fleet? Or would it be a more aggressive, toe-to-toe battle squadron? The direction was by no means clear at the time of *Olympia*'s conception.[9]

Following the "ABCD" experiment, naval experts and politicians had iterated the next step in the modernization process. Plans and authorizations from 1883 to 1886 reflected both sides of the debate and, in fact, mirrored what was going on in Europe at the time. Four monitors, six cruisers, one torpedo boat, and three gunboats suggested the traditional camp, but two "battle-ships" hinted at the early advance of the modern, high-seas combat fleet. While House Naval Affairs Committee and Cleveland administration figures wrangled over numbers and types, they essentially adhered to the traditional coastal defense/commerce destroying navy. Still, in 1887, the influential journal, *Scientific American*, appeared to shift toward advocacy of bluewater navalism. Indeed, to Shulman, the apex of cruiser enthusiasm in the United States occurred about this time. "The demise of America's commerce-destroying strategy" lay with authorization of the battleships *Texas* and *Maine* and the armored cruiser *New York*. But it was also on 7 September 1888 that Congress authorized six light, so-called "protected," cruisers—among them "Cruiser Number 6," the *Olympia*. This class developed from the need to provide some level of protection for cruisers that were "too small to carry heavy side armor," notes naval restorationist Donald Birkholz Jr. It had to do so without "a major sacrifice in speed."[10]

The solution lay in armored deck, extended by British designers for their warships to slope below the water line, that would shield engines, boilers, and magazines. Yet *Olympia* was something more and, like *Texas*, *Maine*, and *New York*, could hardly be regarded as a "commerce destroyer" in the traditional sense of American naval policy. Rather, their heavier tonnage, armament, and faster speed (*Texas* and *Maine* at 7,000 tons, 18.5 knots, with 10-inch and 12-inch guns; *New York* at 8,000 tons, 21 knots, with 8-inch guns; *Olympia* at 5,540 tons, 22 knots, with 8-inch guns) signified a new American resolve.

These warships would be able to give battle to enemy squadrons bent upon their own task of destroying American commerce. "We can not at present protect our coast, but we can return blow for blow, for we shall soon be in condition to launch a fleet of large and fast cruisers against the commerce of an enemy, able to inflict the most serious and lasting injury thereon," Secretary of the Navy William C. Whitney told the public just before leaving office in 1889.

Whitney claimed that, in terms of ships of nineteen-knot speeds and 3,000 tons or more displacement, the United States Navy ranked second only to Great Britain, whose ten ships displaced a total of 56,600 tons. America's eight ships, displacing 32,010 tons, exceeded France's five ships at 24,630 tons, Spain's three ships at 14,400 tons, Japan's two ships at 7,500 tons, and Russia's one ship at 5,030 tons. Thus, Whitney's ships (*Olympia* among them) represented an offensive spirit. But they remained within the traditional framework of naval policy and reflected political and technological realities of the time. Traditionalism was but one of the obstacles to naval progress faced by Whitney and his comrades.

When the Democratic Party had regained the White House in 1885 for the first time since the Civil War, President Grover Cleveland had selected Whitney, a prominent New York corporation lawyer, to lead the Navy Department. While much of Whitney's attention went to departmental administration, his concern for Gotham commercial interests stimulated his concern with building a navy to protect foreign trade. In turn, European developments—as well as the state of domestic industry to support any ambitious naval rearmament—also disturbed Whitney. He investigated production of gun forgings and established a government ordnance factory at the Washington Navy Yard. He encouraged domestic steel production, soliciting bids on armor contracts with a thirty-month deadline for delivery. However, this deadline, plus rigid specifications, frightened the steelmen. Bethlehem Steel Company won the initial bidding only to find itself hamstrung by lack of facilities and technical know-how for producing modern armaments steel.[11]

Whitney, like the steelmen, realized that the American navy remained dependent upon foreign technology for such armaments, an untenable position for any nation. American steel mills had never rolled hull plates before, nor had a vessel ever been built entirely of domestic steel. Shipbuilders lacked skill in application of materials while domestic foundries remained ill-equipped for forging ordnance steel. Therefore, Whitney acquiesced to what would amount to a three-year delay in completing the authorized warships while the government developed the requisite plant and facilities. The Washington gun factory and an imported steel plant for hull plates at Bethlehem were the first steps. Historians have suggested that a drift in policy accompanied this delay for neither the Navy Department nor Congress chose to define specific types of armored fighting craft until after industry showed its capacity to build them.

All of this meant that, in the late 1880s, newly authorized warships like the *Olympia* faced delays through more than just the typical problems encountered during their construction. Rather, from the very beginning the lack of material and withholding of contracts at the secretarial level in Washington postponed their completion for various reasons. The lack of resources plus the development of a learning curve in acquisition, procurement, and fabrication would be manifest across the program. Far too few historians have understood this fact in their rush to analyze merely the policy implications of naval rearmament of the time. The *Olympia* stands as a case in point.

CRUISER NUMBER 6

In his final annual report as secretary, Whitney noted the authorization of a twenty-knot cruiser which was to cost, "exclusive of armament and speed premiums," no more than $1,800,000. His successor, another New York lawyer, Benjamin Franklin Tracy (brought in when the Republican Party regained the White House), noted that the design process for the new vessel had begun. In that regard, the Navy Department had expended a mere $176.00 for draftsmen, writers, copyists, mold makers, and so forth during Tracy's initial period at the helm. The secretary himself "has made the plans a special study," as newspapers and the public delighted in following what the *Pittsburgh Dispatch* pronounced would be "a beauty as well as one of the most efficient cruisers in the navy." Admittedly, that western Pennsylvania city expected its turn in the naming of new cruisers after the nation's cities. But, for the time being, the new warship merely took the title "Cruiser Number 6," being that figure in the construction sequence for this class.[12]

Protected cruisers would form a category between the unprotected version of this class of warship with no armor and what later were styled armored cruisers with vertical side and often superstructure armored plate (and almost akin to a class styled "battle-ships"). As adopted first by the British and French navies (and subsequently, the American), the protected cruiser had the distinguishing characteristic of a sheet of armor plate within the hull, curving upward from one waterline and down to the other in order to protect the ship's vitals from enemy fire. "Cofferdams," or a series of small compartments along the waterline filled with cork or other fiber to slow flooding in the event of hull damage, were another feature. Superstructures and even some gun mounts might be very vulnerable, but the engines, magazines, and lower hulls were comparatively impervious to enemy fire. Principal armament for this category of vessel would range from eight 6-inch guns upward to as high as four 8-inch and twelve 6-inch guns with variants to the scheme, as would be witnessed on the *Olympia*. Cruiser tonnage also would vary from 4,000 to 14,000 with speed in the sixteen to twenty-two knot range. But each vessel would have a certain uniqueness built into her by policymakers, designers, and constructors.[13]

Much of the early work with Cruiser Number 6 centered on the desires of a new "Board on Construction" or, as it was initially known, "The Board on the Design of Ships." Formed by General Order 371 on 25 June 1889, the board consisted of the bureau chiefs for yards and docks, construction and repair, ordnance, equipment and recruiting, steam engineering, and, after 1890, intelligence. Reflecting the navy's attempts to professionalize the forging of the new navy, Capt. George Dewey represented equipment and recruiting before becoming president of the board in 1891. Thus, he would be intimately connected with the fabrication of his future flagship. Dewey would be succeeded as equipment representative by French E. Chadwick. Other early members included Montgomery Sicard (succeeded by William M. Folger in 1890 and William T. Sampson in 1893) from ordnance, George Melville from steam engineering, G. B. White from yards and docks (succeeded by N. H. Farquhar in 1890), and Theodore Wilson (followed by Philip Hichborn in 1894) from construction and repair. Melville was the only continuous member of the board during Cruiser Number 6's construction phase, while the succession of intelligence officers that joined the group undoubtedly reflected the body's desire to have first-rate information ready to hand about naval developments abroad.[14]

It was true that much of the detailed design work on a navy ship was left to the shipyard that built her, but the Navy Department provided basic specifications. In the *Olympia*'s case, the written specifications ran to a hundred and two pages. Twelve plans accompanied them, and an index constituted an additional nine separate pages in and of itself. Little would be left to chance, although the shipyard was required to submit design proposals for the most detailed work and inevitable changes. Negotiations and much anxiety were to be expected between public and private partners in the enterprise. Thus, some four hundred detailed plans of the *Olympia* on file with the cartographic branch of the National Archives and Records Service in College Park, Maryland, attest to the eventual learning experiences of contractor and navy on the building of this ship. Of course, many of those plans reflected rejected design proposals. Little wonder that it would take so long to complete the vessel. The process was one of experiment and exploration for both parties.[15]

Much of the early work centered on selecting a suitable armament for the new cruiser. Never in doubt was the notion that her main battery would comprise the latest model 8-inch breech loading rifled cannon fabricated at the navy's new gun factory in Washington, D.C. In fact, the 14-ton, Mark III, 8-inch .35 caliber breech loading rifle became standard in 1889, and formed the main armament for not only the *Olympia* but for sister cruisers *Charleston*, *Brooklyn*, and *New York*, as well as the battleship *Indiana*. Firing a 260-pound shell, either solid or with a bursting charge of twenty-five pounds of gun cotton, 8-inch gun propellants came from two 90-pound bags of brown powder rammed from the rear of the piece by gun crews. Nearly twenty-five feet in length, the muzzle velocity of a Mark III was 2,100 feet per second. The cruiser's heavy turreted armament led naval historian John Alden to term the *Olympia* "a 'colonial battleship' of sorts."[16]

But the question loomed as to how many of those heavy guns there would be and what would complement them. Moreover, the issue of gun protection (barbette, shield, or turret) was equally fluid, so that weight and number of guns as well as protective composition for gun crews was important in the 1889 board deliberations. The next year additional topics intruded as ship plans reached the bidding and contract selection phase. Under law, the vessel had to be constructed from materials made in the United States.[17]

On 8 April 1890, the Navy Department advertised and two months later (10 June) opened bids for Cruiser Number 6. Only one bidder responded, the Union Iron Works of San Francisco, California, with two distinct bids. One bid ($1,796,000), "for the hull and machinery including engines, boilers, and appurtenances, complete in all respects," was in accordance with the plans and specifications provided by the navy while the second ($1,760,000) was provided by the bidder. Secretary Tracy awarded the contract on the basis of the higher bid. The vessel was to be finished by 1 April 1893 and a speed premium was offered. The Navy Department was anxious to further stimulate warship construction on the west coast, but wanted its own specifications adhered to. Money was no particular object at this point in a period of treasury surpluses available for a naval rearmament program.[18]

The Union Iron Works management immediately asked to lengthen the vessel by ten feet in order to secure more fireroom space, and was willing to absorb the additional cost. The ship would plan out at 340 feet in length with a 53-foot beam and draw about 21.5 feet of water. Both parties signed the contract dated 10 July, which required that Cruiser Number 6 be completed and ready for delivery to the government on or before 1 April 1893. Tracy could report by the end of 1890 that "the vessel has been laid down and the preparatory work is progressing satisfactorily." Moreover, the combination of "sustained speed, exceptional coal endurance, powerful battery, and a certain amount of armor protection make her a cruiser of no ordinary character," he beamed.[19]

Interestingly enough, this was what the navy expected of the new warship. Her greater size would permit "an expansion in those qualities wherein the ordinary cruisers are most defective—coal—endurance and sustained speed." With a planned coal capacity of 1,300 tons (providing an effective range of 13,000 miles) this would be a distance "far in excess of the average vessel of this type." In fact, comparable British cruisers of the period, such as the *Blake* and *Blenheim*, were supposed to achieve a 15,000-mile cruising range although heavier in tonnage than U.S. protected cruisers. But their endurance actually remained in the 10,000-mile range, although trial and forced draught speeds did reach the desired 19–21 knot requirements. The U.S. Navy expected Cruiser Number 6's twin 13,500 horsepower triple expansion engines to achieve similar speeds ("at least 2 knots in excess of that ordinarily maintained by ships of her class"), and felt the additional weight of such machinery would enable her "to reach not only the guaranteed trial speed of 20 knots, but a sustained sea speed of 19 knots."[20]

Tracy also would trumpet other advantages, such as unusual fully-turreted (albeit straight-sided cylindrical turrets, more indigenous to the Civil War–era monitors than the slanted front and overhanging gun house designs that were beginning to appear on European drawing boards) protection for the guns and a powerful battery "in which the rapid-firing feature is distinctly marked." The new cruiser's main armament would settle at four 8-inch and ten 5-inch guns, while the secondary battery would comprise fourteen 6-pounders, six 1-pounders, and four Gatling repeating guns—in all fourteen heavy and twenty-four light pieces. Tubes for launching six torpedoes would supply additional firepower. Four inches of armor protection for the guns and ammunition hoists "make the element of defensive strength one of the marked characteristics of this ship," claimed the Secretary. The distinct armored conning tower could also be counted in this vein. All of this had emerged from two years of Construction Board discussion during which 4-inch, 5-inch, and 6-inch guns had all been considered, with the smallest deemed inadequate and the larger slow in firing. Compromise pointed to the attractiveness of the main 8-inch guns, with weight compensation coming from reduction of turret armor to merely three-inch thickness. (The *Blake*, at 9,150 tons, would mount two 9.2-inch and ten 6-inch guns by comparison as would *Orlando*, more nearly Cruiser Number 6's counterpart at 5,600 tons.)[21]

Placed in care of the Bureau of Construction and Repair by 10 September, a board of constructors had been established in San Francisco to oversee the project. Naval Constructors F. L. Fernald and Joseph Feaster, as well as Assistant Naval Constructor A. W. Stahl, were to ascertain and determine "the amount of increased or diminished compensation that the contractors may be entitled to receive, if any, in consequence of any change or changes in the plans and specifications in the hull of Cruiser No. 6." They were to continue those duties until the end of June 1893. Under their supervision, "Work has begun on the big warship known as Cruiser No. 6 at the Union Iron Works, San Francisco," trumpeted the *Scientific American* on 12 September 1891. She will be "the largest vessel ever built on the Pacific Coast," although the writer noted at the end of his piece that already men were setting up the blocks nearby for the battleship *Oregon*, the keel of which would be laid soon.[22]

But what of the contractors themselves and their capability to construct the new warship? Certainly, Union Iron Works could boast of being the only west coast yard having the plant "for building deep-sea vessels of any size of iron or steel." Located in well protected, temperate San Francisco

Bay, the Iron Works stood at the center of a maritime industry blessed with adequate forging mills, engine works, dry docks, access to cheap coal, and California as well as British iron ore. As early as August 1885, the Works (under the leadership of Superintendent Irving Scott) made proposals to build any of the cruisers then authorized by Congress. The launching of the *Arago* that same year, the first steel steamer built on the coast for deep-water cruising, marked the advent of Union Iron Works as the preeminent yard on the Pacific slope.[23]

In succession, Scott secured contracts for the cruisers *Charleston*, *San Francisco*, a coastal defense vessel, *Cruiser Number 6*, and eventually the famous battleship, *Oregon*. In fact, according to one author in the respected *Proceedings* of the U.S. Naval Institute, "the launching of the *Charleston* marked a new era on the coast, the inauguration of a great ship-building trade." Certainly such an accomplishment had been years in the making. Union Iron Works had paved the way from its humble beginnings before the Civil War as the initiator of castings west of the Rockies, builder of the first locomotive on the coast in 1865, even maker of the engines for the *Saginaw*, the first warship built in that part of the world. By the 1880s, the plant stood as a tribute to Scott's personal energy and sagacity. He had succeeded in creating an industry "that should rival in its completeness and capacity the great shipyards of the Atlantic side of the country."[24]

Scott had toured the world in 1880 investigating and considering all the great shipbuilding works before establishing his own plant in the Poterero suburb about three miles from the center of San Francisco. Here, twenty-eight acres with 1,785 feet of deep-water bay frontage and the tracks of the Southern Pacific Railway Company affording land and sea transport "to all parts of the world" enabled Scott and his plant manager George William Dickie to provide a complete system of manufacturing, from machine shops to hydraulic dock to launching ways. What was not made in the shipyard itself could be provided, in the *Olympia*'s case, by the steel, castings, and heavy forgings for hull angles and beams made at Pacific Rolling Mills, part of Midvale Steel Company of Philadelphia, Pennsylvania. Boiler plate would come from Carnegie, Phipps and Company of Pittsburgh, Pennsylvania. Of course, heavier armor plate had to come from the east, in the new cruiser's case from Bethlehem Steel Company in Bethlehem, Pennsylvania, until that company ran into difficulties fulfilling all of its navy contracts.

Washington had to eventually call in Andrew Carnegie's rival shop in western Pennsylvania to help out with the *Olympia*'s armor.[25]

The Iron Works team (like their east coast counterpart in this business of building new cruisers, Charles Cramp and Sons) already knew the procedures. Having completed the *Charleston* the previous year and about to finish up the *San Francisco* in November, the contractor worked closely with the Navy Department as the new cruiser took shape. As was custom, naval inspectors at the construction site opened the path for official agreement on myriad details from the composition of steel cylinder and valve chest covers to the need for additional electrical energy generators. By May of 1891, reports from government inspectors indicated favorable progress, with the keel laid and frames in course of erection. By September, the navy's Bureau of Steam Engineering optimistically anticipated a completion date of the following April, although the Bureau of Construction and Repair more realistically projected another twelve to eighteen months on top of that.[26]

Cruiser Number 6's construction represented a process of discovery in the art and science of shipbuilding. With so many bureaus responsible for separate parts of the ship, the process involved contractor, the design board, then the bureaus, and finally secretarial approval for literally every change. And there would be many—everything from arrangement of the ice machine to substitution of clothes bag hangers and mesh for wire lockers, from the height of the masts to the dimensions of fighting tops and search light top platforms, even the type of wire for shrouds. The Navy Department decreed substitution of Oregon pine for teakwood decking. The question of cost always bore the simple phrase "to be referred to the Board on Changes." Such was the case when the equipment bureau chief asked to have two 200-amperes dynamos replace two of 100 amperes and one of 200 amperes because of the electrical energy requirement in connection with search lights, motors, and incandescent lighting. Similar procedures would come with the eventual outfitting of the ship in due course. Finally, in October, official references substituted a name for the title "Cruiser Number 6." Henceforth, the new vessel would be styled the *Olympia* in honor of the capital of the new state of Washington. It was an obvious ploy to recognize the growing economic and political importance of the Pacific Northwest.[27]

COMPLETING THE CRUISER OLYMPIA

Then came the moment of actual launch for the new warship—11:25 A.M. on 5 November 1892. Scott and his force had constructed sturdy launching ways to handle the launch weight of 2,400 tons for the vessel (plus a 34-ton cradle). Pilings of Oregon pine, seventy to eighty feet long, fourteen to eighteen inches in diameter, were sunk into the mudflat of the yard, which was covered only at high tide. Soft tallow or sap sufficed for lubricating the hull's passage. A force of thirty carpenters, eight boys, ten laborers, eight riggers, the yard foreman, and superintendent of the site were all present on launching day. The price for the operation was set at $1,618.30 with fully two hours required for preparation time. With flags sent over on 2 November from the Mare Island Navy Yard, all was in readiness for the large crowd on hand that morning. Miss Anna Bella Dickie (daughter of Union Iron Works manager George W. Dickie) christened the vessel while her friend, Miss Elsie Lilienthal (daughter of Philip Lilienthal, manager of the Anglo-California Bank, Ltd.), deftly administered the *coup de grâce* to

USS *Olympia* being launched at Union Iron Works
in San Francisco on 5 November 1892.

the launching rope. The *Olympia* slid silently into the waters of San Francisco Bay to loudly cheering throngs on the shore.[28]

Two more years of effort would be expended in completing the ship. If anything, the finishing process became even more feverish after launching. This would be the period of "filling up the hull" as landlubbers might see the effort. In the process, however, both contractor and patron would learn new things. For instance, *Olympia* was to be outfitted as a flagship for the Far East Squadron. Thus, two major cabins had to be allotted, one for the ship's commander, the other for the admiral commanding the squadron. This meant different appurtenances and wood paneling, as well as accommodation of the fact that officer's space would also contain a 5-inch rapid-fire gun. Moreover, since *Olympia* would be the navy's only turreted protected cruiser, problems arose in implementing the design. The contractor recommended hydraulic, not steam, power for turning the turrets as well as increase in the diameter of armored ammunition tubes therein. In turn this was deemed necessary "to give sufficient clearance between the steam turning tube and the armored tube, thus preventing the possibility of the turret being jammed by a chance shot."[29]

A steam launch and steam cutter had to be constructed, and better means of communication obtained between forward fire room, after boiler compartment, and propeller room. On some items, the Navy Department merely deferred decision, as in the case of specific mess space for petty officers and engineer's force—"until a Commanding Officer be ordered to the ship." Decision making on such minutiae was apparently not eased by provision of additional on-site naval inspectors, as when on 10 April 1893 Equipment Bureau Chief Dewey detailed Cdr. Henry Glass "to occasionally visit San Francisco" in addition to his duties at Mare Island for the purpose of inspecting cutting and fitting of *Olympia*'s rigging. Like other of the new steel ships, she would carry a complement of sail—in this case a seldom-used two-masted schooner auxiliary sail rig.[30]

Such continuous changes necessitated a modified contract before Secretary Tracy left office in March 1893. Nonetheless, Steam Engineer Chief Melville told the new secretary, Hilary A. Herbert, on 2 May that so far as the machinery of the ship was concerned, she would be ready for her official trials the first of the year. Chief Constructor Wilson also told the Navy Department in late May that *Olympia* would be ready for steam in six weeks

Olympia's starboard main engine, built by Union Iron Works, ready for installation circa 1892.

(about 1 July), but could not do her trial trip "until the sponsons, which are necessary to close up openings in the hull," were delivered. At this time, three anchors—two bower, one sheet according to allowances—were being set aside at Mare Island. The little steamer *Sunol* would bring them across the bay.

Some of the delays resulted from difficulties with armor fabrication and even labor disputes. The sponson, conning tower, and barbette armor were being finished by Carnegie Steel Company in Pittsburgh before tests at the navy's Annapolis proving ground and subsequent shipment west with an anticipated June/July delivery. On 10 July, the navy's superintending constructor at Union Iron Works, A. W. Stahl, sent a four-page tally of conditions of work, which suggested that, "In my opinion, this vessel is 81 percent completed, on the basis that 100 percent completion represents her condition when ready for sea in all respects in all matters" as coming within the purview of the Bureau of Construction and Repair. Barring undue delay in the delivery of the turret armor, he estimated the ship would be ready for contractor's trial about 1 December 1893 and for delivery to the government about the first of the year.[31]

Capt. William T. Sampson, Chief of Ordnance (who would later garner fame for his success over the Spanish fleet at Santiago, Cuba, during the Spanish-American War), told Secretary Herbert on 1 October that some 224.25 tons of armor plate had been ordered from the Homestead Works of Carnegie Steel. Of that figure, 150.51 tons had been delivered with 73.74 tons yet to be received at San Francisco. Barbette, conning tower, and sponson, as well as turret and barbette plate, numbered among the orders. The story of delays and missed deadlines mirrored the difficulties of the steelmakers in fabricating this heavy type of steel plate and plagued construction of the New Navy for fully a decade. Later, it would be more a matter of price. But at this early stage, when the *Olympia* awaited completion, the issue was principally technical. The process of heating, rolling, tempering, and annealing the special nickel steel, harveyized armor plate was but dimly understood, as manufacturers and managers Andrew Carnegie, Joseph Wharton, and John Fritz all admitted to the government.

The production registers of the Carnegie company, now preserved at the

Four of *Olympia*'s boilers, made by Union
Iron Works, ready for installation.

Independence Seaport Museum Library in Philadelphia, present an imposing array of dates, statistics, and technical detail on the process. But they also record a litany of problems experienced by the steel industry in responding to naval orders. Even seen in microcosm with respect to the *Olympia* specifically, they reflected the subtleties of a blossoming relationship between military and industrial sectors in the country—predictive of the later-twentieth-century so-called "military-industrial complex." Little of this could be anticipated, much less set in context in the autumn of 1893, when the stakes for both Herbert's Navy Department and Irving Scott's Union Iron Works revolved on a $1,796,000 contract price plus $50,000 bonus for every quarter knot in excess of contract speed.[32]

The machinery placed aboard the new cruiser is in itself a fascinating technical story. Steam power in U.S. warships underwent a relatively rapid evolution by the 1890s, and by the time of the *Olympia*'s construction the vertical-stroke reciprocating engine was in vogue. Cruiser Number 6 was one of the first ships to be equipped with them. Propelled by twin screws driven by two of these three-cylinder triple-expansion engines, each was designed to produce 6,750 horsepower apiece at 129 revolutions per minute and, together, they were ostensibly capable of delivering 16,850 indicated horsepower at 139 rpm. Each of the manganese bronze propellers alone was fourteen feet nine inches in diameter. As for the cylinders, each was supported at the back on an inverted "Y" frame of wrought iron and at the front on two forged steel cylindrical columns. The columns were originally supposed to be cast steel but procurement difficulties led to the substitution, while retaining strength and light weight.[33]

The main pistons, however, were of cast steel and the bedplates of manganese bronze. The intermediate- and low-pressure cylinders were steam-jacketed, while cylinder bores measured forty-two, fifty-nine, and ninety-two inches, and the stroke for each piston was forty-two inches. Steam (at one hundred sixty pounds per square inch) came from six Scotch boilers (four double-ended, two single-ended) with forty furnaces working under forced draft on a closed-stokehold system. Total weight of machinery aboard the *Olympia* numbered 1,239 tons and the coal consumption rate figured at 2.19 pounds per indicated horsepower hour. Forty separate upper and lower tier (above and below the protective deck) coal bunkers, located port and starboard, allowed for 1,169.60 tons of coal. Eight fresh water tanks below and one distributing tank on the upper deck supplied 7,869.58 gallons, mainly for the engines, while a single salt water distributing tank on the upper deck accounted for 1,196 gallons. A separate distilling plant, consisting of two evaporators and two distillers, provided a combined capacity of 8,100 gallons of potable water per day. In addition, seven oil tanks (two for dynamo and lubricating oil each, and single tanks for linseed, lard, and lubricating oil) accounted for 2,085 gallons of that necessary fluid. Of course, condensers, various types of pumps, tanks and filters, dynamos, miles of wiring, ventilating and internal communication systems, munitions and supplies stowage, much less the crew spaces also accounted for the complexity of one hundred fifty-eight watertight compartments aboard this modern man-of-war.[34]

To serve the intricate technical weapons system that would be the *Olympia*, the Bureau of Navigation allocated a force of four hundred eighteen men including a wide variety of specialties from ordinary seamen, landsmen, apprentices, and mates to carpenters, shipwrights, blacksmiths, plumbers and fitters, sailmakers, painters, machinists, boilermakers, coppersmiths, water tenders, oilers, firemen, coal passers, apothecaries, buglers, stewards, cooks, attendants, and chiefs. Thirty-three officers could also be counted. Because of her outfitting as a flagship, she carried thirty-five bandsmen and forty marines. Moreover, the whole ship was a virtual munitions dump, with separate stowage for 8-inch and 5-inch ammunition, combined 6-pounder and 1-pounder stowage and saluting and small arms ammunition each having separate rooms—forward, amidships, and aft. Two gun cotton magazines fore and aft contained thirty-six torpedo warheads and service and exercise torpedoes, pattern D, while twelve dry gun cotton primers and sixteen dry gun cotton blocks were stowed in cabins. Even the admiral's and captain's offices were pressed into storage for twenty-four exploders and thirty-two detonators.[35]

In terms of numbers, the *Olympia* was configured to support her batteries as follows. The four 8-inch turret guns were served by two hundred seventy-two cast iron shell rounds as well as thirty-four shrapnel and armor piercing rounds, each with one hundred seventy ordinary 113-pound charges and one hundred fifty reduced (83-pound) charges. The ten 5-inch rapid-fire pieces were served by nine hundred sixty-four fixed rounds. The 6-pounder ammunition aboard included 3,498 common and steel rounds each and, similarly, 1-pounder ammunition accounted for 1,800 rounds of common and 1,300 rounds of steel, with an additional three hundred rounds each of both (short) common and steel. The small arms ammunition room contained 13,900 .45 caliber ball and 7,000 .45 caliber blank cartridges, 28,800 .38 caliber rounds of ball cartridges, and 89,000 rounds of .22 caliber ball cartridges.[36]

By early September of 1893, the press was reporting that *Olympia* was steaming around San Francisco Bay, although, as one reporter added wistfully, "very little is heard of the ship." Appointment of a trial board was expected momentarily, and it was anticipated that she would follow the pattern set by *Charleston* and *San Francisco* over what was styled the Santa Barbara Channel course. By this time, both contractor and department were spending much time in ironing out wrinkles with the galley, her silver plateware of a new pattern, carpeting and curtains for cabins and wardroom, china and glassware for flag officer and captain, soap and brush trays, even earthenware slop jars, double tin foot tubs, and the first books for the ship's library. These items included diplomatic correspondence, history, and

Running builder's trials near
San Francisco, 1893–94.

biography, even a premier book on naval architecture by renowned English designer William White. On 3 November, the *Olympia* put to sea for the contractor's own preliminary sea trial, where she recorded a maximum speed of 21.26 knots on a run of sixty-eight nautical miles in Found Bay, leaving Scott and the builders confident that she would achieve 22 knots at her official trial and net them a $400,000 bonus.[37]

But Union Iron Works found it necessary to delay the official trial and put *Olympia* into dry dock. Inspection of her bottom disclosed sea grass fouling, requiring overhaul and prompting President Scott to quip that, "If the Olympia made her time of over 21 knots with her bottom in that condition, I have no fear of what she will accomplish when she is clean and just in time for her race against time." This allowed a continuation of outfitting, including a complement of oil lamps and lanterns as insurance against electrical failure. Finally given the "OK," the vessel left San Francisco harbor on Monday 11 December only to face a further three-day delay due to fog in the Santa Barbara harbor. Ultimately, the *Olympia* left her anchorage at 6:30 A.M. on 15 December and took a run of about two hours before starting on her official trial. "The ocean was like a big mill pond," noted one observer, "and was only ruffled by the cruiser herself as she sped through the water, sending spray over her bow until the decks were dripping." Quite a swell was running from Goleta Point to Point Conception, but not enough to retard her headway. The machinery worked perfectly as she made a corrected mean speed of 21.67 knots (netting the Iron Works a bonus of $300,000, the highest premium yet earned for one of the new warships). She generated 17,700 horsepower, or 4,200 in excess of the requirement. Of course, *Olympia* was racing without full complement of armor and ordnance. Still, at one point her speed reached 22.2 knots before she finished her trial trip and turned out to sea for the purpose of testing her steering gear.[38]

Both the navy and the contractors were quite pleased. "In every point of machinery, speed, horse power, and coal consumption, plans and specifications have been beaten," declared one reporter. It would take from seven to eight more months to put the finishing touches on her but, as President Scott of the Iron Works declared, "This means that the Pacific Coast now carries the marine banner and has the queen of the entire American cruiser fleet." In fact, *Olympia*'s competitor, *Columbia*, then being built by Cramp's

Olympia in Dry Dock #1 at Mare Island Navy Yard circa 1895.

shipyard at Philadelphia, had a slightly better speed record (achieved because of her three triple-expansion engines propelling triple screws). Taken together, however, said one commentator, the performance of the two vessels "will make more notable than ever our increasing naval powers and cause shipbuilders in other lands to stare in amazement at the astonishing rapidity of our growth in naval affairs." Or, as Marcus P. Wiggin noted in *Harpers Weekly*, "All that need be said for the *Olympia* is that in her the United States possess an armed protective cruiser which can fight or run, as the emergency demands, and which, with possibly three exceptions, can show her heels to any foreign warship afloat."[39]

Still, the task wasn't complete. The details of acquiring messware, coal baskets, oil lamps, library books, life preservers, and otherwise outfitting and finishing the vessel consumed much of the next year. At various points during the trials and eventual shakedown cruises, minor problems caught the navy's attention. Excess heat in several firerooms, annunciation call bells that could not be heard, and compass deviation that necessitated removal of foremast boom and construction of a nonferrous metal compass platform over the conning tower were among them. Furthermore, the trials were done without ordnance and armor, and a spokesman for the Union Iron Works had complained to Navy Department officials in Washington at the beginning of November that "the failure to provide carriages and guns is accountable for the delay in turning over the Olympia to the Government." Stepped up efforts by the Naval Gun Factory sped the remaining 8-inch and 5-inch pieces west by the end of the month, while test runs at the California Powder Works at Santa Cruz confirmed the viability of guns and propellant charges. At the Mare Island Navy Yard, they pulled twelve Whitehead torpedoes (shipped from the torpedo works at Newport, Rhode Island, in response to the Chilean crisis in 1891) for the new cruiser.[40]

In point of fact, *Olympia's* guns had been arriving piecemeal since mid-August. Receipt of the final 1-pounder piece finished the complement at the end of December 1894. Secretary Herbert happily wired the Mare Island commandant, Capt. Henry L. Howison, on 8 January that "all constructing work" would be completed by the twenty-sixth, with transfer of the vessel to government control anticipated soon thereafter. Additionally favorable reports on testing of the steam training gear for controlling the turret guns pleased officials. Finally, on 5 February 1895, Howison wired Herbert the news they had all been awaiting—"*Olympia* placed in commission this afternoon." Seven years later, on 14 May 1902, California Congressman Victor Metcalf (later secretary of the navy under Theodore Roosevelt) grumbled on the floor of the House of Representatives that the *Olympia* had been twenty-two months behind contract time in construction.[41]

2

The Queen
of the Pacific

The USS *Olympia* (more appropriately dubbed "U.S.F.S." for United States Flagship) undocked at the Union Iron Works shipyard on 9 February 1895. Although only four days had passed since commissioning, this was at least a month overdue, according to navy expectations, and nearly two weeks behind what the contractor had promised. But promises were always overly optimistic at this stage of New Navy construction, and projections still held that the ship would be ready for sea by mid-March. There was still much work to be done before *Olympia* would be truly finished, and it fell to the Mare Island Navy Yard across San Francisco Bay to complete those details. But she already sported her earliest color scheme—all white, with light buff stacks and masts. In February, Capt. John J. Read became the *Olympia's* first commander. The fifty-three-year-old New Jersey native was a Naval Academy graduate and had seen service with Farragut, first aboard the *Hartford* and later on the western rivers and at Fort Fisher during the Civil War. After the war, Read passed through the customary assignments of ship command and lighthouse inspector before coming to the *Olympia*. His later career included commandant of the Portsmouth, New Hampshire, navy yard and chairman of the Lighthouse Board. He reached the rank of rear admiral before his death in 1915.[1]

SHAKEDOWN CRUISE

From procuring an 8,500-pound anchor to repainting her bottom, from securing the correct torpedoes to completing the binnacle stand and procuring plated ware for junior and warrant officer messes, the miscellaneous work continued on the ship. Changes in rugs and carpeting requirements for the admiral's and captain's cabins, as well as substituting numbers of crewman hammocks, occupied yard workers' time. Ordnance work was finished by 20 March, although telescopic sights for the 8-inch guns remained lacking. The ship took on coal in preparation for additional trial runs and tests in home waters. But, as things dragged along, the Navy Department sent orders that all work had to be completed by early June in preparation for *Olympia* going to sea. Meanwhile, during April and May, the crew "began to gradually wear off the 'newness' and slip into the regular routine of man-o'-war life." Part of that routine included complaining about the poor quality of rations, since the executive officer had prohibited bringing aboard any more than a day's supply of vegetables at one time.[2]

Still, there were moments of excitement during this period. The *Olympia* steamed to Santa Barbara in early April for a flower festival, as well as to Sausalito and Santa Cruz, where the crew practiced landing party drill on the hot sand, according to one crewman. The festival particularly proved invigorating for the young sailors. The attention of the local ladies and the presentation of a handsome silk banner spoke to community hospitality and affinity for this newest ship from the Bay area. From Santa Cruz, it was on down the coast to San Diego, where tragedy first struck the ship on 20 April when the initial target practice turned sour. Coxswain John N. Johnson, gun captain of the number 3 rapid-fire 5-incher, was instantly killed in a mishap—the first fatality aboard the ship. According to the Gunnery Drill manual for new armaments, the recoil cylinder had not been properly filled at Mare Island. A shocked crew buried their comrade the next day in a San Diego cemetery with military honors, subscribed to a handsome stone "as a mark of respect and esteem," and composed a rather maudlin memorial poem to honor the young officer.[3]

Capt. John J. Read, USN,
Olympia's first commanding officer, circa 1866.

Both press and Washington officialdom clamored for investigation. A courts-martial board ultimately exonerated Lts. W. W. Buchanan (division officer) and E. J. Dorn (ordnance officer), but Secretary of the Navy Hilary Herbert disapproved. "It cannot be that on board a United States man-of-war, so plain a regulation can be violated and no one to blame," claimed the stiff ex-Confederate veteran and one-time senator from Alabama. Accountability and reliability were what Washington officials like Herbert sought to instill in the New Navy officer corps. So, Dorn became a scapegoat for failing to inspect the piece prior to target practice. Nonetheless, both officers eventually returned to duty with Herbert releasing Dorn from arrest in late July "in view of [his] very high character." But a clear message had been sent for all aboard the *Olympia*. Both the Navy Department and the nation expected her to be an exemplary vessel in every respect.[4]

Some of the crew thought the new ship was "spooked," however. A succession of troubles seemed to follow the Johnson tragedy. Returning to San Francisco, one of the ship's anchor chains gave way, almost severing an ensign's leg. Then, boiler fumes nearly overcame a cleaning crew. Finally, several shipmates were lost in a typhoon when the Pacific Mail steamer carrying them home to the east coast went down. Skies brightened by June when the ship was chosen to take San Francisco naval reservists to Santa Cruz for that city's water festival. *Olympia*'s now-maturing regular crew made short work of these freewheeling dry-land sailors and quickly had them scrubbing down decks and attacking the paintwork, so causing "the very 'holystones' to shudder and the dirt to disappear as if by magic." From Western Union messenger to court stenographer, the reservists were nothing if not enthusiastic "embryo sailors," suffering the injustices of sea sickness as well as jibes from the crew before banding together as a parade party to sample the delights of the festival. It was important to provide the New Navy with citizen-sailors who could be mobilized in case of war. The *Olympia* did her bit for that cause from the start.[5]

The reservists got their revenge by causing the ship's cook, "Nebraska Bill," to be transferred for ostensibly purloining part of their ration of eggs and causing them to verge on starvation. Yet more important things awaited the warship. On 18 June, army general John Schofield came aboard with full honors, including the *Olympia*'s first experience with firing fifteen salute guns upon his departure. Inspection boards, torpedo practice in San Pablo Bay, and an Independence Day open house in which civilians swarmed all over the new craft to gain firsthand acquaintance with a warship were followed by an uproarious parade through the downtown streets of San Francisco. The *Olympia*'s sailors played to the galleries of this hometown crowd for "a good many of our crew had friends and relatives in the city" and many a lad "espied the face of a father, mother, or perchance a sweet-heart gazing at him with worshiping eyes."[6]

On 27 June, the ship made her final test runs under the watchful eye of an official board chaired by Capt. Frank Wildes (who would later command the USS *Boston* at Manila Bay). Board members confirmed her avowed speed, as the run to Santa Cruz was conducted using only two of six boilers and still maintaining better than 15 knots over the four-hour test run. Indeed, at times the smooth seas and light wind permitted a 19.6-knot clip. There had been concern about her stability under varying conditions with some official reports indicating "that she is rather cranky in heavy seas, rolling badly and recovering her equilibrium slowly." Another new cruiser, the *Philadelphia*, had similar proclivities, said the navy. More satisfying were inspection board reports of "zero defects" with tests on guns, electrical and signaling apparatus, searchlights, and general handling qualities, while the overall condition of the ship as to cleanliness was judged excellent. In the florid words of one newsman, the inspection comprised a thorough test of everything pointing to the workings of a modern war cruiser, from "the firing of immense bow chasers down to cutting pigeon's wings within a limited space in mid-ocean."[7]

Returning to Mare Island, *Olympia*'s crew learned that the ship they now dubbed "Queen of the Pacific" would relieve the USS *Baltimore* as flagship of the Asiatic Station, rather than Pacific squadron flagship *Philadelphia* as previously supposed. The latter was in dry dock at the yard and one of her crew claimed to be the champion boxer of this and all navies. That sounded like a hollow boast to the fleet newcomer. So one of the *Olympia*'s firemen, by the name of Dunn, challenged the *Philadelphia*'s pugilist, notwithstanding attempts by the ship's chaplain to instill manners and morals in the young swabbies. A solid $1,000 purse was put on this pivotal match. After a mid-August compass test in San Pablo bay, the *Olympia* returned to the yard and the two fighters met at nearby Vallejo. Alas, the *Philadelphia*'s champion, Tom Sharkey, quickly dispatched Dunn, leaving the fickle crew of the *Olympia* to ponder their loss of coin and turn their thoughts to imminent departure for the Far East. Indeed, waxed ship's chronicler L. S. Young (who for two subsequent years would edit the ship's famous newspaper, *The Bounding Billow,* from a tiny press room in the fantail), Asia was "that 'flowery kingdom,' the land of the almond-eyed beauties who wear pants, but as yet have not mastered the festive bike; the land where the chickens fly in through the port holes and fresh fish beat their brains out on the ship's bottom." So, on 25 August 1895 "we left the land of the free for the land of the Chinee."[8]

BOUND FOR THE ORIENT

On the way out, the navy wanted the *Olympia* to test whether or not she or her sister cruiser, *Columbia,* was truly the fastest American warship. The *Columbia* had recently kept an average speed of over eighteen knots on a run from Southampton, England, to New York City. Now the *Olympia* would try for a record, at least as far as Honolulu. "We believe sincerely that we shall beat the record of the Columbia," opined one enthusiastic officer.

"The distance is 1200 miles, we ought to make it in 4 and $^{1}/_{2}$ days," he added. And so, on 26 August the Mare Island commandant wired Secretary Herbert that "Olympia sailed Sunday morning crossing the bar at six-thirty bound for the Asiatic Station via Honolulu."[9]

Not everyone was mesmerized by the prospective speed race, however. Captain Read, for one, was too busy establishing proper shipboard operating procedures. General Orders Number 4, which he issued on 31 August, would see to that. For example, watch officers would take position on the forward bridge, "where a good observation can be had from directly ahead to around on both bows and abeam." While permitted to visit any part of the superstructure deck while on watch, such officers were not to engage in conversation except with the executive or the navigation officers. Smoking was not permitted and nobody could lounge about on either bridge. Night orders were especially stringent for the deck officers on matters ranging from lifeboats, lookouts, signal lights, police duties, carpenter and gunner gangs, inclement weather operations, handling of collision and water tight doors, charts, anchors, compass, changes of course, and so forth.[10]

It took *Olympia* a week to traverse "the trackless deep" to Hawaii. It was a stormy crossing, and many of the young crew "were spread-eagled, flat on their backs, passive in the misery of, must we say, seasickness," chided Young. But, anticipating shore liberty in Honolulu, they weathered the passage. Then the crew was crestfallen to find that there would be no such leave. Lying off the reef which enclosed Honolulu's harbor, they saw the dreaded yellow quarantine flag sported by the gunboat *Bennington*. Cholera was the culprit, with restocking of provisions almost impossible and shore contact limited to transferring fumigated mail bags, "put in a wooden box" and landed at the end of the breakwater for a 6:30 pickup. On 10 September, the *Bennington*'s captain lamented to Read about being treated like an "infected ship" although there had not been an incidence of cholera aboard his vessel in nine days. Still, there was no way around the impasse.[11]

The *Olympia* proceeded to cruise the islands, navigating tortuous channels and skirting the lepers' island of Molokai before finally anchoring at Lahaina, Island of Maui—"if not Paradise itself, as near as ever any mortal got on this earth." Again, no liberty, but plenty of rest and relaxation on deck, drinking in every evening's portrait of clear waters, sun setting over the mountains, truly "a scene to inspire the Masters," said crewman Young later. Finally, the bark *Forest Queen* came up from Departure Bay on 5 October bearing 450 tons of coal and fifty welcome sacks of Irish potatoes. Then it was back to Honolulu on the thirteenth to find the quarantine lifted but, again, no shore leave. The ship needed recoaling for the next stage of her voyage across the Pacific. Only the occasional "bum boat" (that virtually legendary local purveyor of fruit, Yankee notions, sometimes even beer) broke the monotony of ten further days of grime and the gritty, dirtiest job in the sea navy—before the *Olympia* departed on 23 October. The crewmen were not happy, having been denied a chance ashore, and they let Read know it by taking it "to the mast" with the captain.[12]

But departure came right after dinner, "not waiting to wash down, and with the blooming 'Queen of the Pacific' looking very dingy in their grimy coat of coal dust, we started off on our long trip for Yokohama, Japan, giving the vessel a deep sea drink on the great circle route to our destination," noted Young. This leg of the journey proved far from smooth, a necessity for setting speed records. Typhoon seas and some pesky coal bunker fires made the passage miserable for all aboard. The official report on the fires blamed the poor quality of the 1,200 tons of coal hastily procured during the cholera outbreak. Fumes nearly overcame several crewmen battling the blaze and the berth deck had to be evacuated one night because of the threat. Equally threatening for the ship's safety were the storms encountered soon thereafter.[13]

Read reported later that gale force winds blew steadily for twenty-four hours and for nine hundred miles "we worked against head winds as severe as any I have ever encountered." Young remembered that the vessel "was plunging bows under, taking green seas over the forecastle every few minutes." During one lull, some men were sent out to put covers over the hatches and a heavy swell unexpectedly surged, nearly carrying off boatswain's mate Charles Ross. Although the cry of "man overboard" went up, the life-buoy was dropped, and the lifeboat manned, Ross was found injured and pinned in the angle formed by superstructure and a 5-inch gun. The buoy was subsequently picked up by another steamer plying the route. Read nevertheless claimed that his ship took on little water and "is the best weather boat I ever sailed in."[14]

Speed records proved impossible, although one *New York Herald* correspondent in Yokohama reported later that "there was no time when she could not have fought her 8-inch and 5-inch guns." But the crew was disgusted, and Young fussed also about crossing the 108th meridian on 29 October and "getting to windward of Uncle Sam for two rations of salt pork." Well, he advanced, "Uncle Sammy makes up for it when we go home, for then we will have to hustle, as we get no rations for one day." Such were the logistical regulations in the steel navy. By mid-November, the new flagship and her worn-out crew reached Japanese waters and, early on the morning of the ninth, "the silver tipped peak of 'Fujiyama' the pride of Japan, burst on our sight in all its majestic glory." New sights awaited the ship as soon as she entered Yokohama harbor.[15]

Everything was bustle and confusion as *Olympia* steamed in. Sampans darted about, said Young, "loaded with gesticulating Japanese, Chinese and Indian merchants, all anxious to get on board first and dispose of their wares at fabulous prices to the green and gullible 'Jack Tars.'" The official log entry was more formal, stating merely that they encountered one Japanese, three Russian, and two French warships in port, all flying colors at half mast due to the death of a Japanese prince. Absent were ships of the American Asiatic Squadron. Nevertheless, salutes were exchanged with the Russian and French flagships as their admirals soon came aboard the *Olympia*, "showing much interest in the latest specimen of American naval architecture." To a man they declared her "to be the most warlike looking craft in the harbor," although the Russians actually had two ships present with greater tonnage.[16]

SHOWING THE FLAG

In some people's minds—unofficial, perhaps, as well as official—the *Olympia* was here to advertise American warships and American shipbuilders in the Far East. Irving Scott and his Union Iron Works, Charles Cramp of Philadelphia, Carnegie, Phipps and Company as well as Bethlehem Steel, and the navy and its infrastructure were now all part of a blossoming American military-industrial complex. So why not compete with European (especially British) counterparts for the emerging Japanese naval expansion, if not something similar on mainland China? At least, these were the sentiments of men in the States as well as Special Far East Correspondent of the *New York Herald,* Col. John A. Cockerill. Representatives of this upswing in American interest in trade expansion included shipbuilders, manufacturers, and merchants in general, to whom were now added representatives of the

New Steel Navy. The "Queen of the Pacific" provided the latest "Exhibit A" or manifestation of opportunities afforded by warmer Sino and Japanese-American ties. Of course, none of this was of the slightest interest, perhaps, to the crew of the *Olympia* as they prepared to go ashore and explore the novel land of the rising sun.[17]

Shore leave in Yokohama after the arduous Pacific passage for many meant a sixty cent rail trip to Tokyo. Others stayed closer to the ship, discovering numerous ways to part with money in a strange land. Then, on 15 November, Rear Adm. Charles C. Carpenter arrived from Shanghai in the flagship *Baltimore* and Read saluted the arrival with seventeen guns before paying the obligatory visit. The *Baltimore*'s band transferred to the *Olympia* a fortnight later with the first measures of "Hail Columbia" (the unofficial national anthem) played at evening colors. After this, the evenings passed in dancing or listening to lighter airs or "bum music." The two crews shared traditional Thanksgiving fare before the *Baltimore* and Carpenter left for home on 3 December. The band played "Home, Sweet Home" and "Auld Lang Syne" as she steamed out of the harbor. Later, it was reported that heavy weather had claimed one of her crew on the voyage back to the States.[18]

Visits by the Japanese Minister of War, followed on 18 December by dry-docking at Yokosuka, the fortified Japanese naval base, preceded the arrival of Rear Adm. F. V. McNair, the new squadron commander, via the steamer *Rio de Janeiro*. He soon retired to quarters in the Grand Hotel ashore, leaving Japanese workers to scrape and clean his new flagship. The crew of the *Olympia*, meanwhile, removed her ammunition and were then permitted to tour the facility. They stared at the visible scars of the recent Sino-Japanese war on the emperor's docked cruisers and battleships. It was a good learning experience for navy folks manning America's new fleet, most of whom had not even the faintest idea of what combat meant. Their idea of mission remained showing the flag and providing visible evidence of America's interest in protecting lives and property abroad.[19]

Christmas found a signal flag and flower bedecked *Olympia* still in dry dock. Saint Nicholas failed to visit the ship but, instead, the first mail from home restored crew spirits. Two days later, the cruiser returned to the water and moved off to retrieve ammunition at the yard's magazine before bidding Yokosuka adieu on 30 December. She steamed back to Yokohama, testing her compass en route. New Year's Day 1896 was marked by twenty minutes of customary revelry, bell and gong ringing, and complete cacophony of noise making from purloined mess pans and kettles. Needless to say, galley personnel were not impressed by such intemperate use of their wares. For a time, the ship's company assumed a sedate tone until the men could organize a minstrel show replete with electrically lighted stage, awning, and suitably attired side and stage dressing made from the flags of all nations carried in the ship's signal kit. Key officers and crew provided the butt of many of the jokes in a show which was judged "a grand success."[20]

By 21 January, however, "we determined to change our place of residence," as crewman Young phrased it. This time the goal was to break the record of HMS *Edgar* on the 380-mile run to Kobe. To accomplish this feat, Chief Engineer George J. Burnap directed that the local market be cleaned out of virtually everything edible to bolster the strength and endurance of his "Black Gang" and deck volunteers. Turkeys, ducks, and chickens in profusion came aboard for each day's mess tables. They were washed down "with a little of the 'doctors best' every hour to keep steam up." Departing at 4:00 in the afternoon, however, the ship ran into heavy winds and seas as usual, to everyone's discomfort. There wasn't a dry spot aboard as swells even invaded ventilator space (designed to cool the fire rooms where temperatures soared to an average 180 degrees). Despite thirty-foot waves, the cruiser plowed on through seas that smashed pilot house windows, tore bridge railings, and wrecked the brass indicator, as well as bending one of the four-inch stanchions just under the winch house. Had she not slowed to five knots, "everything would have been carried away."[21]

Despite Japanese press skepticism, the *Olympia* claimed to have made over twenty-two knots on the passage to Kobe. Reaching that city at 6:00 the next evening, she stopped only long enough to pick up a pilot before entering the Inland Sea, bound for Nagasaki. The beauty of the season's first snowfall on the surrounding mountainous islands soon vanished when a new challenger caught up and audaciously passed the "Queen of the Pacific." It was the Canadian Pacific steamer *Empress of India*. The sea's surface was glassy and everyone on board both vessels anticipated a race. It was not to be. Officered by Royal Naval Reserve personnel, the glistening white steamer quickly glided abreast of the warship and then passed at a sixteen-knot clip. British travelers lining her rails chided their American comrades aboard the passenger vessel. Pointing to the sluggish *Olympia* they quipped "finest of her class in the world I believe you said, may I ask what class?" The *Empress's* captain quickly commandeered one passenger's Kodak camera with pictures of the feat to send to the *London Graphic*.[22]

Crestfallen, *Olympia's* crew wondered what was wrong with their "hoodoed" craft that supposedly had been sent over to Japan for the purpose of advertising Yankee genius and skill at shipbuilding. Quickly refuting any notion that her men below decks were too played out to race again, crewman Young claimed "we were all willing and able to help her out." Every man and boy in the deck force would have volunteered his services rather than see her beaten, suggested Young. Yet, after this insult to American pride, "the grandeur of the scenery [of the Inland Sea] lost its charm for us." Little did they realize that the *Empress* was engaged in her own mission— making up time with the English mails—while the *Olympia's* captain, constrained by customary naval pecuniary peacetime caution chose to steam at reduced speed and lowered boiler pressures. The behavior of the "Queen of the Pacific" and her speed received great prominence in Japanese official circles. But, noted Young, the glory of the *Olympia* soon melted away between Kobe and Nagasaki, for it was the *Empress of India* of the Canadian Pacific steamship line "that brought the *Olympia* to grief."[23]

That night, the *Olympia* dropped anchor off "Pagoda Point" at Nagasaki harbor and next morning moved closer to the city. Other foreign warships filled up the harbor giving deck officers anxious moments contemplating collisions. But one crew member wrote home how there was "lots of saluting going on" and how they had fired over one hundred times upon arriving. "Almost every day, we are firing salutes," noted Apprentice Wayne Longenecher, and he went on to admit that "they are drilling us like the mischief." Sister ships *Yorktown* and *Charleston* were laying there, the latter with a broken shaft, and the *Concord* and *Detroit* arrived soon after the *Olympia*. Departure of a homeward bound Russian warship gave the Americans an opportunity to cheer themselves hoarse as a gesture of comradery, and the *Concord* likewise soon departed for the States and a well earned rest. "A good many of us would have liked to be going with her," noted Young. At this point, however, Captain Read had other things in mind. The ship had ducked required gunnery and target training since leaving Hawaii and arriving in the Far East so as to conserve coal. Furthermore, internal discipline had grown slack as several directives attested—proper saluting procedures for passing ships, the routine of leaving and boarding ship, and shipboard hygiene of airing crew hammocks all needed attention.[24]

Needless to say, *Olympia*'s sailors looked more to Washington's birthday celebration, when boat racing, tug-of-war, three-legged, spud, and sack races, and the indispensable pie-eating match—all for generous prizes—held more allure. Every vessel in the harbor received an invitation to join in and make merry. The boat races were particularly anticipated as *Olympia* excelled at barge, cutter, gig, dinghy, catamaran, and shovel contests. Only the twelve-oared cutter race, won by *Charleston,* marred the otherwise unblemished *Olympia* record. The pie-eating contest was anything but sweet, as government socks, potato skins, and orange peels lent a note of comedy to the proceedings. The day passed too quickly, it seemed. Colors came, the visitors left, and so ended "one of the most enjoyable days spent on this ship," concluded one Tar. But the next day the *Charleston*'s boat crew challenged their counterparts aboard *Olympia* to a return race over a four-mile course for twenty dollars an oar and forty dollars in the coxswain's box. The *Charleston*'s reputation for having never lost a race caused the *Olympia*'s crew to go into training immediately.[25]

Read and his officers set up procedures for instilling good order and discipline aboard the flagship. At some point, they published a mimeographed memorandum relating to duties and honors of the officers, marine guard, band, and ship's company when dignitaries came aboard or left and when other ships passed and necessitated salutes. On 23 February 1896, the captain issued an order that all officers and men on deck would stand at attention when other warships passed and that everyone would salute at the band's playing of the national air until finished. Other directives were issued periodically from then on concerning orderly airing of bedding on deck, the apparently perennial problems attending smoking aboard ship, time gun firings at mid-week, and announcing the arrival of mail steamers when in port. The band especially received explicit instructions concerning protocol for visiting American as well as foreign dignitaries. It was all part of daily shipboard development during peacetime.[26]

CHINA STATION

Meanwhile, other duty called. On 3 March, *Olympia* left for Woosung, China. Bad weather again attended the passage, with crew members recalling rolling decks and more time spent headfirst in sauce pans and pickle barrels while partaking of mess than salutary sea breezes. But new sights, sounds, and smells awaited them in Chinese waters with native boats "of the same pattern as the Nina, Pinta, and Santa Maria of the Columbus era," Chinamen "sleek and greasy" but enjoying the best of health, and a town of Woosung so foul that "it could be smelt twenty miles at sea with the wind off shore." Admiral McNair and his retinue quickly departed for Shanghai, only thirteen miles distant by water, while the flagship left for target practice on 9 March at a group of islands called "the Saddles" about sixty miles offshore. Frankly, the Americans were quite ready to leave Woosung, "about the dirtiest town, or rather hole, on the face of the earth."[27]

After placing their targets and blasting away with the 8- and 5-inchers, *Olympia*'s tars went ashore for small arms practice and fraternization with the few inhabitants of the island. They found goat herders and fishermen, like the fellow they dubbed "Old John," who quickly made himself quite ill on the strong and slightly sweetened ship's chewing tobacco. Tobacco smoking, in fact, would become such a heavy pastime aboard the ship that by May Read had to issue strict orders about places and times for such activities as well as code of conduct. He would be particularly snappish, declaring that the practice of carrying lighted cigars, pipes, and so forth in the mouth when between decks or going up or down ladders "is unmilitary and not in accordance with the customs of the service, and must be discontinued." Frankly, there seemed to be more concern about such affairs when in port rather than when off "the Saddles" range practicing.[28]

Returning to Woosung at 3:30 P.M. on the twentieth, the *Olympia* once more enjoyed a change of pace. McNair and his wife gave a ball in the American Consulate at Shanghai three days later. So the officers, decked out in dress uniform—"claw hammers and cocked hats," according to the slang of the day—traveled by the steam launch. Crewmen, afforded liberty of the city, went ashore in the gaudily painted sampans and were landed in about six inches of soft, oily Chinese mud. Except for the few rice fields, the country between Woosung and Shanghai seemed to be one continual graveyard. An occasional idol kept lonely watch and ward but the Tars' education took a distinctive upturn upon reaching more modern Shanghai.[29]

Laid out in distinctive districts for international residents of the place, the refreshment houses and tea gardens, the "Bubbling Well," shade trees, lepers, and "Joss houses" captured many an American sailor's fancy. Quite a few of the crew missed the boat scheduled to take them back to the *Olympia* and, seeing that they were "in for it," determined to make their stay a good one, some of them remaining four and five days beyond their leave. Later, they would be called before the captain, who doled out their punishment "with misplaced generosity and munificence" according to the extent of their misdemeanors. The average dose was "three and four" which meant three months restricted to ship and fourth or lowest conduct rating, which in turn meant plenty of time to reflect upon the error of their ways.[30]

During their stay at Woosung, the Americans performed humanitarian service when two steamers collided a short distance from the *Olympia's* anchorage. About 1:00 A.M. on 30 April, the quartermaster reported that he had heard a crash and, as the tide was running like a millrace, the water was full of floating debris and Chinese yelling for help. All hands turned out, manned lifeboats, and brought numerous survivors back to sick bay, seamen's hammocks, blankets, and dry clothing. It turned out that the *Newchang* and *On-Wo* had collided, the latter sinking. In all, perhaps fifty lives were lost. But countless others were saved due to "the humane spirit and seamanlike ability of officers and men of the Squadron present," in the words of Admiral McNair's appreciative general order of 1 May 1896. The Chinese governor of Shanghai province added his thanks, with the *Olympia* particularly singled out for promptness and skill in helping with the disaster. The Viceroy of Nanking ordered a tablet made and sent to Read with an inscription commending him for his humane action.[31]

Then it was off to Chefoo for "fleet evolutions and target practice in company" with fellow squadron member cruisers *Charleston*, *Detroit*, and *Yorktown* and the gunboat *Machias*. More welcome than the drills was an epicurean round of milk, cake, fruit, candies, "eggs by the yard and chickens by the dozen" provided by local purveyors as well as the long-awaited boat race with the *Charleston* crew. The latter's barge crew were well rested and excused from drills "while ours was excused from nothing and were ashore with the rest, drilling in the hot sun and heavy sand" groused L. S. Young. Nevertheless, the race on 14 May was neck and neck until after the finish, when reward of the stakes was made to the coxswain of the *Charleston* "owing to some misunderstanding" about the finish line. The disgusted crew of the *Olympia* listened while their band played "You'll never miss your money, till it's gone."[32]

The *Charleston* left for home several days later, along with the prize purse, but the crewmen of the "Queen of the Pacific" consoled themselves that "it was going to a good country to be spent." More consoling for some was the handsome silk "Cock," a racing flag of blue silk with a rooster in a triumphant attitude crowing over his victories, each of which was represented by a star brought to the *Olympia* by the *Charleston*'s barge crew as a gesture of appreciation and sympathy. One might have taken it as a thumbing of noses, but by this time the Jack Tars on both vessels were thinking of other things. *Olympia* was now bound for Vladivostok and celebration of the Czar's coronation.[33]

NORTH TO RUSSIA

Stopping to clean and paint ship "so as to make a respectable showing" before entering the Russian harbor on 23 May, "we went in just before sundown and the usual burning of gunpowder occurred." However, there were so many salutes to be fired that some had to wait until the next morning. Nonetheless, since the *Olympia* was the only foreign warship present, great respect was shown the Americans. This delighted the boys, apparently, for visitors were continually coming on board ship to be shown around. Coronation day was 27 May and, at 11:30 A.M., all the vessels "dressed ship" at once, making a majestic rainbow-like spectacle while one hundred one guns thundered a salute to the new ruler, covering the harbor in a dense cloud of smoke. In the evening, incandescent lights and Chinese lanterns replaced the day's flags and bunting. Not to be outdone when they could not effect similar lighting, the ingenious Americans simply raised the Russian flag at the mainmast, turned the searchlight on it and then ran their own ensign up to the fore and turned another searchlight on it also. "The Russians cheered like mad," recorded Young.[34]

The evening proved most memorable with the whole town a mass of fireworks, every vessel sporting some artistic grouping representing the Czar's coat-of-arms, the Russian Bear, Throne, or Imperial Title, and Crown, and music and song wafting across the water from each ship's band. Cheers and "tigers" rent the air from enthusiastic young throats, with the result that next day crew members spoke in whispers. But the festivities lasted three days, with balls, parties, dinners, and fêtes galore. One of the *Olympia's* cutters was rigged out with spars and yard arms, covered with Japanese lanterns and, on the evening of the twenty-eighth, was given over to the flagship's band in the cutter cruising from ship to ship serenading each with "good old songs" like "Annie Rooney," "Daisy Bell," "Sweet Marie," and "Come Where my Love Lies Dreaming."[35]

Dinner invitations from the Russian ships *Rurik* and *Pamiat Azova* for fifty *Olympia* sailors apiece on 31 May meant the Yanks' first introduction to barrels of vodka. Ladled out by their hosts, "no ordinary person could drink a dipper-full and live," but "Johnny de Roosh" led the way, taking it "like ice cream soda." Toasts and early conversations revolved around use of hands and feet doing the talking, but L. S. Young reported after fifteen minutes that "our boys could speak Russian like natives." Everyone began to feel sociable and settled down to business amid cheers on both sides for the "Americanos" and "Johnny de Roosh." Even the fierce looking guns took on "an aspect of good nature," as flags and evergreens lavishly and picturesquely hid the commonplace bulkheads. After all this, a few of the lads were laid away to sleep it off in the chain lockers or under the "to'gallant fo'cas'le" while those still standing frolicked on the beach. The party boys returned to *Olympia* the next morning heavy-eyed and tired but happy, agreeing that the reception was a "peach" and always remembering with gratitude the hospitality of Vladivostok.[36]

Officers aboard the American flagship, from McNair down to lowliest midshipmen, like William H. Standley (later an admiral himself), also came in for their share of the entertainment and gaiety. Vodka-inspired singing by Standley and several of his Academy mates (taking their post-graduation obligatory cruise aboard the *Olympia*) scandalized their seniors until the Russians indicated their pleasure at the Americans' jollity during one shoreside fête at the town hall. A reciprocal party hosted aboard the flagship (that normally boasted only Scotch whiskey and English ale) ended up with the ship's boats depositing Russian army and navy officers and civilian officials indiscriminately up and down the bay in the post-midnight darkness. With that and the difficulty of language, "it took a couple of days to sort them out and get them back to their proper ships and army camps," Standley remembered years later.[37]

Indeed, those *Olympia* sailors not fortunate enough to dine aboard the

Russian warships enjoyed the liberty of the town, but found lodging nonexistent and the terminus of the great Siberian Railroad about the only item of tourist interest. By 2 June, the Americans were ready to move on. Even then, matters proved a bit shaky in implementation. Standley recounted how the *Olympia* had hosted a large party the night before. The ship was then scheduled to depart at mid-morning on the next day, but at noon "considerable confusion still existed." One head of a department aboard ship "noted for an ingrown disposition" lost his cool and reported a junior officer as being intoxicated and unfit for duty. Hauled before Read that morning, the young officer admitted to having imbibed too freely at the gathering but disclaimed incapacity for duty. On the contrary, said the junior officer rather proudly, he thought that he had stood up pretty well under his liquor, better in fact than most of the Russians he had been entertaining. An amused Read looked at him with a twinkle and told him, "Well, young man, had you remained cold sober during the party yesterday, I would certainly have had you court-martialed for neglect of duty." He dismissed charges and everyone resumed preparation to take the flagship out of port.[38]

At about 4:00 P.M., Read finally got the *Olympia* under way, steaming around the harbor while crew cheered each ship and the band played their national anthem—to which the recipients returned such courtesy. "It was a sight worth seeing to observe the dexterity with which our captain handled the ship," recorded Young, "zig-zaging between the various vessels in a manner that made the Ruskies stare, and spoke well for the promptness with which the vessel answered the call of the helmsman." After this exhibition of seamanship, the American ship moved out smartly, bound for the most northern port of Japan, Hakodate, where she dropped anchor on the morning of 4 June, and prepared for the much dreaded "Admiral's Inspection" which had been anticipated for most of the year.[39]

BACK TO JAPAN

The inspection was a repetition of that held by the Board of Inspection with the exception of gun firing. There was "arm and away," "clear ship for action," "Fire quarters," and "man overboard," all of which made the crew jump sideways. The next day, they had "collision drill," indicated by a mournful blast of the ship's steam whistle followed by short blasts to tell the location of the injury—one, starboard bow; two, port bow; three, starboard; and four, port quarters. This was followed by "abandon ship," indicated by continued application of the whistle while the boats were provisioned and rigged out. Promptly at midnight, the fire alarms sounded to see if everyone could spring quickly enough to put out the possible blaze. Done properly to "the Queen's or rather the Admiral's taste," the Tars were again permitted to seek "our downy couches." Having satisfied the powers that be as to their proficiency, the crew watched wistfully as, at 11:30 on the morning of 5 June, *Olympia* slid away from Hakodate without its crew having had a chance to see anything "but the combers on the wave-washed front of the town." Two days later she once more dropped anchor inside the Yokohama breakwater.[40]

The weather was warm, swimming became a favorite pastime, and the *Olympia*'s baseball nine gave a Japanese team (who thought they knew all about America's favorite sport) "a few pointers on playing the game." The

Olympia's baseball team, the Asiatic Squadron champions, at Yokohama circa 1895–96.

ship was dressed in honor of Queen Victoria's birthday and the Glorious Fourth came and went as usual with "many of the boys in a retrospective mood, meditating on how many bunches of fire-crackers they would have fired by this time had they stayed home." Since there were French warships in the harbor, the Yankee Tars helped celebrate "the Fall of the Bastille" on the Fourteenth by dressing ship and firing a 21-gun salute. That night, the *Olympia* sent two boat crews to help Yokohama authorities put out a blaze that threatened the city. Soon thereafter, the intrepid editor of the ship's newspaper recorded a 9 August eclipse of the sun, which tantalized everyone and was soon followed by a great tidal wave which wreaked havoc, "leaving in its wake thousands of homeless starving human beings."[41]

Boat races with the crew of HMS *Grafton*, unexpected deaths of comrades like bandsman De Lucca (whose assumed name made it impossible to notify any kin) and Charles Nelson, captain of the after-guard, caused mourning aboard ship rather less for their passing than for the unpaid debts they left behind. Still, Nelson was widely respected as an expert coxswain and an indefatigable, generous worker. They both were buried in the cemetery at Yokohama with full military honors. The arrival of the little Mexican corvette *Zaragosa* after a three-year world cruise occasioned additional excitement. By 17 September, the *Olympia* was in the Yokosuka dry dock having her bottom scraped and repairs made but she returned to Yokohama two weeks later "as clean as a new pin." By mid-October, the flagship had set off again "to make another round of the 'station,'" visiting Kobe, and traversing the Inland Sea (where a sighting of the America-bound Pacific Mail Steamer *Rio de Janeiro* prompted caustic remarks about the soft life of civilians) before reaching Chefoo harbor and another round of small arms practice, battalion drill, and torpedo exercises at nearby "Drill Island." Technical deficiencies of the latter weapon proved particularly vexing, requiring diving to the bottom to retrieve at least one of the wayward devices.[42]

Rough weather in early November scrapped "great gun practice," but all hands soon fell to wagering large sums on the impending election between William Jennings Bryan and William McKinley back in the States. News of the latter's election was signaled on the night of 5 November from the *Yorktown*, but "no bets were paid over" until more authentic information

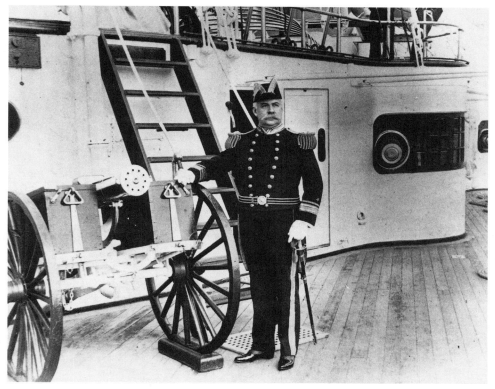

Rear Adm. Frederick V. McNair, commander Asiatic
Squadron, on board *Olympia* at Nagasaki in 1897.
Note the 1894 Gatling gun to his right.

was obtained. Little did *Olympia*'s crew know what the election of McKinley would mean for their future fate at the time. Soon it was off to Nagasaki
and coaling ship "a job that had no more terrors for us," said chronicler
Young, as it was "all done by the natives" this time (mostly women and
young girls as it turned out). Arrival of the Russian warships *Rurik* and
Pamiat Azova permitted *Olympia*'s sailors to return the Vladivostok hospitality, and Thanksgiving came and went with customary turkey dinners and
"youthful poker," many visitors, but no sports. That evening, *Olympia*'s
band played "the same old moss-grown tunes for the benefit of the few

whose musical education had been neglected." Even the many "that boasted a classical ear sat around, sowing evident thankfulness for the past and a hope that if it would not inconvenience the creator of circumstances, they would be more than pleased to spend their next Thanksgiving, 'back among the old folks once again,'" added Young.[43]

Yet life was hardly dull or unpleasant at Nagasaki. Arrival of a young fourteen-year-old lad, on his way home from Elsie Adair's Theatrical Company stranded in Shanghai, opened a round of musical festivities that included more fêting of the Russians with music, feasting and a performance ashore two days before Christmas by "Olympia's Minstrels" for the benefit of Nagasaki charities. The latter must have truly been a sight to behold for the packed opera house. Glee club singing, the Grand Cake walk, string quartet performances, blackface comedy, gymnastic exercises, and what was billed as "the longest speech in the shortest time" by talented Boy Orator, W. J. O'Brien, assisted by "the world's Famous So So's (Sub) Marine Band under the leadership of J. Phil So So" reached a climax with Songs of All Nations and Grand Tableau, "Columbia the Gem of the Ocean," by the entire minstrel troupe. Christmas Day itself was anticlimactic, although cooks "with their dyspepsia laden eatables" and shore liberty were not avoided.[44]

The "Olympia's 400, burnt cork comedians" repeated their show on 5 January 1897 for the benefit of the men who had missed the one given ashore, and Admiral McNair and Captain Read had seats in the "bald head row" and seemed to enjoy the performance as much as anyone. The next day a challenge from HMS *Undaunted* for a boat race led to predictable Yankee victory. Several ensuing days passed in transferring men whose service time was to expire to the USS *Detroit* which was going to New York via the Suez canal. "We would all have liked to have made that trip as she would touch at a great many ports of interest on her way, and we all had an ambition to circumnavigate the globe, to say nothing of getting home," noted L. S. Young. Instead, 23 January found the *Olympia* bound for Hong Kong with a smooth sea, plenty of good things to eat on board, and a desire to meet the *Empress of India* for a return engagement race. "Sad to say we missed her," noted the future editor of *The Bounding Billow*. However, "we came to anchor in Hongkong having made the trip in sixty hours from light to light, beating the fastest record by twelve hours hitherto held by the steamship 'China' of the Pacific Mail Steamboat Company." Obviously, the USS *Olympia* was still trying to prove her reputation as fastest of her class of warship.[45]

VISITING HONG KONG

There then followed the next round of formalities and welcoming dignitaries. The Governor of Hong Kong came aboard to honors on the twenty-seventh, and admirals were all too common, since five flagships lay in the harbor at the time. HMS *Grafton* and HMS *Centurion* represented the British Royal Navy, *Rurik* the Russians, *Kaiser Wilhelm* the Germans, and, of course, America's own "Queen of the Pacific." Together, the foreigners witnessed "the pleasure or rather torture" of a boisterous Chinese New Year on 2 February, with tons of fireworks of all descriptions and streets so crowded with merry makers that it was almost impossible to walk. Several desertions from the *Olympia* and the suicide of the *Grafton*'s Royal Marine captain at the height of a combined regatta created a sensation. "It's a bloomin' shame he couldn't bloody well wait till to-morrow," was the British Tars' reaction and the program went on as if nothing had happened. Highlight of these festivities was a cosmopolitan pie-eating match between one of the *Olympia*'s crew, an Englishman, and a German—won by the Brit, possibly enticed by his captain's promise of an additional five dollar reward.[46]

The month of March passed in target practice in Mirs Bay (with generous prizes offered for beating previous records) and a repetition of the ill-fated torpedo practice at Chefoo. The torpedo went to the bottom again, stayed there despite sailors and natives diving for it, and, said Young, "Uncle Sam is about twenty-five hundred dollars out in the transaction." Then, back to Hong Kong to anxiously await the results of the famous Corbett/Fitzsimmons prize fight, departure of a flock of young Midshipmen for the States, examinations to see who would remain in the navy and who would not, and the customary retirement to dry-dock at Kowloon for cleaning. Arrival of one hundred sixty replacement seamen in mid-April and the gunboats *Yorktown* and *Petrel* in early May attended *Olympia*'s return to Yokohama and more target practice.[47]

Once more, *Olympia* honored the Queen's birthday in June as the crew trimmed the ship to commemorate Victoria's Diamond Jubilee. But they even more zealously prepared for the American birthday celebration two weeks later. Reveille sounded at 4:00 A.M. on 5 July (the fourth, having fallen on a Sunday, precluded celebration that day) and the ship was dressed ten minutes later. Sampans began arriving with greens and flowers and the warship soon looked like "a floating conservatory." Everything was green "from truck to keelson," claimed L. S. Young. An artificial waterfall was built amidships, surrounded by trees and flags and in front of the bank on which this work of art rested were the figures "1776" and "1897." In the background surmounting the fall was a reproduction of the "Liberty Bell" made from greens and flowers. Apparently, it was all so realistic that even the birds hanging in the drooping branches in their cages did not tumble and kept up a continual chirping and singing all day long.[48]

Daytime fireworks began at 8:00 A.M. and continued all day while the air was full of representations of Uncle Sam, Stars and Stripes, 1776, the Liberty Bell, and so forth. A few of these pyrotechnics "came near putting a few of the boys on the road to the undiscovered country." One hummed

Officers, men, and band in full-dress uniform salute
Commo. George Dewey as he comes aboard *Olympia* in 1898.

a tune like an 8-inch shell and struck the *Olympia*'s side within a foot of where some of the crew were standing, but they escaped. Sporting events began at 12:45 P.M. with the boats towed out to the light-ship off Honmoku. Hefty prizes, ranging from $22.00 to $26.00 per winning crew, awaited the 10- and 12-oar cutter, as well as gig and whaleboat races. Sampan races garnered but $2.00 and $3.00 by comparison. Deck sports—including tug-of-war, mast head racing, swimming, a 10-minute "Go as you please" race, cake walk, three-legged race, greasy pole, pie eating, horizontal bar, high jumping, threading the needle, and boxing—similarly promised anywhere from $3.00 to $20.00 to winners. Funding resulted from subscriptions, and there was even a fencing contest between Japanese sword masters. HMS *Grafton* and the French barbette battleship *Bayard* (which had come on station again) sent representatives. To the Yankees' chagrin, perhaps, "the Monsieurs" captured a prize for some excellent work on the horizontal bar. Any American pique dissipated a fortnight later when fifty *Olympia* crewmen went to dinner aboard the *Bayard* to help celebrate Bastille Day. If not a repetition of Vladivostok, the festivities must have been anything but dry.[49]

Sometime during the *Olympia*'s visit to Hong Kong, Read made a singular contribution to both the flagship's operational capabilities and posterity's knowledge of the details of his ship. Ever since coming out to the Far East, he had been actively compiling a *Hand Book* on the vessel. Now, he had it printed by Kelly and Walsh, Ltd., presumably in Hong Kong (although the firm had establishments in Shanghai and Yokohama as well). Perhaps it was to be a parting gesture to the officers and crew, since Read was due to leave the ship and return home. But from "A" to "V," his little sixty-one-page handbook was a delightful—even eclectic—potpourri of statistics and details about the ship and her equipment, the men and their prescribed rations, drainage and pumping, defending against torpedo attack, the ice machine, and finally, a rundown on her actual performance since going into commission. If nothing more, it was surely a godsend indeed for his replacement, Capt. Charles Vernon Gridley who arrived aboard the mail steamer *Gaelic* on 25 July.[50]

ENTER A NEW CAPTAIN

Nearly a month and a half earlier, Gridley had been ordered by Secretary of the Navy John Long to take the San Francisco steamer leaving on 5 July for the Far East. After a hasty courtesy call, Gridley went ashore to see friends, as he was well-known and liked in Yokohama, having captained the USS *Marion* there in 1890. The formal change of command ceremony took place on 29 July with crew mustered on the spar deck. Everyone wore dress blues, the ship's band complement aligned for its presentation, and Read issued his detachment order "appearing much affected and nearly losing control of his voice." Gridley commended the crew and ship, but failed to say anything about "whitewashing the books" (the traditional promotion of all hands to First class) to the crew's dismay. He read his relieving directive, took formal charge, and shortly before dinner Captain Read's gig pulled away from the *Olympia* for the last time as the crew rendered three rousing cheers as he passed abreast of the ship.[51]

Charles Vernon Gridley, Annapolis '64, had seen duty late in the Civil War, participating in the battle of Mobile Bay under David Farragut and displaying what his biographer later termed two prominent traits—"a quiet, dependable attention to duty" and a "certain decency and consideration in his dealings with others regardless of their position or status in life." His postwar service was typical for a cruising, slowly obsolescing wooden fleet, with duties occasionally ashore at the Naval Academy, the lighthouse board, and as ordnance officer at the Washington Navy Yard. "Capt. Gridley was not a 'dress parade' officer," declared one eulogist upon the captain's untimely death the following year. Enjoying a reputation among his peers as "one of the best equipped officers of the navy," he was a superb navigator through knowledge of all its details and requirements, pronounced Chief of Navigation Rear Adm. Francis Munroe Ramsay. Gridley was "one of the brainiest and pluckiest officers in the naval service," he added.[52]

Foreign eastern service aboard the USS *Marion* from 1892 to 1894 had acquainted Gridley with Asiatic waters. Avowedly more enamored with the quieter if older sailing ships of the *Constellation* type, he could no longer escape duty aboard vibrating, dirtier steam vessels. In this respect, he certainly had fellow spirits among the *Olympia*'s enlisted force. Seaman Gilbert H. Purdy—seventy years old at the time of the battle of Manila Bay the following year—had shipped out aboard whaling vessels before becoming a seaman in the navy. His tales of almost sixty years afloat were legendary. Now, he was definitely one of the old sailing salts remaining aboard the flagship. But Gridley, most especially, could not overlook one salient fact.

USS *Olympia* firing the George Washington's
birthday salute at Hong Kong in 1898.

While having to share his new ship with the squadron commander, his was a plum job. The *Olympia* was one of the most desirable new ships in the navy at that time.[53]

So, Gridley quietly took over the captain's stateroom and quarters from Read and by mid-month was busy digesting his predecessor's final "state-of-the-ship" report, sent to McNair on the sixteenth. Therein, Read chronicled the *Olympia*'s movements, noting 5,040 tons of coal consumed (at $55,950.86 U.S. money), the various military, gun, and torpedo drills, and a series of twenty-four turning trials conducted in Sendai Bay in June at speeds up to fifteen knots. But, Read also cited vital facts about the *Olympia*'s crew. Their health was good with only a 1.6 percent (129) sick rate going to the hospital (one invalided at home) and two deaths. There had been thirty-seven enlistments (of which twenty-six were reenlistments), thirty-two discharges, twenty-two desertions, and twenty courts-martial. Read had ordered some 916 punishments on his own, however.[54]

The summer of 1897 was a full one for the *Olympia*'s crew. Morale was high; comradery among the men of the Asiatic Squadron was strong. One of the sailors started an ice cream parlor on the *Olympia*'s berth deck, and L. S. Young decided that navy icons David Farragut and John Paul Jones would turn over in their graves at such frivolity. But, he quickly added, "why not have a few of the luxuries of civilized life when they can be had at the modest price of 15 cents a plate." Besides, he noted "the plates were shallow and the measure slim." Discovery of gold in the far off Alaskan Klondike caused everyone to include a visit there in their post-service plans. Sadder events claimed the lives of one of the marines and a young apprentice (the latter falling through an engine room hatch to the gratings above the cylinders), thus reminding everyone of the hazardous duty aboard ship. In fact, apprentice Wayne Longenecher's letters home to his brother were a litany of barroom and brothel battles with civilian Japanese, and Read, before he left, had been forced to publish a general order against throwing "heavy pieces of coal" at Japanese policemen "upon their leaving the ship's side after having delivered on board men for whom rewards had been offered." So the period was one of unruliness and high spirits. Then, on 15 September, *Olympia* left again for Chefoo to transfer all the time-expired men to the *Yorktown*, bound for San Francisco, and to the tiny gunboat *Machias*, bound for New York. When the Far East squadron rendezvoused for this purpose, McNair found he had the *Boston, Yorktown, Machias,* and *Petrel* together with the *Olympia* all ready to shift incoming and outgoing personnel. This time-honored navy tradition always proved to be sheer madhouse for the duration of the exercise.[55]

In the autumn, the cruiser moved to Woosung, China, where McNair temporarily transferred his flag to the old side-wheel gunboat *Monocacy*, whose light draught enabled her to go far inland up rivers in China to protect American and European interests. The *Olympia* remained saltwater bound during his absence while her boys honed their team skills at football, baseball, and boat racing against teams from Shanghai as well as the fleet. Somebody told the press that the son of an English peer was among the flagship's crew and a group styled the "Regular Army and Navy Union" invited Olympians to a 10 P.M. "Entertainment and Banquet" at the Central Hotel on 23 October. Then, returning to Nagasaki in early November, the ship gave birth to her famous newspaper *The Bounding Billow* with

L. S. Young at the helm. The first edition was filled with chatter about shipboard life, including pictures of galley crew, "the hurdy gurdy brigade" or sewing machine attendants, as well as newsy items about happenings elsewhere in the squadron or aboard other nations' warships, such as the drain burst aboard HMS *Narcissus* which nearly flooded the ship. Tongue-in-cheek advertisements for specialists in tailoring, barbering, and even the Concordia Restaurant ashore in Nagasaki edified the *Olympia*'s sailors. One item surely struck their eye—announcement that their genial admiral was due a replacement on the day before Christmas. Taking his place would be Commo. George Dewey, under whom the *Olympia* would secure, perhaps, her greatest moment in history.[56]

First Read and then Gridley began making a trim ship of the *Olympia*. True, there were a few overly zealous junior officers, including one lieutenant who boasted that "he would make a redhot flag ship out of us," one seaman wrote his brother in October 1897. But he quickly overstepped his charge by putting the headstrong young Americans on report too frequently and they bucked him on at least one boat drill, causing Gridley himself to intervene and warn his young subordinate about his heavy handedness. Gambling, smoking, and whoring ashore are predictable of sailors in most eras, and given the steam and steel's typical cramped quarters, sooty and often overheated interior space, shore leave could naturally produce its share of brawls and brushes with local authorities. Pictures of the time, however, portray robust, biceps-bulging, handlebar-mustachioed young Tars like landsman and coal passer Frank Seideman. Years later, he responded to a government survey about his naval service aboard the *Olympia* with glowing comments about clothing, equipment, and rations as well as discipline and what he thought of the ship's officers. Having enlisted in November of 1896 at age eighteen, he would have three years to develop his opinions of life aboard the "Queen of the Pacific."[57]

As for the *Olympia* herself, the public press as well as the professional naval community had followed her story across the Pacific. Enthralled by this new American warship, in March of 1896 the *Scientific American* proclaimed boldly that the cruiser could easily challenge comparison with any other protected cruiser in the world in one respect. "There is no other ship which can show on a given displacement so high a development of the various qualities which go to make up the efficiency of this type of warship," claimed the writer. Pointing to the "Genius of the designer" as the key, especially in weight distribution, he suggested that the most successful ship would be that which secured a high all-around efficiency without the sacrifice of any other essential feature. That is, it would be relatively easy to build a ship which should be at once the fastest, and best protected, most heavily armed, and have the greatest coal endurance of any ship in the world—provided there were no limits upon displacement. The *Columbia* therefore could steam at 23 knots speed against the *Olympia*'s 21.68 knots. But, to get the extra speed, she had to sacrifice her offensive power to such an extent that she would be easy prey to the smaller ship in a naval duel.[58]

The *Scientific American* then compared the *Olympia* (5,800 tons, 17,363 horsepower, 21.68-knot speed, 2–4³/₄-inch protective deck, 400 ton coal capacity [sic], and thirty-eight guns including 6-pounders, both 5-inch and 8-inch calibers) with two British-produced warships from the Armstrong company of Newcastle-upon-Tyne. These ships were the *Eclipse* (5,600 tons, 9,600 horsepower, 19.5-knot speed, 2¹/₂-inch protective deck, 550 ton coal capacity, and twenty-five guns including 3-inch, 4.7-inch, and 6-inch calibers) as well as the *Blanco Encalada* (4,400 tons, 14,500 horsepower, 22.78-knot speed, 1³/₄–4-inch protective deck, 900 ton coal capacity, and twenty-four guns including 6-inch and 8-inch calibers). Yet, in the end, despite his quotation of numerous statistics, what the author seemed to be pointing to as the *Olympia*'s defining difference rested with the nickel steel turrets and conning tower armor, superior variety and range of armament, the triple-expansion engines, and an expandable coal bunker capacity for 1,093 tons.

Later that same year, Lt. John M. Ellicott regaled a prestigious Naval Institute audience at Annapolis regarding the composition of the fleet. Suggesting the need for an "armored cruiser class to fall upon the enemy's communications, to strike at his outlying possession which might form bases of operations against us, or to send quickly to our neighbor's aid if foreign powers attempt by force to encroach upon their territory," Ellicott also envisioned them in a fleet engagement as "reinforcement of the fighting line, to destroy or capture crippled adversaries or to pursue and destroy the individual vessels of a routed enemy." He advocated a one-to-one ratio between such a class of vessel and battleships. "As many *New Yorks* as we have *Indianas*," was the way he put it. Commo. C. C. Todd agreed, but in subsequent discussions, he noted that "I would prefer an enlarged Olympia of not exceeding 7,000 tons, which would give her a light armor belt to keep out light projectiles." And, said Todd, for twenty battleships there should be "twenty armored cruisers—improved Olympias," if admittedly for coast defense (as the official policy of the time had it). This idea of an advanced *Olympia*-class never gained momentum and her design was never replicated. Still, even at this point, the *Olympia* was being thought about less as a raider indigenous to her class and more as a fighting ship with wider possibilities.[59]

3

The Heroes of
Manila Bay

THE BEST GIFT

The highlight of the winter should have been Commo. George Dewey's succession to command of the Asiatic Squadron aboard the *Olympia* on 3 January 1898. Having just turned sixty-one years old, the Civil War veteran sailor, whom Pulitzer Prize–author Margaret Leech once described as that "fit, ruddy little Vermonter with frosty hair and mustache and an authoritarian manner," had arrived at Yokohama on Christmas Day aboard the Pacific mail steamer *Gaelic*. As he had told a family member back in November, "I have received what is to me the best gift the President could make"—a command in the Far East. A week later, he went on to Nagasaki, passing New Year's weekend sequestered with Rear Adm. F. V. McNair and getting briefed on his new duties and command. Promptly at 9:00 A.M. on Monday, amid dress blue uniforms, cocked hats, frock coats, and gold-knotted swords, the band played "the Admiral's March," Capt. Charles Vernon Gridley of the *Olympia* read the proper order of the day, and Dewey announced his directive from the Navy Department. The top brass saluted one another and a broad blue pennant with the single star of a commodore replaced the two-star rear admiral's pennant atop *Olympia*'s main mast.[1]

AN UNSETTLED FAR EAST

McNair had prepared a long official letter transmitting the files and records of the command to Dewey. In it he discussed the situation in the Far East and the condition of the squadron. Only four ships were on station, he told Dewey, the modern cruisers *Olympia* (alternating between Japanese ports Yokohama and Nagasaki) and *Boston,* one of the original "ABCD" New Steel Navy ships of the previous decade and assigned to safeguard American interests in Korea. The others were the smaller gunboat *Petrel* and the ancient paddle steamer *Monocacy,* good only for riverine duty at Shanghai. The gunboat *Machias* was even then transiting the Indian Ocean en route home. Two additional cruisers were due out in the new year—the *Raleigh,* coming via Suez, and the diminutive *Concord,* steaming across the Pacific from Mare Island. McNair anticipated few problems. True, there was a "distinct lack of friendliness on the part of the Japanese," he concluded, and the German seizure of Kiaochow the previous November as part of imperialist moves in China "require[s] careful watching." But he discounted rumors about other European intrusions on the Asian mainland at China's expense. Besides, McNair was a lame duck, going on to other duties. It would be Dewey's responsibility to keep an eye on the British, Russian, French, German, and Japanese activities in the region.[2]

Indeed, Dewey was quite aware of the strategic situation. He had written his son in January that everyone was "playing a big game of bluff" over who would carve more territory out of China. All were hungry for mining concessions, commercial zones, naval bases, and inland railway construction designed to open the heartland to trade. So, commenting upon the arrival of a Russian squadron at Port Arthur later that winter, Dewey opined that he would not be surprised to see a "general war at any time." The commodore further wrote his sister in February that "England, Russia, and Germany have largely increased their naval forces in the Orient," and the United States was doing likewise. American ships were largely in Chinese and Korean waters "looking out for a right to protect American interests," of which there were many. "What we all want is Chinese trade, and we are gradually getting more and more of it, all of which we would lose were it not well known that we are ready and will protect it." Still, as he admitted, meeting the Russian and English admirals while at Nagasaki had been unsettling. While both were most agreeable and able men, "the former has no less than twenty, and the latter thirty, vessels of war under their command." Therefore, Dewey maintained a steady correspondence with the *Monocacy*'s commander in order to be kept abreast of political affairs via the Shanghai listening post.[3]

McNair and Dewey differed on another point. The departing admiral held little notice of events in the Spanish Philippines. In fact, recalled Dewey, the only reference to the Philippines in McNair's transmittal letter was a short paragraph to the effect that newspaper accounts from the islands told of a rebellion in progress but that no official information had been received on that matter. Further, there had been "no information of any sort that shows American interests to be affected." Dewey, by contrast, went to the Far East not only with greater knowledge of and interest in the islands (he had spent his last days in Washington and the passage out reading and reflecting on the situation there), but with a keen awareness of his own responsibilities in that region. From his recent tours with the Navy Department (the last being as Chief of the Board of Inspection and Survey) and membership in certain political salons of the American capital, Dewey knew of contingency planning that had been going on for several years concerning possible war with Spain. While Spanish Caribbean possessions seemed to be the primary target of American interest, the Philippines also featured in war schemes. Moreover, in some circles the energetic Dewey's name was thought to have been put forward as point man by navalists and expansionists, like Asst. Secretary of the Navy Theodore Roosevelt and his friend Sen. Henry Cabot Lodge, for aggressive action against Spain. In the end, however, even Secretary of the Navy John C. Long recognized Dewey as best able to implement a decisive naval strike at the Philippines—should it come to that.[4]

In retrospect, at least, it appeared that George Dewey had been quietly but steadily preparing for war from the moment of his appointment. Aware of the unsatisfactory condition of the squadron's ammunition supplies from his stint with the Inspection and Survey Board, Dewey secured departmental permission to have the *Concord* bring out a partial allotment, with the rest to come with the *Baltimore* later in the spring. Then he made a stopover at Mare Island Navy Yard before departing the West Coast to ensure that Cdr. Asa Walker understood the urgency of the *Concord*'s mission in that regard when it joined the squadron early in the new year. That was a sensible precaution for a relieving officer to be properly prepared for any emergency in his new command. Dewey was aware of strained Spanish-American relations, and the distinct possibility that hostilities could break out in the new year.[5]

A PERIOD OF UNCERTAINTY

Dewey's most immediate duty upon arriving in Japan was to take the *Olympia* through the straits of Tsushima to Yokahoma from which he would go to Tokyo for an audience with the emperor. This custom of each new commander in chief on station had fallen into neglect, but Dewey determined to reinstate the practice. It was part of the commodore's building of good will given the incendiary nature of Asia. Yet, if *Olympia's* shipboard newspaper was any indication, the men in the fleet were more interested in several deaths among their comrades, various sporting bouts that attended peacetime duty on station, and various humorous incidents that enlivened the male cloister that was the navy of the time. No one on the *Olympia* or anywhere else in the squadron was too concerned that war might break out thousands of miles from Asia in the Caribbean. Except that Dewey received Secretary Long's short but portentous 27 January telegram, "Retain until further orders the crew of the squadron whose terms of enlistment have expired." Obviously, seasoned crews could be important in the event of conflict.[6]

Dewey was more worried that he was about to lose Gridley and the *Olympia* in the customary rotation of ships on station. This "will be a great sorrow" to me, he wrote an old friend, Capt. William H. Emory, soon to go to the European station on 5 February. The *Baltimore* was due to exchange stations with Dewey's flagship unless, of course, the international situation deteriorated in some manner. Meanwhile, the commodore seemed to enjoy his life in the Far East far more than he expected. On 29 January, he had hosted "ten ladies and gentlemen at 'tiffin', as they call a luncheon in the East." The three-hour fête aboard the flagship was resplendent with Chinese stewards robed as if they were Buddhist priests while Bandmaster M. Valifuco had the *Olympia's* band entertain the party with a full program of marches, overtures, waltzes, polkas, and other pieces, ending with "The Star Spangled Banner" (not as yet the national anthem but symbolic nonetheless).[7]

Arrival of the *Concord* on 9 February, after a peaceful fourteen-day voyage from Honolulu (with thirty-five tons of much needed ammunition), meant spelling the *Boston*, which had been observing Russo-Japanese enmity at Chelmpo (Inchon), Korea, for some time. Following ammunition transfer the next day, the "Queen of the Pacific" left for Hong Kong on the eleventh. She was to rendezvous with the tiny gunboat *Petrel* (affectionately dubbed the "baby battleship" because of her four outsized 6-inch guns), under orders to reach Canton in time for expected anti-foreign demonstrations attending Chinese New Year celebrations. Dewey recounted in his memoirs that his decision to change base to Hong Kong came "without any hint whatever from the department that hostilities might be expected [with Spain]." Of course, he added retrospectively, it was certainly evident that in case of emergency "Hong Kong was the most advantageous position from which to move to attack" the Spanish Philippines.[8]

Before leaving Japanese waters, the *Olympia*'s crew managed to batter the local Yokohama rugby team 24 to 10, and that sent everyone off in happy spirits. The *Olympia* arrived at the British crown colony on 17 February in a thick fog. That night, all hands learned that the battleship USS *Maine* had blown up half a globe away in the harbor of Spanish-owned Havana, Cuba. "We were just preparing for Washington's Birthday" noted *Bounding Billow* editor L. S. Young, "but this terrible news cast a gloom over the crew and of course pleasures were laid aside." War, and nothing but war, with Spain became the topic of the day, he added. Still, contemporary photographs show the ship firing salute guns and festooned with flags for the holiday. Her superstructure still bore stark white paint while her stacks were now a darker buff with black bands at the top. A black stripe adorned her sheer.[9]

On 25 February, Asst. Secretary of the Navy Theodore Roosevelt sent Dewey his famous (if slightly premature and presumptuous order, given Secretary Long's absence that day) to concentrate the squadron at Hong Kong (except for the *Monocacy*) and "keep full of coal." Dewey was told that, in the event of a war declaration, "your duty will be to see that the Spanish Squadron does not leave the Asiatic coast, and then offensive operations in Philippine Islands." He could keep the *Olympia* until further orders. When Long returned the next day he canceled all of Roosevelt's directives but the one to Dewey. Quietly making war preparations on his own, Long again wired Dewey that same day to "keep full of coal—the best that can be had."[10]

In fact, the uncertainty of news from the outside world caused the crew of the *Olympia* to collect $340 for their own cable link (via *The Army and Navy Journal*) to provide information on the deteriorating situation. War preparations seemed active, the country greatly excited, was the message reaching the sailors. But Congress was delaying action pending investigation into the *Maine* disaster. Mails from the States in early March confirmed this information, as well as word that homeward-bound orders for the flagship had been shelved. Then the war fever tapered off, although the *Baltimore* was still coming out from Hawaii with additional ammunition. Meanwhile, the *Olympia*'s crew concentrated on a scrum of rugby with a combined team from the fleet at "Happy Valley," the local sports park out on the Queens Road about three miles from Victoria. Cuba's woes had never truly bothered the Americans, but "we were now every man anxious to avenge the Maine and our slaughtered shipmates," for nobody doubted that it was an act of Spanish treachery.[11]

Far East tensions remained high. Soon after the arrival of the Americans in Hong Kong, they were followed by the German cruiser *Gefion*, flying the pennant of the Kaiser's brother, Prince Henry—"a thorough sailor who had really worked up through all the grades from midshipman to rear-admiral," recalled Dewey. But, when some of that ship's crew came aboard the *Olympia*, one of them was recognized as a deserter from the "Queen of the Pacific." The German rear admiral refused to yield him over to the Americans, declaring that he was a German subject. A nasty little impasse ensued, further stoked by slights (at least in Dewey's opinion) to the American head of state and national air (confusion reigning at the time as to whether the latter was "Hail Columbia" or "The Star Spangled Banner"). All of this suggested future trouble with the Germans, except that even the American commodore acknowledged pleasant social engagements with the Crown Prince, where the two bantered about what each other's country really wanted out of the imperial scramble in the region. "We only need a bay," the cocky Vermonter told Prince Henry in jest.[12]

WAR PLANS AND PREPARATIONS

By April, developments took a decided turn toward hostilities—not with Germany but with Spain. East coast newspapers in the United States had been speculating for some time that the *Olympia/Baltimore* exchange would devolve into retention of both ships due to the onset of war. Besides, the second cruiser had far too much ammunition picked up from the USS *Mohican* in Hawaii for the squadron unless both warships remained on station. Meanwhile, Long wired Dewey several times in early April about provisioning his ships and purchasing several extra supply vessels for an expeditionary squadron. Dewey at first chartered then purchased the collier *Nanshan*, followed three days later by the steamer *Zafiro* as Long now counseled the urgency for action. They were towed to the American squadron's anchorage and loaded with coal. That evening, a draft of fifty sailors arrived from the *Monocacy* (thought too old for combat and left on "Pie Row" at Shanghai).[13]

The *Olympia*'s seamen placed bets that war would begin within two weeks. Carpenter crews began turning out toboggan-like stretchers. The quartermasters likewise busied themselves making new flags as signal codes were changed in keeping with heightened security. Engineer and medical inspections of the flagship reported universally good structural and sanitary conditions although there appeared to be a chronic problem with continuously wet provisions in the hold that prevented compartment D-4 from ever being in perfect order. Pres. William McKinley's war message to Congress finally arrived on 12 April, and all ships were coaled and made ready to move at a moment's notice. Still, the crews of *Olympia* and *Raleigh* managed a boat race between them with thousands of dollars riding on the outcome. The flagship's boat "The Yellow Kid" won handily.[14]

The revenue marine cutter *McCulloch* stood in from New York on 17 April. She had been on her shakedown cruise to the Bering Sea via San Francisco. But, due to the situation, she was held over awaiting developments. Two days later, Dewey's squadron plus the *McCulloch* doffed war paint—a dark slate color, with the faintest tinge of green. It made *Olympia* seem cool and big, said Young, adding that "she looks as though she could ladle out steel passports to that warmer clime where quarter sections are given away gratis." Meanwhile, a confident Dewey wrote his sister on 18 April that while still awaiting the declaration of war "to begin our work here," his seven ships were ready for action and "should war be the word, I believe we will make short work of the Spanish reign in the Philippines." Filipino insurgents were ready to rise "at our first gun," he suggested and long before the letter would reach her, "we may be masters at Manila and other Philippines cities." He felt that "with the force under my command, I could enter the bay of Manila, capture or destroy the Spanish squadron and reduce the defenses in one day."[15]

Rough weather did not hamper the *Baltimore's* arrival on the evening of 21 April, and all hands breathed easier fearing that she might have been intercepted by the Spanish far eastern squadron from the Philippines. Her arrival rounded out Dewey's battle fleet just as the latest telegram from Washington announced that, even though war had not yet been declared, the North Atlantic Squadron was blockading Cuba. The *Baltimore* went into dry dock on the twenty-third, and the very next day the long-awaited telegram arrived from Washington. "War has commenced between the United States and Spain," wired Long. Proceed at once to the Philippines and commence operations, "particularly against the Spanish fleet." Dewey was to "use utmost endeavors" to capture vessels or destroy them. Then the Americans received their "walking papers" from Hong Kong's governor as no combatant vessels could remain over forty-eight hours in a neutral port after a declaration of war. Farewells were made among the professionals at the crown colony and, as Dewey recorded in his autobiography, a certain pessimism pervaded their hosts as to the Americans' success. "A fine set of fellows, but unhappily we shall never see them again," was the rather pompous send-off by one set of British regimental officers.[16]

Dewey later told John Barrett (sometime U.S. minister to Siam and consul general at Singapore who accompanied him to the Philippines aboard the *Olympia*), that his subsequent success in the Philippines "was won in Hong-kong Harbor." The period spent at the British possession had been well used by the commodore and his ships' captains. True, his own personality was strong, prompt, and decisive in action, but he was also deliberate and sure in preparation. Knowing that his squadron was thousands of miles from any home base, he had to ensure its survival. Logistics assumed a primary importance. But so too was the forging of a battle team—a team that allowed subordinates to provide their impressions and opinions, suggest alternative preparations for combat and tactics, and then congeal around a final plan that was Dewey's alone. The period also afforded an opportunity to obtain intelligence from civilian ship captains arriving from the Philippines as well as Dewey's own agent in the Spanish colony.[17]

Given the British ultimatum, *Boston, Petrel, Concord, McCulloch, Nan-*

shan and *Zafiro* left immediately on 24 April to the cheers of a passing English hospital ship, recounted one *Olympia* crewman, Wayne Longenecher. As Chinese officials had as yet not clamped similar neutrality restrictions upon the belligerent, they found temporary sanctuary thirty miles north of Hong Kong in Mirs Bay. The *Olympia* and *Baltimore* remained behind to keep company with the *Raleigh*, experiencing engine trouble (our port circulating pump, said Asst. Surgeon Dudley Newcomb Carpenter, broken by "a careless oiler just as we were about to leave on Sunday"). Even then, according to marine Lt. Dion Williams, aboard the *Baltimore*, "The English authorities were very kind to us and allowed us to coal even after war was declared." By the 25th, however, these remaining American warships had also moved to Mirs Bay to finish combat preparations. Gridley wrote home that "Of course, we really have no right here, but China, poor China, can't help herself." All she could do would be to protest, he told his wife, and "that we would pay no attention to." Furthermore, he told his wife to keep his son in school and not to let him enlist as "there are plenty of older people to attend to that." Besides, "I fancy the war will not last long."[18]

Two years earlier, during one of the periodic flare-ups with Spain over Cuba, Gridley had told a Buffalo, New York, group that Spain was hardly a worthy enemy. Poorly manned and uncared for, "in her navy, as in everything else, Spain is far behind the times." Based on personal observation during his cruises, "everybody knows that Spain is 150 years behind the age," a third-rate power and bankrupt, "a true Bourbon country—learns nothing, forgets nothing," he had sneered. "So far as the discipline of the men and esprit de corps are concerned her navy compares with ours about as the Chinese navy compared with that of Japan during the recent wars," he continued. Besides, the Spanish are very poor sailors—"not at all like they were two centuries ago." He then regaled his audience with a rundown of American warships—including the *Olympia*—which would be mustered as a powerful battle fleet to overwhelm any Spanish threat to Atlantic coast cities or American commerce. Granted, "we can't do without coaling stations of our own, as coal is contraband of war, the same as powder." But, "on the whole, I think a war with Spain would be a picnic for us," Gridley had concluded.[19]

That had been in the spring of 1896. Now, two years later in far eastern waters, a mere squadron—not a whole battle fleet—prepared to make good

Gridley's prediction. Missing were those American coaling stations alluded to by Gridley. Still, as the *New York Sun* suggested on 6 March 1898, the Asiatic Squadron's concentration at Hong Kong was "a significant move, since this southerly rendezvous is so near the Philippines as to make the short run thither, followed by active operations, practicable without anxiety to coal supply." For the moment, however, more immediate concerns occupied captain and admiral aboard the *Olympia*.[20]

Almost all navies at this point in time were terrified of torpedo boat assault. And so, Dewey's men had their first war scare in this regard as they made their preparations in Mirs Bay. About midnight on 25 April, a tug boat or launch was seen coming in and everyone suspected a torpedo boat attack. The flagship turned a searchlight on her and sounded general quarters. But it proved to be a dispatch boat from Hong Kong and, after establishing a quarter watch to guard against future surprises, recorded Young, "we piped down." Nevertheless, observed Longenecher, "The people on the tug told us they thought their time had come when the search light we turned on them and they saw the guns swing around on them." Subsequently, everyone was more alert when, according to Dewey, the tug *Fame* arrived on the morning of 27 April. Aboard were reporters and Consul O. F. Williams, late of Manila, with the latest intelligence data from the Philippines. A command conference of ship captains convened aboard the *Olympia*. Signal flags fluttered up the mast to prepare to get under way and fires stoked to get up steam. By 2:00 P.M., Williams was safely aboard the *Baltimore* and each captain back on his own ship. The squadron was in motion. Long's telegraphic orders in hand, Dewey and the *Olympia* led the way out of Mirs Bay.[21]

RENDEZVOUS WITH DESTINY

Dewey and his nine ships put to sea from Mirs Bay shortly after noon on 27 April. When John Barrett, acting now as a special war correspondent, queried one 8-inch gunner on the *Olympia* as to their destination and purpose he got back the clipped answer, "Go and do? Damn little did I or any one else on this ship care as long as the old man was ordering it." We knew we were going to a hot place and meant to make it more so, he continued, "but, man, we would have sailed straight into hell after him!" Under sealed orders and with "nine crews bursting with expectancy," the Olympians in particular were piped to quarters at 5:00 P.M., where they listened to the reading of Long's 24 April dispatch to Dewey. "Proceed at once to Manila; engage and destroy the Spanish fleet, when and where you find them," was the way Landsman John T. ["L. G. T." or "Lieu"] Tisdale remembered the moment. "We went mad with joy," he added. The news was quickly signaled from ship to ship, and before "lights out" that night, a new battle flag was begun—and finished. The placing of each star proved that every state in the Union had its representative aboard the flagship. Tisdale carefully marked California and his name on the back of one and then sewed it to the blue field.[22]

Of course, there was more to the preparations than flag sewing. The next morning, orders came from Gridley and his officers to "clear for action." This meant shedding anything that might duplicate Sino-Japanese war experience, where flying wood splinters from battle damage had caused frightful casualties. So spars, hatch covers, chests, and other removable woodwork was taken apart and either thrown overboard or stowed carefully aboard the *Nanshan* and *Zafiro*. From wainscoting to bunks, turpentine, shellac and varnish chests, and wooden ceilings, everything wooden in nature went overboard. The sea, observed Lt. John Ellicott of the *Baltimore* "was strewn for fifty leagues" (150 miles) in the ships' wakes. Even the most prized possessions of the sailors—their ditty boxes—were rumored to be in jeopardy. But Dewey—"the little Commodore, with the fate of a nation fluttering in his hand"—came to the rescue. He thought it an outrage to take from the men the only thing the navy allowed them to hold sacred. So he asked Gridley to let the crew stash their ditties below the protective deck, to the everlasting gratitude of Tisdale and his mates. "Good-by, Diddy, until—until we meet again," were Tisdale's parting words.[23]

Ironically, Dewey, the fastidious member of Washington's fashionable Metropolitan Club, probably saved the *Olympia*'s interior appearance for future appreciative generations by his unwillingness to see his flagship ripped apart. As Apprentice Seaman Longenecher remarked to his brother, the *Boston* tore out everything as did most of the other ships, "but us, we didn't tare [sic] out any wood work at all only covered it with canvas and splinter nets." Most of his mates "are growling about it as they would sooner have seen all the wood work go so that there would be no chance of a fire being started by an exploding shell." But it turned out all right, he noted, "as the Admiral knew just what we were going up against and their [sic] is no more criticism no matter what he does."[24]

At this point, Consul Williams, who had slipped out of Manila one step ahead of Spanish officials, a mob, or an assassin because of his espionage activities, injected a new tidbit of information. It was a piece of inflammatory propaganda calculated to prompt the ire of all the American lads in Dewey's fleet. The Spanish governor general at Manila, Gen. Basilio Augustin y Davila, had issued a proclamation designed to spur resistance and war spirit in the islands. Claiming that "the North American people constituted of all the social excrescencies" had exhausted Spanish patience and provoked war with their "acts of treachery" and "outrages against the laws of nations and international treaties," the governor claimed the resulting struggle will be short and decisive. "The God of victories," he noted, "would provide a victory as complete as the righteousness and justice of our cause." Claiming the sympathies of all nations, he then blasted the adventurers from those States who "without cohesion and without a history, offer to humanity only infamous traditions and a Congress in which appear united insolence and defamation, cowardice and cynicism."[25]

None of this propaganda would have necessarily enraged the *Olympia's* sailors when posted on the ship's bulletin board, had not the Spaniard attacked them directly in his diatribe. A squadron manned by foreigners, "possessing neither instruction or discipline," he continued, was bent on coming to the Philippines to rob us of all that means life, honor and liberty. Pretending to be inspired by "a courage of which they are incapable," the North American seamen were undertaking a Protestant crusade against Catholicism, a blatant move to "treat you as tribes refractory to civilization" and to take the Filipinos' property and enslave their people. Suggesting the courage and valor of the islanders would suffice to punish and abuse the people that "claiming to be civilized and cultivate, have exterminated the natives of North America instead of bringing to them the life of civilization and progress," the governor called on everyone to prepare for the struggle, unite under the glorious flag of Spain, "and oppose with the decision of the Christian and the patriot the cry of 'Viva Espana.'"[26]

This "unjust and cowardly manifesto prompted the anger and indignation of every man in the fleet," noted *Bounding Billow* editor Young. Many and deep were the growls and threats, he claimed, and the learned Spanish governor general would have "fared badly" had he been at hand. Apprentice Longenecher was even more colorful, claiming "Everybody swore that if we captured him we would print 2,000 copies [of the proclamation] and make him eat every one of them." Young felt compelled to respond in kind through the squadron's newspaper so as to whip up fighting spirits in Dewey's flotilla. Predictable counterclaims concerning Spanish colonial brutality, Old Glory's honor, and "crimes that none but the lowest of Lucifer's emissaries would commit" spewed forth from Young's pen in turn. "It is to avenge these wrongs, to give blessed liberty to an oppressed and down-trodden nation, and to uphold the honor of our country, that we are going to war with Spain," he trumpeted. Finally, he suggested to his shipmates that when they got to Manila and met the Spanish murderers, "let our battle cry be—'Remember the *Maine* and down with Spain!'"[27]

In the meantime, Dewey and his ships' captains continued more practical preparations for the impending contest. Steaming silently through the South China Sea, they drilled and trimmed both ships and crews. Barbers shaved each crewman's hair close to the scalp, since the surgeons "say hair is as dangerous as cloth in a wound." It was news to Tisdale, he observed, that the order "Clear for Action" necessitated that sacrifice. But the medics themselves, ghoulish in their pre-battle gallows humor, prepared *Olympia*'s wardroom as an emergency hospital. One junior surgeon, taking a cigarette from his mouth while sitting on the edge of the long table, warned one work gang, "God pity any of you poor devils who come under this" while brandishing an ugly surgeon's knife.[28]

There were countless other duties and drills at this point. The flagship's band struck up "some of our old war songs" on the twenty-eighth, and everybody was singing and having a good time in general," noted Longenecher. Battle stations could be cleanly manned and final preparations undertaken. The apprentice noted that the cooks had thrown all the mess tables overboard except six or seven before they were stopped and, on 29 April—"We got up the sheet chains and staked [sic] them up and down on the for[e] part of the superstructure in [the] wake of the ammunition hoists to serve as armor." Awning stanchions were also lashed, he said, in the wake of the other ammunition hoist, and iron shutters were lashed in the fore rigging to keep the small-caliber bullets from raking the upper decks. At the same time, boats, spars, and booms were similarly lashed, while hoses were connected with hydrants and laid along the deck.[29]

Ammunition stood at hand everywhere, the guns were soon loaded, and the order "cast loose and provide" occasioned the metallic sounds of breech blocks closing around the ship. There was a new sound now, claimed Tisdale—not the customary click of steel that had attended the hundreds of practice drills in the past. Rather, "a muffled something that shut in a full charge" rippled through each gun crew's very being. "I cannot tell what it was," claimed the landsman, but "I know that every man who fought a gun that day realizes what I mean, and it was impossible to make one who has never heard it understand." From the moment the guns were loaded and trained, there wasn't half the excitement manifested by every boat race and other competition, said Tisdale. Yet no pen could portray "the sensations that alternately raged and slept within our breasts that night" before Manila Bay.[30]

The 628-mile trip southeastward to the Philippines passed uneventfully, despite earlier American fears that the Spaniards might sortie to intercept their flotilla. As Assistant Surgeon Carpenter aboard the *Raleigh* wrote his mother, "The squadron sailed very auspiciously and [a] gorgeous trip of three days was made; moonlight nights, calm seas, and all that sort of thing." The Spanish, it seems, were concerned with defensive preparations in the islands and harbored no offensive thoughts of any kind in their war planning. There was probably very little that they could have done anyway. Their colonial troops were engaged in constabulary and counter-insurrectionist duties. From 1885 (updated seven years later), the defense of Manila, the capital, rested with massive, archaic masonry fortifications mounting a veritable museum of antique artillery pieces and a landward string of fortified strong points to deter insurrectionists. Sea defense remained with Rear Adm. Patricio Montojo y Pasaron's small hodgepodge squadron of rotting wooden and obsolescent steel warships, hardly the equal of other rapidly modernizing world-class navies and certainly incapable of Mahanite high-seas combat.[31]

Too late into the escalating imbroglio with the United States, Spain's liberal home government in Madrid realized that it needed to strengthen its overseas possession. The *Isla de Mindinao* was dispatched with modern ordnance, underwater mines, and other munitions. It would arrive almost on the eve of the American attack and too late for rapid emplacement by lethargic colonial and military officials in the Philippines. By contrast, the administration in Washington was bent on using newfound American naval power to win a quick victory over Spain once war was declared, thereby forcing independence of Cuba but little else. "No annexationist aims were contemplated" for Dewey and his expedition, concludes historian David Trask. So the issue revolved around the navies.[32]

Steaming along at eight knots over a smooth sea, the *Olympia* and her sister ships ran at night with only stern lights showing. They were "just sufficient to gauge distance," opined seaman Tisdale, and such precautions took on an intensity as they approached the Philippine coast. Dewey anticipated making landfall at Cape Bolinao, a Luzon headland about thirty-five miles north of the entrance to Manila Bay, near Subic Bay where Consul Williams had earlier indicated Montojo planned to force the Americans to do battle. Indeed, Subic lay on the flank and rear of any expedition advancing directly to take Manila. Thus, it had to be dealt with. Well considered in prewar Spanish planning, Dewey and Montojo missed meeting in Subic Bay by perhaps twenty-four hours. The Spaniard had taken his squadron there from Manila over the night of 25/26 April only to discover the unreadiness of the place for planned battle. Despite easily six weeks of lead time, local engineers and naval Captain Del Rio had accomplished practically nothing. Insurgents had robbed submarine mines of explosives, four 5.9-inch guns had not yet been mounted, and the Spaniards generally had wasted precious time, displaying little energy and enthusiasm for any impending battle.[33]

It was about this time that the Spanish consul in Hong Kong wired Montojo that Dewey had departed Mirs Bay headed for Subic. Montojo reported later that he "had still held a hope that the Americans would not go to Subic, and give us time for more preparations," but "this telegram demonstrated that the enemy knew where they could find my squadron and that the port of Subic had no defenses." His options evaporated as the hours ticked away. Actually, he had been most desirous of confronting the Americans at the very entrance to Manila Bay where a combination of mines and shore batteries might have best denied passage. But the water was deep at this point (thereby adding to lifesaving difficulties in any combat), he

claimed. Electrical wire for the mines proved lacking and the available ordnance on Corregidor near Boca Grande or the main entry could only briefly
deter a determined invader.[34]

Subic had been the first alternative. Barring that option, however, the
Cavite naval station or even under Manila City's fortress guns offered possibilities. However, political concern for a battle's impact upon the capital
should it take place in adjacent waters negated that option. Far from
defending the city, said Montojo, "this would provoke the enemy to bombard the plaza, which doubtless would have been demolished on account
of its few defenses." True, he might have led the Americans on a running
"hide and seek" game elsewhere in the islands had he planned better. This
approach might even have helped save the Spanish possession. But coal
and provisions had been stockpiled only at Subic and, in the end, Montojo
was simply forced to take his meager flotilla back to Manila and anchor in
shallow water in the Gulf of Canacao (within Manila Bay proper) off
Cavite where his naval guns could be joined by those of batteries at Sangley Point and Ulloa. So, he had left Subic at 10:00 A.M. on the twenty-
ninth in such shaky condition that the transport *Manila* had to tow the now
inert *Castilla* (her leakage having been sealed with concrete thereby rendering her engines inoperable). Arriving at his anchorage that afternoon,
little wonder that the Spaniard projected a rather defeatist, lethargic
defender of Crown rule in the Philippines.[35]

LANDFALL

Meanwhile, Dewey remained unaware of all this. Lookouts in *Olympia*'s
crow's nest spied the outline of Cape Bolinao at 2:45 A.M. on the last day
of April. The flotilla "kept about five or six miles from the coast line, keeping a bright look-out for men-o'-war or other craft of the enemy," reported
the *Bounding Billow*'s editor. About an hour and fifteen minutes later, Dewey
directed the *Boston* and *Concord* to reconnoiter Subic Bay. Anxiously awaiting the result, the report came back in mid-afternoon that Spanish ships
were nowhere to be seen. "Now we have them!" shouted Dewey at the
news. By 5:30 P.M., he had convened the other ships' commanders in his
cabin aboard the flagship. The brief meeting disclosed that the commodore
planned to lead them into Manila Bay that night—single file behind the
Olympia—to achieve surprise. When Dewey's nephew, Lt. William Winder

Commodore Dewey's fleet entering Manila Bay
led by *Olympia*. Painting by F. S. Cozzens.

serving aboard the *Baltimore*, pointed out that a lead ship might set off any
mines in the channel, his uncle bluntly answered: "Billy, I have waited sixty
years for this opportunity," and mines or no mines, "I am leading the
squadron in myself."[36]

Shades of Dewey's Civil War hero, David Glasgow Farragut, running
past forts Jackson and St. Philip below New Orleans and later proclaiming
"damn the torpedoes, full speed ahead" in Mobile Bay. And so it was that
the ghostly American squadron set off about 6:24 P.M. aiming to enter the
Boca Grande Channel in column behind the *Olympia*. Once again, with
all lights extinguished except a small one on each ship's stern, there was
nothing to see except the dim outlines of the ships and the distant coast-
line two or three miles off. "Let me tell you, we were scared," remembered
Olympia crewman Edward Russell sixty-eight years later. Only the swish of
water along the ship's sides and the sound of the engine cut the quiet,
according to Lt. Bradley Fiske aboard the *Petrel*. They were sailing blindly
where no charts had been made in years. Nobody knew if the waters had
been mined or not—later, some Spanish officers thought the Americans
had captured the plans for their torpedo defenses, so flawless was the pas-

sage. "Any minute could have been our last," said Russell, a sentiment echoed by his comrade Wayne Longenecher that the "hardest part of the fight [was] running the gauntlet of both mines and forts, not knowing which moment a mine or torpedo would send you through the deck above." For this, they had thrown overboard mess tables and could expect a paltry $16.00 a month in pay![37]

Rumors later held that a British pilot had guided the flotilla into Manila Bay. Ensign (subsequently Rear Admiral) H. V. Butler vehemently denied that assertion years later. He noted that only Lt. Carlos G. Calkins as navigator of the Olympia and assistant navigator Ens. Arthur G. Kavanagh—both of the U.S. Navy—had done the job. The crews went to quarters at 9:45 P.M., having loaded their guns but carefully leaving the breech blocks open so as to prevent premature firing. They caught naps beside their guns. Then, passing about a half mile from El Fraile, there were some anxious moments concerning both mines and land batteries.[38]

Due to the channel's depth, both contact and electrical mines would have deteriorated rapidly in tropical waters, Dewey concluded. The seventeen guns located on various promontories—especially six 4.7-inch breech loading pieces on El Fraile—promised a hot quarter hour should the Americans be discovered. Yet, only the last vessels in the column drew fire, receiving in quick response fire from one of Raleigh's 5-inchers and McCulloch's 6-pounders. Signal flares and rockets blazed briefly from on shore, but then it was dark again. Either the Spaniards had not anticipated night passage by the Americans or everyone ashore was as defeatist as their commanders. At any rate, the Olympia and her sister ships slipped past the entry point and entered Manila Bay shortly after midnight.[39]

Dewey continued at a slow speed so as to do battle only after daybreak. Watch officers spied the lights of Manila about 3:00 A.M. Twenty minutes later, Olympia crew members remembered, word was passed to "lay by your guns and take it easy"—easier said than done given pre-battle anxiety. Decks sprinkled with sand irritated the lounging men's eyes, noses, and ears and, since everything was pitch black, restless Tars would trip over one another as they stumbled around trying to relieve the tension. Coffee, beans, and hard bread were served about 4:00 and the "stillness was broken by the clashing of bowls and the merry laughter occasioned by collisions in the dark." The commodore himself disdained the beans but not the bread and coffee, which apparently did not mix well with the cold tea that he had been imbibing all night. Newspaperman James Stickney, who had signed on as Dewey's volunteer aide, reported later that the Vermonter was as completely agitated as if he had been a "youngster going out of port into a heavy sea on his first cruise"—throwing up nearly everything.[40]

By contrast, the *Olympia*'s crew down below were as happy as though on an excursion, observed L. S. Young. Jokes and witty stories made the rounds and "some pensive nightingull" would strike up the lilting tune of "Just Before the Battle Mother," before being suppressed by a hot quantity of java spilled over him by less appreciative shipmates. Dressed in "war clothes" (which, said Young, consisted of almost nothing) and, despite the levity, a determined gleam in the seamen's eyes showed that everyone meant business. Reportedly, it was the same on the other ships and, with first light, crews calmly prepared for general action. They attended to last minute chores—sanding decks, ensuring extra signal flags aloft, and getting extra coffee and crackers from galleys. Dewey himself would eventually make his way to the forward bridge, smartly attired in white uniform and tweed "morning" or "golfing cap." It was about this time, according to Asa Walker aboard the *Baltimore*, that "the folds of 'Old Glory' were given to the morning breeze" from every ship in the column.[41]

Still, the Americans remained edgy as the fleet trolled up the bay at six to eight knots. Relegating the *McCulloch* to squire the supply ship *Zafiro* and collier *Nanshan*, Dewey also directed the cutter to protect the American battle line from surprise attack and to offer aid to any casualties from the main action, replacing them in combat if necessary. There was a momentary scare when two lighter craft crossed the path of the oncoming Americans. Torpedo boats, everyone thought, but they turned out to be merely English-owned fishing boats bent on plying their wares in the city. No warships could be seen in the early May dawn as the Americans drew abreast of the Manila breakwater and the Passig River. Dewey now had Gridley swing 90 degrees to starboard and head south toward another possible enemy anchorage at the Cavite navy yard. As if on grand parade, the Americans swept past the city and its Lunetta promenade, drawing desultory fire from some guns ashore. Luckily, nothing hit (although one 9.4-inch shell passed uncomfortably close between the *Baltimore* and *Raleigh*, noted one junior officer aboard the latter). *Boston* and *Concord* lobbed a

Dewey in action during the Battle of Manila Bay. *Left to right:* Apprentice Signal Boy Samuel Ferguson, Marine Orderly John A. McDougall, Dewey, and Chief Yeoman Merrick W. Creagh.

couple of shells in reply just "to let the enemy know that we were not there solely to become targets." The time was about 5:05 A.M.[42]

BATTLE IN MANILA BAY

Obediently, every ship had turned in *Olympia*'s wake, keeping a four hundred yard distance between each of them. The column—*Olympia, Baltimore, Raleigh, Petrel, Concord,* and *Boston*—presented a formidable looking battle line, despite their drab attire. Packing just over 19,000 tons of American iron or steel cruiser force (Montojo later tried to claim the figure was over 21,000, compared with half that tonnage for his own squadron), they carried fifty-three guns of 5-inch caliber or better (ten were 8-inchers). Four of the vessels had protected or armored decks. Moreover, the fleet's complement of 1,611 officers and men were well-trained, disciplined, and enthusiastic. Above all, they possessed the impetus and elan for battle. Steaming through the tropical waters of Manila Bay, they must have seemed as some primeval cat on the prowl for its prey. Suddenly, there they were, the Spaniards, in a slightly ragged, inward bent line "in front of the white buildings of the arsenal" at Cavite, noted Lieutenant Calkins aboard the flagship.[43]

"Clustered in the bight of Canacao Bay" behind Sangley Point (in the colorful phrase of historian Ivan Musicant), Montojo had positioned his line of battle behind a boom protected with chains and lighters filled with stones and water covering the water lines. From west to east (Sangley Point to Las Pinas) they waited—two unprotected cruisers, *Reina Christina* and *Castilla* (now little more than a floating gun platform) and five gunboats, *Don Juan de Austria, Don Antonio de Ulloa, Isla de Cuba, Marques a Duero* and *Isla de Luzon.* Two other disabled gunboats, *General Lezo* and *Velasco,* as well as the transport *Manila,* were in nearby Bacoor Bay. Displacement for the Spanish squadron was about 11,300 tons and they mounted thirty-one major guns, the heaviest of which were seven 6.2-inch rifles. There were also, of course, the guns of the Sangley Point battery: two 5.9-inch rifles and one 4.7-inch gun in the Canacao battery, or thirty-four pieces total. Some one hundred light guns aboard the Spanish vessels vied with one hundred thirty-five such pieces aboard Dewey's ships. Then too, according to one American naval officer who inspected them later on, the Manila batteries numbered two hundred twenty-six guns of all types including one hundred sixty-four muzzle loaders. Since Montojo chose to fight where he did, however, the Manila guns were mostly irrelevant to calculations.[44]

Over all stood the issue of the men behind the guns. Montojo counted almost as many sailors as Dewey. The difference lay with training, leadership, and morale in combination with the condition of his squadron. The Americans were told later that nearly all the Spanish warships had double crews, many of them conscripted from among the citizenry. By comparison, some of Dewey's ships had people such as Asst. Surgeon C. P. Kindleberger of the *Olympia,* Capt. Frank Wildes and Gunner J. C. Evans of the *Boston*— all of whom had volunteered to "remain after orders detaching them had arrived," noted Dewey in his after-action report. In the words of Gridley's

Olympia opens the Battle of Manila Bay.
From a colored lithograph.

biographer, "The Spanish situation at dawn on 1 May 1898 was just about as dismal as Montojo and his men assumed it to be."[45]

Indeed, the battle of Manila Bay was neither battle nor skirmish. It was more a turkey shoot; a carnival shooting gallery for the Americans. At 5:15 A.M., the guns on Sangley Point and aboard the Spanish ships opened an inaccurate fire. Dewey, anxious to conserve his ammunition until close enough to ensure hits, did not respond. "Our hearts threatened to burst from desire to respond," recalled "Lieu" Tisdale aboard the flagship as they listened to the calling of the ranges. "I sat upon the gun-seat repeating to the rhythm of the engine's throb, 'Hold your fire . . . hold your fire . . . hold your fire until the bugle sounds,' while my fingers grew numb upon the spark," he continued. Several Spanish mines exploded ahead of the *Olympia,* and the naval and fortress guns seemed to be probing for range.[46]

Dewey had instructed Gridley to go to the armored conning tower and direct the ship's gunfire in the impending fight. The commodore, together with Lieutenant Calkins would stay on the bridge or possibly climb to the raised compass platform above that bridge in order to direct the entire squadron's activities. Gridley obeyed reluctantly. Obviously, it would not have been wise to have both fleet and ship commander together on the same bridge in the event of an enemy hit. While not in good health,

Gridley's sense of duty held him close to the helm. At approximately 5:22 A.M., with the range still a distant 5,500 yards, the flag officer turned and spoke into the brass communication tube between bridge and conning tower those simple but immortal words, "You may fire when you are ready, Gridley." According to *Olympia*'s logbook, the starboard 8-inch gun in her forward turret fired the first shot at 5:35 A.M., soon followed by her companion. The battle of Manila Bay had been joined.[47]

"We at once bore down on them," Gridley wrote his wife the next day, "this ship leading," referring to the *Olympia*. Briefly stated, the American warships passed the Spanish line three times to the west and twice to the east, blasting away at steadily diminishing ranges from 5,000 to 2,000 yards (some observers claimed 1,500 yards). Discovery of greater water depths than indicated on available charts facilitated such closure. But it also led to subsequent criticism that Dewey "had surrendered a tactical advantage," for if he had kept at the maximum range of his 8-inch guns, the Americans would have remained completely beyond the reach of the Spanish guns. Such hindsight of course fails to consider either Dewey's natural aggressiveness or the fact that any good combat commander seeks to employ full firepower against an enemy. Frankly, Dewey needed every one of his guns to effect a swift victory.[48]

At about 7:00 A.M., Montojo suddenly counterattacked. Several ineffectual Spanish torpedo boat sorties had already been beaten back by the *Olympia*'s rapid-fire guns. Now, the Spanish admiral ordered his flagship to leave its mooring and assault Dewey's counterpart just as the Americans made their second sweep westward. "As the Reina Christina came out from the yard to meet us she planted a shell into the side [of the *Olympia*] right at my gun port," recorded Longenecher, "but, it was spent and did not come all the way through, it burst." The Spanish flagship's slower speed, as well as the full fury of all the American guns, quickly cut short her sortie. Dewey's ships raked her from bow to stern, said Gridley, his own ship obtaining range by cross bearings from the standard compass and the distance taken from the chart. *Olympia* crewman Tisdale in the ship's aft turret remembered how one of their 8-inch shells ripped "through and through" the enemy ship, yet "like an enraged panther she came at us as thought to lash sides and fight us hand to hand with battle axes, as in the olden Spanish wars." Swathed in fire and smoke, the Spanish vessel limped back mortally wounded to her moorage. Tisdale noted how the Spanish admiral soon transferred his flag from his dying flagship to the *Castilla* (Montojo said it was the *Isla de Cuba*).[49]

Then, about a half hour later, Dewey received disturbing news from Gridley. The *Olympia* had only fifteen rounds of ammunition left for each of her 5-inch guns. "It was a most anxious moment for me," the commodore recorded in his memoirs. The battle seemed far from over; the enemy remained essentially unbowed. In fact, the Spanish ammunition supply seemed to be "as ample as ours was limited," thought the Vermonter. Assistant Surgeon Carpenter opined that "It did seem as though we had wasted a lot of ammunition for the true state of affairs was not obvious till later." Besides, Dewey knew that fifteen rounds could be used up in five minutes of sustained fire. He immediately broke off the action so that his flotilla might count its remaining supply of shells. The tired and dirty Tars also welcomed the respite to enjoy a hot breakfast. As it turned out, Gridley's communiqué had been garbled. Only fifteen rounds had been expended and, with the smoke of battle temporarily lifted, Dewey and his ships' captains now could see the results of their fire—death and destruction were clearly evident aboard the enemy ships.[50]

At this point, the battle assumed a more leisurely tone. All of Dewey's captains had assembled aboard the *Olympia*, and it wasn't until 11:16 A.M. that "the fleet stood in to silence the batteries on Sangley Point." The flagship permitted the other units to lead this action. Meanwhile, Montojo had ordered all of his warships still afloat to retire from Canacao Gulf to Bacoor Bay, just to the south behind Cavite. There they were "to resist to the last moment" and "should be sunk before they surrendered." All the while the distant Manila batteries banged away ineffectually until Dewey dispatched a message to Governor General Augustin warning that he would fire on the city if such annoyance did not cease. Then, he and his squadron methodically resumed the task of finishing off Montojo. The second phase of the battle of Manila Bay would be over by about 12:30 that afternoon. In Gridley's last letter to his wife, he told her that "We sank, burned or destroyed their entire fleet, killing and wounding great numbers" as "they could not stand our fire."[51]

Only gunfire from the *Don Antonio de Ulloa* and two modern guns from the Sangley Point batteries provided effective resistance to the final

Capt. Charles Vernon Gridley, USN, recipient of Dewey's famous command, "You may fire when you are ready, Gridley," which opened the Battle of Manila Bay.

onslaught of the Americans. The other Spanish ships had been moved into shallow waters, scuttled, and abandoned by their decimated crews, "taking care to save the flag, the distinguishing pennant, the money in the safe, the portable arms, the breechplugs of the guns, and the signal codes," according to Montojo. Longenecher thought otherwise, however, for "none of their ships struck their colors, in fact I do not think they had time, for they left their ships with their guns loaded in too big a hurry to fire them, so I think they forgot all about their colors." No matter, as *Olympia*'s logbook noted tersely: "At 12:15 the Spanish admiral surrendered." A white flag fluttered out at Cavite while Dewey sent the *Concord* and *Petrel* to finish off the Spanish merchant ship-transport *Mindanao* anchored at Bacoor as well as to police up the other burning warships. So, the attack ended in Dewey's words, with the Spanish "batteries being silenced and the ships sunk, burnt and destroyed." Cheer after cheer echoed from the *Olympia* and her sister combatants of the Asiatic Squadron.[52]

Nevertheless, remarked L. S. Young aboard the flagship, "Even amidst the horrors and cruelties of war, one cannot help remarking and admiring the valor of those heroes, Spaniards and enemies though they may be." By 2:00 P.M., Dewey brought his squadron to rest, guns trained shoreward, just off the Lunetta at Manila City. Such intimidation paid off and, in Young's words, "When the sun set that night its last rays rested like a benediction on 'Old Glory' waving proudly from mast head and peak of Uncle Sam's doughty arbitrators." Then, darkness was further lit up by the burning vessels that "threw a lurid glare over the rack and ruin ashore and the wrecks afloat." Periodically, a magazine would explode "like the eruption of a volcano," heaving flaming debris high into the air and making a picture of the "horrors of modern warfare." One explosion sent debris four hundred feet into the air. Noted Apprentice Longenecher, "it was a beautiful sight to see; besides about 12 or 13 ships all in flames, small magazines were going up all night." Such a scene naturally left a lifelong impression on all who witnessed it.[53]

The horrors of Manila Bay proved disproportional. Enamored with blood and gore, the young and impressionable American seamen like Longenecher remembered Spanish decks covered with dead and dismembered bodies. The chief engineer in one ship was "laying across a rail in the engine room with his hand on the throttle, with intestines torn out." Not only was Spain's far eastern fleet destroyed, but Manila's shore guns were silenced. Dewey's landing parties soon remarked that "the effect of our deadly fusillade was simply frightful, the dead and wounded strewing the ground and buildings like leaves in the autumn." One Spanish sailor, with both legs shot away, thought the true number of deaths in the fleet would never be known due to the double crews and that "no sooner had a gun been loaded than a storm of projectiles would sweep away the gun's crew." Some one hundred sixty-one Spaniards killed and two hundred ten wounded at a cost of only nine Americans injured (one or two aboard the *Olympia* seem to have escaped that statistic) memorialized the human cost of the battle.[54]

While *Olympia, Baltimore, Raleigh, Boston,* and *Petrel* were all struck, the *Baltimore* suffered the most significant Spanish hit. One enemy shell penetrated a 6-inch gun sponson, disabling piece and crew. Yet, Gridley claimed that his ship "received the brunt of the fight and [we] were struck seven or eight times." They had been lucky and it had been a weird sight to see his men stripped to trousers and shoes, he told his wife. Certainly, the American fire got the job done but at the expense of only one hundred forty-two hits for 5,859 rounds expended. The *Olympia* alone accounted for 1,617 shots fired and still retained six hundred thirty unexpended rounds at battle's end. Lt. Bradley Fiske, later an American gunnery expert who invented a range finder, took it all in from the *Petrel*. His observation was that uncertainty of range and the individual zeal of each gun captain in the squadron to fire as rapidly as possible had hampered good firing discipline. Another witness, Lt. John M. Ellicott, thought that the *Olympia*'s 8-inch guns were more effective per caliber in terms of damage than the others, notwithstanding the whole issue of range closure and the enemy's stationary posture.[55]

Of one thing, however, there could be no question: Manila Bay belonged to the Americans. Dewey, the *Olympia,* and the rest of the squadron commanded the soft tropical waters off Manila. But they did not control Manila City nor any other part of the Philippine archipelago. As the commodore

Olympia's gunners cleaning a .40 caliber 5-inch rapid-fire gun in 1898. Cyanotype photograph by George Grantham.

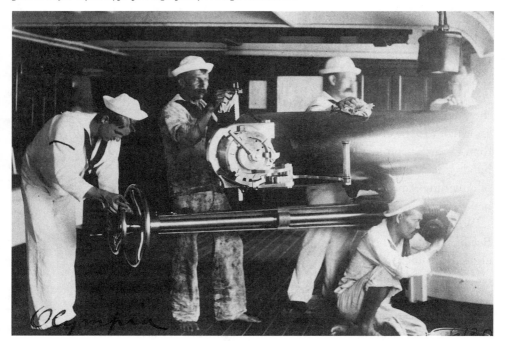

himself later observed, the blockade of the city had to be "established and enforced" and "immunity from surprise attack by the Spanish insured." Moreover, the Cavite arsenal had to be occupied, policed, and its contents secured. Most of all, said Dewey, "American supremacy and military discipline" generally had "to take the place of chaos." Indeed, the war with Spain was hardly over; it had scarcely begun. Still, for the moment, the flag of America flying atop Olympia's main mast, seemed to have supplanted the Spanish banners in this distant outpost of empire. Dewey and others intended it to stay that way.[56]

In 1910, the prestigious United States Naval Institute Proceedings published a translation of a French naval commander's multipart study of naval strategy. Although dated and superseded to some degree by the Russo-Japanese war of 1904–5, Cdr. R. Daveluy's piece accorded space to the Spanish-American contest six years earlier. Proportionately, he gave more attention to Caribbean operations. But the succinctness and perspicacity of what he had to say about Dewey, the Philippines, and Spanish actions was illuminating. Frankly, he painted a picture of Spanish ineptness and irresolution against which American action had been decisive. He concluded that, "If ever a war might have been foreseen and discounted in advance, it is truly this one."[57]

When Spain "was driven to rupture," declared Daveluy, "it was still ignorant of what to do with its forces." Threatened at both extremities of her empire, with two colonies in full revolt, her position was not promising. Everything depended upon Mahanite command of the sea. Yet, naval forces available to Montojo in the Philippines "were not equal to contending with Commodore Dewey's modern cruisers," and the Spanish colonial army was too involved with holding in check the insurgents to "pretend to repel a landing" from the sea. In short, he concluded, the geographical situation was clearly unfavorable, military circumstances markedly inferior.

What then resulted was the appearance of the American Asiatic Squadron at the end of April and the climactic naval victory on the first of May. This event destroyed the Spanish opponent "anchored at Cavite under the feeble protection of two batteries of two guns each." Here, Daveluy implied that it need not have happened that way. While events depended on Spanish actions, coolness deserted Spanish decisions. Montojo could have checked Dewey simply by positioning his interior flotilla in Subic Bay. Since the appearance of American warships off Manila was what was feared, the Spanish could have kept them away "much more surely by sending away the Spanish [flotilla] which was the object of the enemy's pursuit."

Since Dewey lacked a landing force, Daveluy observed, his range of action was limited to bombardment of Manila and Cavite. As long as the Spanish vessels were afloat, they protected those two locations. "The one thing of importance," concluded the French naval officer, "was to place them where they had the best chance of resisting the enemy's attack." Of course, this comment presumed Subic Bay's superiority or Montojo's tactical abilities—things left unaddressed in Daveluy's evaluation. Still, what he said was that Montojo, by retiring under the shore batteries of Manila and Cavite, had simply made Dewey's job too easy. "Commodore Dewey covered himself with glory cheaply," Daveluy concluded, but it could not be denied that "he showed a spirit of decision that reveals in him the qualities of the true warrior." Underlying that spirit was American confidence in the superiority of their ships and their commander. Dewey and his flagship were as one at Manila Bay.

4

Herald of Empire

The *Olympia*'s work was done by sunset on 1 May; Commo. George Dewey's was not. The Americans had established command of the sea in the waters surrounding the Philippines. Manila Bay had been, arguably, the most lopsided naval victory in history. But, six thousand miles from home port, with dwindled supply of ammunition, coal, and food, the squadron needed refurbishment even in victory. Even the indefatigable editor of *The Bounding Billow* lacked paper to recount the glorious Yankee victory until, "through the kindness of a few of our shipmates who brought us some which the Spaniards left on evacuating Cavite," he was able to print the June issue. Still, he proclaimed, "the fact of the 'Bounding Billow' being printed on captured paper will certainly enhance its value as a memorial of this occasion."[1]

CLEAN-UP AND CONSOLIDATING GAINS

Chief petty officer with the *Olympia*'s Engineer Force, Murray S. Holloway, had been one of eight Union Iron Works machinists enlisted to fill the complement of technicians for the ship. They had assisted in her construction and trials and were familiar with the operation of her machinery. But, during Dewey's self-imposed blockade of the bay after the battle, Holloway recalled that "our life on board ship became rather monotonous." The only source of news from the outside world, he recalled, was through the mails, which would come every week by dispatch boat. The most direct link had been severed late on 1 May under Dewey's orders, when Spanish Capt.-Gen. Don Basilio Augustin had refused use of the Manila–Hong Kong cable. The commodore promptly ordered the *Zafiro*'s commanding officer to drag for the cable and sever it.[2]

While alternate means of communication with both Madrid and Washington would be effected, the cable would not be mended until late August—ten days after the war ended. Dewey biographers Laurin Healy and Luis Kutner thought this act "one of the most controversial of all Dewey's actions in the Philippines." Eventually, correspondents like John T. McCutcheon of the *Chicago Record* and Edward W. Harden of the *Chicago Tribune*, who witnessed events aboard the cutter *McCulloch*, were able to get their stories to the United States before Dewey's official dispatch. But, of course, the blackout left Dewey master of his own fate, undeterred by dictates from Washington. Everyone in the Asiatic Squadron considered their commodore a consummate diplomat. Nonetheless, tension filled the air in the immediate aftermath of the naval battle. Would the Spanish government send a relief force to retake the Philippines? More immediately, would the American warships bombard Manila City? Would the Spanish resist? What about the insurgents, hovering on the edge of the Spanish-American confrontation but anxious to exploit the sudden turn of events?[3]

For the moment, however, Dewey and his ships merely set about methodically consolidating their gains. Both in his initial dispatch of 1 May and a follow-up of 4 May (sent via the *McCulloch* and wired from Hong Kong on the seventh), the commodore noted that he had destroyed the enemy squadron, taken possession of the Cavite naval station, and destroyed its fortifications. Likewise, works at the entrance to Manila Bay had been neutralized and the cable with the mainland cut. "I control bay completely and can take city at any time," he boasted. But he lacked sufficient men to hold Manila and desperately needed a fast steamer sent to him with ammunition. That same day, unbeknownst to the Vermonter, news of his victory having reached Washington and other world capitals, Secretary

Olympia in battle dress in the
Philippines, 1898–99.

of the Navy John Long wired back that a grateful government had promoted Dewey to the rank of acting rear admiral and that he was to hoist
the flag, wear the uniform, and "affix that title to your official signature."[4]

The days immediately following the battle were given to consolidating
position, expanding control of the Bay area, and writing after-action
reports. The Cavite arsenal commander was cowed into abject submission
on 2 May. The place was evacuated the next day. Shore parties from the
squadron discovered death and destruction all over the arsenal grounds and
Catholic nuns pleaded that the Yankees not execute the horribly burned
and mangled wounded. "The idea that we might be guilty of such inhu-
manity" incensed American sailors like Lt. Hugh Rodman of the *Raleigh*
(later rear admiral and commander of American battleships in European
waters during World War I). He was shocked that the governor general and
archbishop had spread that rumor before the battle. Then, on the third, the
Raleigh and *Baltimore* made a circuit of the harbor entry forts, like those on
Corregidor, taking surrenders and paroles, disabling shore guns by removing breech blocks, and destroying stockpiles of ammunition. They also
swept the Boca Chica channel between Corregidor and Bataan for mines,
finding some eighty feet down on the bottom—completely useless. Mean-

while, for the benefit of the trembling population of Manila City (many anticipating bombardment of their homes and work places), the *Olympia*'s band soothingly played refrains from "La Poloma" and other Spanish tunes. Winning the hearts and minds of civilians was as important as destroying their military protection force.[5]

Meanwhile, Dewey awaited the reports of his ships' captains. By the 4th, they were all in, glowing with accomplishments, low battle damage, and singing the praises of American ingenuity, pluck, and technical proficiency at constructing those hearty vessels of war. Typical was that of the *Olympia*'s captain, Charles Vernon Gridley. After recounting the heroic lady's deeds, he broke into details of his ship's particular experience. Following the ordinary preparations of clearing ship for action, he recounted, "the heavy sheet chains were slaked up and down over a buffer of awnings against the sides in wake of the 5-inch ammunition hoists," thus affording a stanch protection, while iron and canvas barricades were placed in various spots to cover gun crews and strengthen moderate defenses. Nevertheless, Spanish fire had struck the ship in eight places, as he recounted the specific battle damage.

Gridley recited the details. One shell had made a 1.5-inch dent in the starboard superstructure plate just forward of the second 5-inch sponson. Three planks had been torn up slightly on the starboard side of the forecastle behind the forward turret. The port after shrouds of fore and main rigging had been shredded. The strongback of the gig's davits was hit and slightly damaged. A 6-pounder shell had made a hole in the ship's frame between frames 65 and 66 on the starboard side below the main deck rail. Other shot had carried away the lashing of the port whaleboat davit and one of the rail stanchions outside the port gangway. Finally, *Olympia*'s hull had been dented on the starboard side one foot below the main-deck rail and three feet aft of the number 4 coal port. Trivial compared to the destruction wrought by *Olympia*'s own guns on the enemy, Gridley could have echoed colleague J. B. Coghlan, commanding the *Raleigh*, who reported that "This vessel at the close of the engagement was in as good condition as when it began, and without any preparation could have fought it over again."[6]

Gridley further noted that the forward 8-inch pieces had fired twenty-three shells, but that the ammunition hoist had been knocked out of commission by a blown fuse. The right gun worked well with the electrical batteries, but the battery of the left gun failed to explode the primer after the first shot and the resistance lamp in the dynamo circuit had broken. So, the gun crew simply employed percussion primers after the first shot—with good results. Similar problems and results obtained in the aft turret—which fired thirteen shots during the battle. In addition, one shell jammed in the left gun, "after which [we] used half-full and half-reduced charge, which fired it." One primer failed to check gas, Gridley concluded. Still, the "battery of this gun gave good results."

Residue from gunsmoke clouded the object glasses of the telescopic sights in both turrets, requiring frequent cleaning. Yet, said Gridley, "these are considered good sights for heavy guns," and he merely recommended adding bar sights for emergency, as there was no provision for sighting other than with telescopes. His observations concerning the 5-inch guns were also useful. The batteries were unreliable, although dynamo circuits on three guns produced good results. The ammunition was poor, and many shells became detached from the cases on loading and had to be rammed out from the muzzle. Several cases jammed in loading and extraction. All in all, the guns and gun mounts worked well, concluded the captain, for about two hundred and eighty-one 5-inch shells were fired. Ironically, it was the 6-pounder battery that "worked to perfection," firing one thousand rounds. In addition, some three hundred and sixty rounds of 1-pounder and a thousand rounds of small-arms ammunition were expended on the *Olympia*.[7]

As for the crew's performance, Gridley simply recounted the facts. From 9:42 P.M. on 30 April until 12:40 P.M. the next day, two divisions of the engineer's force worked the boilers and engines, keeping up steam and "working well, notwithstanding the heat of the fire and engine rooms." The third division had worked at their stations in the powder division. One 6-pounder was manned by a crew of marines, and two relief crews for the 5-inch guns and two for the 6-pounders acted as sharpshooters under Capt. W. C. Biddle, USMC. Gridley also singled out Pay Inspector D. A. Smith, Fleet Pay Clerk William J. Rightmire, and Pay Clerk W. M. Long, all of whom had "volunteered for and performed active service not required by their stations." Even Dewey's secretary, Ensign H. H. Caldwell, had volunteered for combat duty and served with a subdivision of the 5-inch battery. Finally, he cited *New York Herald* correspondent J. L. Stickney ("formerly a naval officer of exceptional ability") who served as a volunteer aid to the squadron commander in the battle, carrying messages and keeping an accurate account of the battle.

Almost as an afterthought, Gridley volunteered the data that "the range was obtained by cross bearings from the standard compass and the distance taken from the chart." Only *Petrel* captain E. P. Woods reported Lt. Bradley A. Fiske's testing of his innovative theories of gun spotting by stationing himself on the fore cross trees of that vessel with a stadimeter to measure the range and report on the fall of shots. Later analysis would bring to light the major failings of the Yankee victory—woefully weak American marksmanship. To Gridley and his fellow commanders, they were quite content to tell Dewey that "This ship needs no immediate repairs and is in excellent condition to engage the enemy at any time."[8]

One tragedy struck the *Olympia* during this period: the loss of the respected Charles Gridley. In declining health with what was phrased at the time as "affliction of the liver so common in the Orient," he had reached "semi-invalid" status after the battle. Chronic dysentery seems to have degenerated into "nearly continuous hemorrhages," and one modern commentator has suggested that Gridley had liver cancer. In any event, neither his determination to command his ship in battle nor his personal dedication to Dewey and the *Olympia*'s crew could any longer hide the fact that the intrepid sailor needed better medical care than was obtainable with the American squadron at Manila. Perhaps the fault lay with a stubborn Gridley himself or even Dewey might have been reluctant to relieve him of his command. Whether or not proper care could have actually been found ashore in the Spanish city, from subsequent events it sounds as if Gridley's malady had reached its terminal stages. Still, a medical survey board for Gridley wasn't convened until 23 May and, not surprisingly, their findings led to his replacement by Cdr. Benjamin P. Lamberton and transfer to the *Zafiro*, which would carry him to Hong Kong and transport home.[9]

Gridley's send-off on 25 May befitted that of a flag officer. Twelve of the *Olympia*'s officers, with his executive officer Lt. Corwin P. Rees acting as coxswain, rowed him from his ship to the waiting transport. Then, as the *Zafiro* steamed down Manila Bay that evening, carefully escorted by the gunboat *Concord*, *Olympia*'s crewmen, as well as those of every other ship in the squadron, manned the rigging to cheer the departing captain. The last we ever saw of our dear Gridley, reported one of the *Olympia's* seamen, was sitting out in a chair on the *Zafiro's* quarterdeck, "apparently 'listening to the old band play.'" Another sailor observed that Gridley was in great pain and had urged the *Zafiro's* captain to hurry so that he could get away from the station as soon as possible since "it was not very healthy for any person out there."[10]

Gridley died within a fortnight. Bedridden but lucid after leaving Hong Kong on the Occidental and Oriental Steamship Company's *Coptic* on 27 May, Gridley had resignedly told one interviewer at Nagasaki on 4 June, "I think I am for it personally." But "I could not leave the ship before the battle." Early the following day, as the *Coptic* entered the harbor of Kobe, Gridley succumbed and his body was cremated at Yokohama prior to shipment home to his family in Erie, Pennsylvania. Today at Lakeside cemetery, four captured Spanish guns guard what is styled "Gridley circle." "The news of his death came like a thunder bolt, filling our hearts with grief and pain," recorded editor L. S. Young in the June edition of *The Bounding Billow*. "Death it cast a sad gloom over all of our ships for many a long day," was the way *Olympia* Master at Arms Harry Kay expressed the crew's sentiments to Gridley's daughter.[11]

As Dewey himself wrote Gridley's widow on 12 August, the captain's loss "is mourned by all who knew him, and especially by me, whose friend and trusted and gallant assistant he was." The admiral told her that he felt personally gratified in "obtaining for him an advancement in his grade for highly distinguished conduct in battle, which he richly deserved, although he did not live to enjoy it." Still, Congressman Albert Todd of Michigan may have said it best in his eulogistic remarks to the House of Representatives in Washington on 21 February 1899. Seeking $5,000 for a memorial shaft for Gridley in Arlington National Cemetery, the legislator suggested that while his death resulted from illness, it was more realistically attributable to "his unswerving fidelity to his country and anxiety to serve her cause." Gridley had sacrificed his health to remain at his duty station on that "Fateful 'first of May.'" History offered "no greater example of unfaltering heroism and patriotic devotion than that shown by our dear departed captain," Todd intoned about *Olympia's* departed commanding officer.[12]

Olympia's "smoking lamp" in use in 1898. Cyanotype print by George Grantham.

ENTER OTHER GLADIATORS

As Gridley's biographer duly noted, Gridley died before final resolution of the Spanish-American War. For that matter, the situation even remained unresolved in the Philippines, and Gridley's ship, the *Olympia*, assumed the mantle of facilitator as well as herald of empire. Assuredly, the Spanish were unable to mount a relief expedition from home waters. Not that they did not attempt to do so. But the voyage of Adm. Manuel de la Camara's relief squadron from Cadiz on 16 June was virtually nipped in the bud by American naval feints and operations in Atlantic waters and adroit information warfare carried on by naval attachés in Europe. Camara got no further than

Suez before being recalled by a fretful home government. Badgered by events in the Caribbean theater of operations (where the squadron of Adm. William Sampson successfully threatened capture of Cuba and Puerto Rico) and the rumor that a separate American force would cross the Atlantic to wreak havoc and destruction among Spanish coastal cities, Spanish politicians were already beginning to seek a peaceful resolution to the conflict. Still, according to historian David Trask, had Camara's battleship *Pelayo* and armored cruiser *Carlos V* reached the Philippines "they would have posed a serious danger to Dewey."[13]

This particular drama—the threat that a Spanish squadron would force the Americans out of Manila Bay since Dewey had no armored ships—led to dispatch of the 4,084-ton monitor USS *Monterey* (yet another of the Union Iron Works–built warships of the New Navy), and a second heavily armored craft, the *Monadnock*. The first monitor sported two 12-inch and two 10-inch turreted rifled cannon plus six 6-pounders, four 1-pounders, and two Gatling guns. The second warship counted four 10-inch, two 4-inch, two 6-pounder, two 3-pounder, two 1-pounder, and two 37-millimeter guns. But the key factors were the 13- and 9-inch side armor plates and the 7- and 8-inch turret armor plates on the two ships, which definitely bolstered American fighting capabilities in the Far East.[14]

It promised to be a Union Iron Works show since the protected cruiser *Charleston* (4,040 tons, with two 8-inch, six 6-inch, four 6-pounder, two 3-pounder, and two 1-pounder cannon, commissioned in 1889) was also en route from San Francisco, with three troop transports under orders to both resupply Dewey with ammunition and complete the conquest of the Spanish colony. Dewey, well aware of Camara as well as his government's efforts to reinforce him, guessed that the Spaniard would never appear in Philippine waters. Yet there were contingency plans, including temporary withdrawal from Manila Bay, if he did. Dewey hoped that the American monitors would arrive first. They did, and Camara was recalled on 7 July after reaching the Red Sea. But the reinforcing ships from America continued to the Far East. It was just as well, for Dewey had new problems to worry about as the *Olympia* rode lazily at anchor off Cavite.[15]

Other nations' warships began to appear in Philippine waters after the American victory at Manila Bay. The British gunboat *Linnet* arrived on 2 May, the French cruiser *Bruix* followed three days later, and the Imperial

German cruiser *Irene* joined the day after that. None of these ships posed much of an individual threat to Dewey's squadron. The British "composite gun vessel," as she has been styled, dated to 1880 and mounted two 7-inch muzzle loading and three 20-pounder breech loading cannon aboard her 788-ton displacement. The *Bruix* however, was a newer and more formidable, albeit small, armored cruiser completed in 1896. She bore twenty-two guns, ranging from 7.6-inch and 5.5-inch turret guns to 1- and 9-pounders, with four torpedo tubes aboard her 4,736-ton displacement. The German cruiser *Irene* (1887), similar in size to the *Bruix,* was a protected cruiser like the *Olympia*, mounting fourteen 150-millimeter guns, six revolving 37-millimeter guns, and three torpedo tubes for her 4,947 tons. The British 5,600-ton armored cruiser *Immortalité* (1886) joined the *Linnet* on 7 May, adding her twenty-eight 9.2-inch and 6-inch guns, 6- and 3-pounders, and torpedoes to the crowd. Even the 4,217-ton Japanese protected cruiser *Itsukushima* (1891)—with a formidable Canet 12.6-inch turret gun, eleven 4.7-inch secondary armament, eleven 3-pounders, and four torpedo tubes—came in on 10 May.[16]

Far more troublesome for the Americans, however, was the fact that by 27 June the Germans had a more formidable squadron sitting in Manila Bay than Dewey. Their squadron counted five warships displacing 24,600 tons—under Vice Adm. Otto von Diedrichs. In addition to the *Irene* and the light cruiser *Cormoran* (completed in 1892, and sporting eight 105-millimeter guns, five revolving cannon, and two torpedo tubes on her bantam 1,838 tons), the admiral had his flagship, a triple-screw wood-sheathed protected cruiser *Kaiserin Augusta* (completed in 1892, with four 150-millimeter, eight 105-millimeter, and eight 88-millimeter guns, four revolving cannon, and five torpedo tubes aboard 6,218 tons). Also, von Diedrichs had the *Irene's* sister ship, *Prinzess Wilhelm,* as well as the old central battery ironclad *Kaiser,* which dated to the mid-1870s but was still considered a good seaboat. In fact, she had been rebuilt as a heavy cruiser at Wilhemshaven in the early 1890s. She boasted her original eight 260-millimeter guns, as well as one 150-millimeter, six 105-millimeter, and nine 85-millimeter pieces for her 8,799-ton complement. Berlin had ordered von Diedrichs to go to the Philippines and ascertain the state of Spanish rule in the wake of American actions. Whether or not he needed quite so many warships to accomplish this task remains debatable.[17]

In truth, the German presence greatly agitated the Americans. Problems were more procedural than substantive, however. The German ships ranged Philippine waters at will and Manila Bay in particular. On occasion they seemed to interfere with the trammels of Yankee authority. One sticking point concerned measures that could legitimately establish the identity of a neutral ship in the harbor. Dewey, who had declared a blockade, expected more than mere genuflection to his presence. The *Olympia* became the site for various posturing and minuets between Dewey and German officers about interpretations of international law, as well as neutral rights and obligations until, on 7 July, the American admiral lost his cool and told von Diederichs's hapless aide, Capt.-Lt. Paul von Hintze, "Does Admiral von Diedrichs think he commands here or do I? Tell your Admiral if he wants war I am ready." Von Hintze muttered to Dewey's flag lieutenant, Thomas M. Brumby, "Mein Gott! What is the matter with your Admiral?" Brumby calmly replied that there was nothing wrong with his superior, but that he meant exactly what he said and that von Hintze better tell that to his commanding officer.[18]

Historian David Trask suggests that "The German-American tempest in a teapot began as a misunderstanding and ended as an enduring myth." Neither party wanted war. In the best tradition of the age of imperialism, both newcomers to the great power stage wanted respect (and, one suspects, more territory). But as yet, Washington had sent no guidance as to the fate of the Philippines. Pres. William McKinley depended on "the self-controlling nature of war" and, technically, that war had not ended. So, a nervous Dewey chose to see sinister intentions behind German actions, a mistrust that would only simmer and grow in his postwar years as the navy's top admiral. The *Olympia* and her sister ships continued to ride the soft summer waves of Manila Bay, clad in their war paint and awaiting some direction of fortune. The German question soon melded with the larger issue of finally wresting Manila from the Spaniards and the much thornier question of what to do about the Filipino insurgents or nationalists, like Emilio Aguinaldo, also waiting to supplant Spanish rule in their homeland.[19]

On 13 July, the German cruiser *Irene* was thought to have interfered with insurgent attempts to take a Spanish garrison at Isla Grande. Inasmuch as the Americans seemed happy with any help in ousting the Spaniards from their remaining positions, Aguinaldo sent Dewey a document the very next day which set forth the formation of a provisional government of the Philippines by the Filipinos, independent of the United States. Dewey forwarded the document to Washington and prepared to assist army general Wesley Merritt's final capture of Manila City. Then, on 17 July, the Japanese protected cruiser *Naniwa* (two 10.3-inch, six 5.9-inch, two 6-pounder, ten 4-barrelled Nordenfeld guns, four Gatling machine guns, four 14-inch torpedo tubes, 3,650 tons, finished in 1885) brought news of American victory in the Caribbean. After a "cornet" or fleet signal was run up on the *Olympia*'s signal halyard indicating a message for all the vessels of the squadron, a signal boy appeared on each of the flagship's gun turrets. Wig-wagging the message, "Cervera's entire fleet destroyed off Santiago harbor. Americans lose one man killed. Ships uninjured," cheers went up from every vessel in the fleet "that must have been heard in Manila, seven miles away." Captain-General Augustin was so nonplussed that he arrested the Spanish officer bearing this same news on his return from the *Naniwa* and then threatened to have him shot. The way was clear for a final solution to Spanish rule in the Philippines.[20]

MANILA CITY AND THE INSURGENTS

The matter was settled on 13 August 1898 in an opéra bouffe "battle of Manila" between Filipino-American forces and the Spanish. By the first of the month, American army and navy forces were poised to take control of Manila and its environs, an endgame that few had foreseen prior to Dewey's victory. But, at the same time, the insurrectionists were also poised to finish their rebellion against Spanish authority, a rebellion that had commanded little attention in Washington until now. True, Filipino leaders including Aguinaldo had conversed with American representatives prior to the onset of Spanish-American hostilities. But Dewey and others simply pirouetted past them, although the acting rear admiral had allowed one Jose Alejandrino to go along with the squadron for its appointment with destiny. Still, Dewey's apparent naiveté concerning insurgent intentions and their understanding of American help in establishing an independent nation would prove troublesome later on.[21]

The admiral's avowed desire to courteously permit Aguinaldo's return to the Philippines from China and then to exploit his presence in weakening the Spanish "in every way" led to the insurgent leader's appearance at

An *Olympia* crewman with his parrot, which lost a leg during the Battle of Manila Bay. Cyanotype print by George Grantham.

Cavite by 19 May. From this point on, notes Trask, "the American war with Spain became intertwined with the Philippine revolution" because of Dewey's carelessness and the overzealousness of various American consuls in the Far East. Aguinaldo, resplendent in uniform and carrying a gold cane (symbolic of some authority in Spanish eyes), soon conferred with Dewey aboard the *Olympia*, even spending the night there. Dewey treated him indulgently but Aguinaldo chafed at restrictions placed by the admiral upon insurgent activities. Still, Dewey told him to go ashore and start his army of liberation. Aguinaldo understood this to mean independence, while Dewey did not.[22]

In any event, while the U.S. Navy controlled the water Aguinaldo's men cleaned out the hinterland and the newly arrived American troops laid siege to the Spanish garrison bottled up in the city of Manila. Fearful of what the Filipinos might do, the American and Spanish authorities anxiously negotiated a way out of the thorny issue of Manila City. Aided by Belgian consul Edouard Andre, Dewey, Merritt, and Augustin (and his replacement Don Fermin Jaudenes) agreed upon a token battle for honor—a "show of resistance," as Hugh Rodman phrased it—after which the Spaniards would surrender. The *Olympia*, *Raleigh*, *Petrel*, *McCulloch*, and the refitted *Callao* would mount a modest bombardment of Fort San Antonio Abad while Dewey's other ships, like the *Monterey*, would exert a show of force and mock bombardment in conjunction with an army-insurgent land assault of Spanish blockhouses and trenches. Spanish batteries along the city's waterfront would remain silent, thus avoiding destruction by Dewey's warships.[23]

The whole farce was completed in less time on 13 August than Dewey had needed to dispatch the Spanish fleet on May Day. Dewey's flotilla left its moorings about 8:45 A.M. Soon, HMS *Immortalité*'s band blared forth the strains of Dewey's favorite march, "Under the Double Eagle," before switching somewhat playfully to "See the Conquering Hero Comes." The English Tars cheered on their American cousins as their ship carefully interposed itself between Dewey and the German squadron (also with steam up, headed ostensibly out of the battle zone). Dewey, comfortably puffing a cigar on the *Olympia*'s bridge, told Lamberton, the ship's new skipper, to commence firing about 9:35 A.M. For an hour the American ships methodically blasted Fort San Augustin, with no reply from the forts. Ashore, Wesley Merritt's American troops advanced as planned against generally token Spanish resistance. By 11:00, Brumby and several signal boys had conveyed "the largest ensign to be found aboard the *Olympia*" to the city's citadel and hoisted it high above a milling throng of distraught civilians and Spanish soldiers. Three hundred and seventy-seven years of Iberian rule had ended. Perhaps only the insurrectionists were chagrined at being denied their share of the victory.[24]

What was even more ironic was that all of this occurred after a protocol had already been signed in Washington providing for cessation of general hostilities. Due to Dewey's original severance of the Hong Kong cable, no word of the war's end reached the Philippines until 16 August (the cable was re-spliced on the twentieth). By this point, American and Spanish soldiers were fraternizing, military bands were playing afternoon concerts on the Lunetta, and Manila civilians had returned to their peaceful pursuits. American soldiers and sailors busily safeguarded Spanish property and citizenry in the captured city. But, since the Filipino insurgents had been craftily prevented from sharing in the final assault on the city, Aguinaldo soon transferred his enmity from the Spanish to the Americans. Above all else, the restless insurgents had to be contained and managed as the United States government grappled with the ultimate question of sovereignty or annexation.[25]

Final peace negotiations between Spain and the United States took several additional months, and the Philippines would stand at the center of the negotiations. Meanwhile the McKinley administration tasked Dewey with appraising the islands—their people, resources, strategic condition, and any "other information which may be of value to the Government in their negotiations." Within a week of Manila's capture and the dispatch of this directive, Dewey had complied, briefly outlining strengths and weaknesses, suggesting the importance of Manila and the island of Luzon for retention, but failing to indicate the nature of the insurgent problem. He hinted that he really did not want to leave the islands "while matters

Olympia's barbershop in 1898.
Cyanotype print by George Grantham.

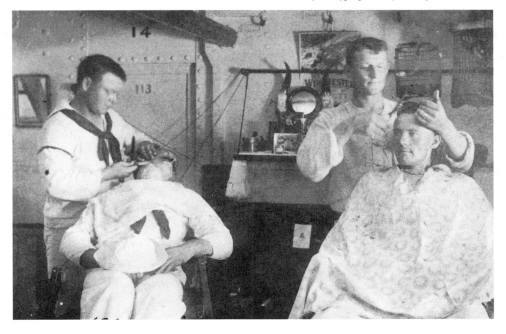

remain in present critical condition." Wisely, Washington allowed Dewey and the *Olympia* to remain, especially as other dispatches were soon forthcoming from the admiral suggesting the desirability of resuming normal commercial intercourse in the region, the need to remove hundreds of Spanish civil and religious leaders ("an element dangerous to the United States," noted Assistant Secretary of the Navy William Allen), and the escalating insurgent problem. Dewey received strict orders with regard to the latter. Insurgents had to recognize the military occupation and authority of the United States and the cessation of hostilities as proclaimed by McKinley. The admiral was "to restrain insurgent hostilities toward Spaniards, and while maintaining a position of rightful supremacy as to the insurgents to pursue, so far as possible, a conciliatory course to all."[26]

Dewey and the *Olympia* remained in Manila Bay for a year after their great victory. When his flagship went to China for a change of scene at the end of August (Dewey allowing every one of his ships to rotate there for rest and recreation), the admiral temporarily transferred his flag to the *Baltimore*, which he found as efficient as the flagship. Singly and in pairs, the American ships returned to Hong Kong and the Kowloon dry docks. There they had their bottoms cleaned and painted, hurriedly in the case of the *Olympia*, which arrived about 7:00 A.M. on 28 August and started back for Manila on 3 September. Naturally, *Olympia*'s sailors were delighted with even this brief period of shore liberty, tributes paid the victors by the city's garrison troops like the Scotch Brigade, West Yorkshire, and Queen's Own, as well as fellow sailors from the Royal Navy, boxing and wrestling matches, and the band concerts for enthralled residents of the city.

Inevitably there were brawls, especially when one of the Kaiser's warships made port at the same time. Along for the good time were the two "mascots" "Boots" and "Searchlight," young boys who had come out to the Philippines with the 10th Pennsylvania Volunteers and then endeared themselves to *Olympia*'s sailors and, with Dewey's permission, went with the ship to Hong Kong. Upwards of a hundred *Olympia* sailors, such as "Lieu" Tisdale, had too good a time and failed to respond to the *Olympia*'s general recall whistle. They held over as "stragglers clean and sober" (to be counseled each day upon reporting to the American State Department representative until retrieved when the *Concord* came into port). Tisdale likened it to returning to school after vacation, but their passage back to

Manila aboard the *Concord* was all work for their truancy. The tardy crew members drew all the dirty details and slept on the bare deck; *Concord's* Tars laughed at them all day and slept comfortably in their own hammocks all night.[27]

Once back at Manila on 6 September, the party was over. "Searchlight" Willie Doran returned to the Pennsylvania regiment. He soon succumbed to pneumonia and was buried in the U.S. cemetery at Maracabon, with full military honors, in the blue jacket given him by the *Olympia's* crew. Other crewmen, such as Ordinary Seaman Edward W. Johnson and Landsman Michael Carr, were also lost to drowning and dysentery respectively, thus saddening their comrades but earning them immortality through citation in *The Bounding Billow*. It wasn't long before some of the *Olympia's* crew, like Tisdale, were homeward bound, their service tour over. Others settled back into "our regular grooves, performing our tasks like so many automatons." There were seventeen ships now under Dewey's command in Manila Bay and some new missions were unfolding for all of them.[28]

Some of Tisdale's "grooves" related to occupation and pacification duties as the fall of 1898 saw increasing resistance by Aguinaldo and his followers. While the representatives of Spain and the United States wrangled over final peace treaty terms in Paris and the Great Powers danced around who might purchase the Philippines from Spain, McKinley and company (stoked by public opinion) determined that there could be no turning back. What Dewey and the *Olympia* had wrought at Manila Bay solidified its possession, even at the expense of paying Spain $20,000,000 for the privilege. Such were the provisions of the final treaty signed on 10 December—despite pleas for help from Aguinaldo for real and imagined wrongs to his people through centuries of Spanish rule. To Dewey biographers Laurin Healy and Luis Kutner, "The toil of consolidating an empire remained ahead."[29]

Various inspections of the *Olympia's* machinery and space aboard ship during the months following Manila Bay showed her to be in fit shape. Meanwhile, the crew of the *Olympia* were having a high old time of it. They watched the comings and goings of the army troopships before and after the farcical capture of Manila City. The *Charleston's* arrival relieved the *Olympia* and her sister ships of manning the *Nanshan* and *Zafiro*, as well as the captured *Callao*, and the launches used for river service. Relief crews came in on the *China* in late June, preceded slightly by a cold-storage ship carrying Australian beef, "which the admiral bought on sight," noted Tisdale. It was the first fit beef the crew of the *Olympia* had eaten since leaving San Francisco. This commodity apparently came from a species of carabao, Tisdale sneered. But with all of this also came a tightening of discipline. There had been much prize taking ashore, apparently, even among junior officers like the *Raleigh's* Lt. Hugh Rodman. Hardly a boat arrived back at ship that wasn't loaded with spoils from Cavite, the accumulation "gradually changing the appearance of our decks into those of pleasure yachts." But one morning down came an order that cleared ship "and left the bay afloat with rocking chairs, sofas, and gilt-framed saints."[30]

Rodman's self-confessed caper in purloining a silver service ashore netted him little more than the short end of a three-way split of this loot between his captain and Dewey and nothing more. But the *Olympia's* liberation activities netted many crewmembers a stint in the brig. Only, regaled Tisdale, the ship's brig having been declared unfit by the ship's doctor, the prisoners went into double irons and were chained prominently about the decks. So the flagship took on something "suggestive of a human kennel." Still the ever-ingenious American sailors devised some good out of the whole business of captured material. Unable to bring their laundrymen from China or Japan, the *Olympia's* bluejackets merely liberated thousands of white sailor suits from Cavite storehouses, wore them until soiled, and then cast them adrift for a fresh suit. Even Spanish cork helmets acquired new owners, happy to have them guarding heads and necks in the savage tropical sun. The most complimentary greeting exchanged on shore became "Halloo, is that you? I thought it was Stanley in Africa."[31]

By Thanksgiving, when young Tisdale learned that he was going home, he confessed to having tired of the sights and sounds of the Philippines. He was now a veteran, boasting tattoos of his ship and its battle to prove it. Small-arms drill, salvage of the sunken Spanish warships, and small-arms practice had vied with the highlights ashore—dusky beer-dispensing senoritas, a gaggle of press corps from the States reporting on everything, and the comical sights of local policemen, barefoot with fighting cocks under arm, going about their business but arresting no one for any transgression. But those things were fleeting fancies to sailors who wanted to get on with their lives. Chief Petty Officer Holloway, sensing there was no further promotion in the navy, was so anxious to get discharged that he waived transportation and paid his own way to San Francisco soon after the new year to avoid being held over because of the outbreak of the Philippine insurrection. Back in the navy later, he reflected that this was a major mistake, "for had I returned home on either the *Olympia* or the [USS] *Buffalo*, I would have been advanced to the grade of warrant machinist two years earlier than I was eventually."[32]

The months after Dewey's famous victory were important ones for the new admiral as well. Voted a bejeweled sword and reintroduction of the rank of Admiral of the Navy in recognition of his success, Dewey remained at his post in Manila harbor, mixing cooperation with the army ashore and concern about foreign intervention, but also following closely the deteriorating relations with Aguinaldo and the insurgents. A fact-finding expedition into the interior of Luzon in November of 1898 by Paymaster W. B. Wilcox and Naval Cadet Leonard R. Sargent altered Dewey's earlier conclusion that Filipinos would accept some form of American governance, and he reported this to Washington. When McKinley acknowledged acquisition of the islands in December, the die seemed cast for trouble, although Dewey held out hope for accommodation and recommended that a special commission be sent to rectify matters.[33]

If he had misled Aguinaldo as to independence earlier, Dewey now used his squadron to police the little steamboats used by the Filipinos in anticipation of further opposition to the American presence. Meanwhile, back in the United States, partisans of imperialism and their opponents waged their own war of words. Still, Dewey was popular, with sheet music such as "Dewey Did March Two Step" appearing and his ship already the model for soap dishes and pictorial reproductions. There was even a "Dewey cocktail" to quench dry throats. Dewey's own dispatches written in his stateroom aboard the *Olympia* exemplified crisp and modest communication of information to superiors. Only later, after he had gotten home, would Congress call upon him to explain any promises of independence to Aguinaldo. Dewey would consistently deny that he had deceived the natives. He readily admitted using them to oust the Spaniards, but that they wanted independence never entered his head.[34]

Certainly the autumn and winter months of 1898–99 passed rather quickly. Ships constantly moved in and out of Manila Bay, and intra-ship

transfers of personnel continued to accommodate shifting staffing requirements. Antipathy toward foreigners, hence fear for Americans and Euro-
peans residing in the Chinese capital of Tientsin, led to Dewey's dispatch
of the *Boston, Petrel,* and collier *Nero* to those waters in October, where
they landed marines who marched to the city under arms. The intrepid cutter *McCulloch* left for San Francisco in mid-November, finally destined for
her Alaskan assignment. Similarly, the *Nero* left for Frisco two weeks later
upon her return from China, filled with expired service men like Tisdale
from the *Olympia.* The *Raleigh* similarly took another one hundred and
twenty-six of *Olympia*'s crew when she headed to New York via Suez in mid-
December. The collier *Brutus* left for the West Coast at this same time with
overtime men from the *Baltimore*. Most importantly for American interests
in the Far East, arrival of the powerful battleship USS *Oregon* (*Olympia*'s sister from Union Iron Works days) on 18 March 1899 answered Dewey's
prayer for more firepower. One battleship alone "shifted the balance of
power in the Far Pacific," suggested the *Oregon*'s chronicler.[35]

Meanwhile, the *Olympia*'s crew stood to their duties while periodically
enjoying another round of Burnt Cork Minstrelsy gotten up by the chaplain, Father Reaney, from the crew. They posted a splendid 5-and-2 baseball record against army teams from the Eighteenth Infantry and Colorado
and Utah volunteers, and took in customary merrymaking at Thanksgiving and Christmas. Here "palm leaf decorations greeted the eyes everywhere." Boxes of sweet meats came in on every steamer for the boys, noted
Bounding Billow editor L. S. Young, and they were "studies of the culinary
comforts of the 'Old home'—jam, jelly, cookies, candy, fruit cake . . . "
Things of which only mothers think, he added, but to the delight of every
American sailor on the flagship. W. L. Sneath, aboard the *Raleigh* at Manila
Bay but with time left to serve when that ship went home, transferred to
the *Olympia* on 13 December in time to play Uncle Sam at the traditional
New Year's stunt. With all the wardroom officers paying his bills for this
activity, he and his mates rigged the catamaran brig and painted "A Happy
New Year" on the foremast and the dates of the Spanish-American War—
1 May, 3 July, and 13 August—on the sails of the mainmast. He was ready
to do his gig when the new year turned.[36]

There was more to the story than a simple New Year's Day party, however. At noon on that day, Sneath and his crew had pulled away from the

port gangway of the flagship and went around the bow and down the star-board side of the ship and, when amidships, the boatswain of the party called "All hands bring ship to anchor." They threw out a wooden anchor occasioning a great laugh from the ship. The gunner of the party fired off a salute of 19 guns from old .45 caliber rifles lashed to the side of the cata-maran. They were then ordered aboard as the band played a march and the marine guard presented arms. Dewey greeted "Uncle Sam" Sneath and thanked him for coming from such a great distance as Washington, D.C. But the admiral chided him for making a great mistake since he only rated a 13-gun, not a 19-gun, salute. Huffily, but with a twinkle, Sneath pro-claimed that Uncle Sam never made a mistake and informed Dewey, "never mind, I will see that you get them." After lunch came a songfest and story telling, and the party went off to visit other ships of the fleet and put on a little show for the army troops stationed at Cavite, returning about 2:00 A.M. for a good night's rest. Still, the story was not over.

The next August, Sneath (now back in his lowly swabbie station) was walking along the *Olympia*'s deck when Dewey's orderly beckoned him to see the admiral. Dewey recalled the Uncle Sam 19-gun salute and handed Sneath a cablegram, which when translated noted that Congress had accorded Dewey the rank of "Admiral of the Navy." "My flag lieutenant and I have figured it out and your words have come true," the Vermonter told Sneath. "Your words have come true and you are the first man to know that I have been made Admiral of the Navy. I will now get the 19-gun salute you promised me on New Year's Day." He then got out a bottle of Cyrus Noble and two glasses and the enlisted man and the admiral drank to his success. On leaving, Sneath noticed the chief signal quartermaster going into the cabin and, when he came out, he started cutting out an admiral's flag from the blue and white bunting. When it was completed and hoisted, the gun crew fired a 19-gun salute and the ship's whistle blew and everything that could make a noise did so. The ships of the fleet took up the cheering and the noise started the foreign warships and merchant ships cheering. Sneath never forgot either the incident or his "clairvoyancy" with respect to the hero of Manila Bay.

Meanwhile, by late in the year 1898, the squadron's restlessness could be sensed in "Situations Wanted" and "Help Wanted" columns carried by the *Olympia*'s newspaper. Mostly in jest, sailors from the squadron listed their preferences from cook to water tender, from dishwasher to "a man who has traveled with a circus, to juggle dish rag and broom." Another line read "Wanted: a neat, clean, old man, to dump the swill and carry coal to the galley." Another desired "A young man who can win Christmas turkeys; play the guitar and piano; lend a hand to make homeward bound biscuits, and Spanish chest protectors (pan cakes); keep the fore castle sitting room in good order, and see that the 'second mate,' does not get left at mess gear." Yet the most poignant of all wanted "Information of the whereabouts of General Liberty, an old veteran, lost some where between Mirs Bay and Manila." Editor Young, who was responsible for the humor and news stories, was already hawking a book entitled "Story of the Cruise" and "Bounding Billows" complete. He billed this offering as "an authentic story of the eventful cruise of the beautiful cruiser from the year 1895 to 1898, and a complete and succinct history of the part played by the Asiatic squadron

Torpedo maintenance aboard *Olympia* in 1898.
Cyanotype print by George Grantham.

in the war between the United States and Spain." Every man, woman, and child should possess one of these fine books, he proclaimed. It was a sure sign that *Olympia's* bluejackets, at least, were looking for a departure from the Philippines in the new year. Apprentice 2d Class William Ammand went so far as to petition the Secretary of the Navy for an early discharge based on the ill health of his parents and the fact that his time had been extended three months as punishment for remaining ashore at Santa Barbara back in April 1895. In any event, the November–December edition was the last for *The Bounding Billow*.[37]

Dewey and Lamberton sensed the restiveness of the *Olympia's* crew, as a number of the men "went to the mast" when one lieutenant told his men there would be no liberty on Christmas eve. They got it for twenty-four hours. In fact, the admiral decreed that there should be no more quarters until after the holidays. During this period, the navy continued a busy supporting role in the Philippines as one year passed into the next. Joint operations with the army, investigating the far reaches of the archipelago in the interest of determining popular sentiment, as well as ending all vestiges of Spanish control and merely showing the flag were among its functions. Not that the *Olympia* engaged in all such endeavors. Rather, her role now was that of command-and-control ship for the navy in those activities. At home, meanwhile, the McKinley administration wrestled with a peace treaty and what to do about retaining the islands. By February 1899, open defiance had turned to combat between Aguinaldo's people and the United States Army. A civilian commission, dispatched at Dewey's suggestion (he thought the Filipinos "little more than children" but greatly feared that both sides would lose heavily in an all out war), arrived at Manila to find just that on their hands. The so-called Philippine Insurrection would continue for years, despite Aguinaldo's capture in 1901. By then, however, both Dewey and his flagship would be long gone from Philippine waters. Washington would have decided to keep the islands, and America, like other Great Powers of the age, would have opted for empire.[38]

"Sphinx-like, immovable, the *Olympia* always surveyed us," recalled Dewey's friend, writer Frederick Palmer, speaking of this period. "She had become an institution like the cathedral and the Bridge of Spain." And Dewey liked it this way. Having hoisted his new admiral's pennant above the *Olympia* on 4 March, he basically remained aboard his flagship after the fall of Manila, attending to business from there. Much of that business related to policy, more to the daily tasks involving logistical support installations ashore such as a marine hospital and coaling station. Later, he even avoided attending the meetings ashore of the commission which deliberated the fate of the islands. Arising early in the morning for a short constitutional around the deck with his faithful companion, a big chow dog named "Bob," he then returned to his cabin and stateroom for breakfast and the morning's squadron business. After lunch and a short nap, he was off by his steam launch to the city for a daily drive. There he was the object of great curiosity from both city residents and the lounging servicemen waiting to catch a glimpse of the great man. Almost like a viceroy, Dewey rode through the streets, stopping mainly to visit the family of H. D. C. Jones, local manager of the Hong Kong and Shanghai Bank, whose sister-in-law was perhaps the reigning beauty of the moment among the foreign residents. At any event, opined Dewey's most recent biographer, "the Joneses undoubtedly helped to ease the monotony of the admiral's last months in the Philippines."[39]

Olympia's placid demeanor may have resulted from a long-overdue boiler cleaning which was done by Chinese laborers working day and night from 4 January to 5 February 1899. Paymaster Daniel A. Smith, at least, noted some 180 pounds of turned beef, 1,522 pounds of rice, 150 pounds of biscuits, 20 pounds of tea, and 105 pounds of sugar issued to those laborers for their work during this period. Certainly the climate was wearing down both ship and crew, and quarterly survey reports for condemned provisions that spring and early summer listed quantities of meat, vegetables, butter and biscuits simply thrown overboard because of spoilage. Dewey, in addition to Gridley, suffered health problems. But, aside from the nine men wounded in the battle the year before, the flagship itself reflected the Navy Department's overall assessment that the health of Dewey's squadron generally varied little from that of 1897. Actually, the ratio per thousand of daily sick was less on the flagship, or only 12.87 for 1898 compared to 13.87 the previous year. Only thirty-two of the average daily compliment of four hundred fifty-four officers and men had been admitted for disease or injury in the year ending 30 June 1898.[40]

When the Navy Department subsequently tallied the costs of maintaining its ships in commission for the fiscal year ending 30 June, the *Olympia* came in as the third most costly among one hundred ninety-four ships, totaling $11,063,393.82. Discounting the destroyed battleship *Maine* that topped the list at $713,918.06, only the armored cruiser *New York* at $387,871.21 cost more than Dewey's flagship. Yet, of the $372,487.59 chargeable to the *Olympia,* accrued pay of officers, crew, and marines and commuted rations accounted for $224,323.50 of that figure. Medical stores and navy yard repairs were not factored in and the $4,4214.73 spent for repairs at private establishments was the highest in the fleet, due, undoubtedly, to the absence of any U.S. Navy establishments in the Far East. Supplies and accounts added $23,149.49, and incidental expenses such as freight, pilotage, postage, and so forth contributed another $9,695.63. The largest costs directly related to the ship included steam engineering ($69,563.65), ordnance ($23,815.77), construction and repair ($9,585.28), equipment ($5,562.56), and navigation ($2,376.98). The "Queen of the Pacific" ranked above the battleships of the Spanish-American War.[41]

On the first anniversary of the victory at Manila Bay, Dewey received a telegram from President McKinley expressing the gratitude of the American people for his squadron's "brilliant achievements [that] marked an epoch in history which will live in the annals of the world's heroic deeds." By 1899, the United States had forged a new empire. Its herald had been the *Olympia* and George Dewey. America, said its master strategist, Alfred Thayer Mahan, now looked outward. It would be for others to transition that empire to eventual self-determination. A new role beckoned for the hero of Manila Bay and his flagship. Word to that effect finally came on 20 May, and *Olympia's* crew readied her for departure. That morning, photographer William Dinwiddie captured a final shot of the heroic ship in the environment of her famous victory. Dewey's pennant atop the aft mast and his white clad sailors on deck conducting their last minute preparations contrasted with the ship's continuing dull gray battle dress. Dewey himself had gone ashore to pay final respects to army commander Maj. Gen. Elwell Otis as well as the Philippine commissioners. Then, in the afternoon, every ship in the squadron (to be temporarily commanded by the *Oregon's* captain, Albert S. Barker, until Rear Adm. John C. Watson could arrive and officially succeed Dewey), hoisted the signal flags from mastheads. "Bon Voyage," "Good By," and "Happy Sailing," they read. Cheer after cheer went up from bluejacket throats across the squadron as steam whistles added to the din.[42]

Up came the *Olympia*'s anchor at eight bells, or four o'clock, as Dewey, in immaculate, starched white uniform, told Lamberton simply, "Weigh Anchor." Cheering crews lined the rails of every vessel, and ship's bands vied with salute guns as the famous ship slipped out into the bay. Majestically, her rear-sloping bow cut smoothly through Manila Bay's waters one final time. Each American ship honored her passing with a 17-gun salute—proper for Dewey's rank. The black-hulled protected cruiser HMS *Powerful,* lying farthest out, added her cheers and gun salvos as the two ships' bands serenaded one another with "God Save the Queen" and "Auld Lang Syne" in passing. Down the bay ran the American warship until only a few puffs of white smoke on the horizon behind her showed that adieus were still being made. Soon she passed Corregidor and El Fraile, while Dewey and his veterans said their individual farewells to the green hills of Luzon. New York was their new lodestar and they would make a triumphal voyage via Europe for their route. But first stop was Hong Kong, to get rid of that drab war paint.[43]

5

Flagship in a Great White Fleet

Hong Kong was the first stop for the returning heroes of Manila Bay. Reaching the British crown colony three days after leaving the Philippines, the USS *Olympia* went into dry dock once again. Her crew scrambled ashore, their tired admiral facing a new round of social obligations. "I am not sorry to leave," he had told a reporter back in the islands, "I could not stand the care and responsibility much longer." In Hong Kong, the accolades and hoopla served as a fillip. No wonder, he was now Admiral of the Navy and, as salute guns from HMS *Tamar* and the Italian cruiser *Aetna* proclaimed his arrival, Dewey began the obligatory visits to the other ships while in return hosting the governor of the colony and the commander of the garrison, as well as captains of various other national warships in the port, aboard his flagship. As the *Olympia*'s logkeeper duly registered for Tuesday 23 May 1899, "fired a salute to U.S. Consul General. Expended 120 pounds of saluting powder and 64 primers." This would be quite typical over the next few weeks.[1]

HAIL THE CONQUERING HERO COMES

Indeed, while Dewey and his men were entertained by the British, it took two weeks of work to return the *Olympia* to her peacetime luster. The vessel was found to be in good condition and, after cleaning, she went back to a normal livery of buff and white (although without the black stripe that had adorned her sheer in early 1898). Then, promptly on a rainy 6 June, with cheers, whistles, and salute guns again filling the air and her band blaring forth "Auld Lang Syne" and "God Save the Queen," the pride of the American fleet left for her leisurely homeward voyage. She reached Singapore five days later. Here again, the social whirl of sight-seeing, races, colonial teas, and dinners proved fatiguing for the admiral and his crew, especially since he wished not only to pay respects to the governor general but to lend support to an embattled outgoing American consul, Spencer Pratt, who was under severe fire at home for supposed mishandling of the Aguinaldo matter. Here too, the *Olympia* encountered a Spanish army transport, late out of Manila with troops aboard—destitute of resources. Many of them clamored aboard the American warship "and we fitted them out in blue cloth," Apprentice Wayne Longenecher wrote his brother. The "poor fellows didn't have any clothes except what they had on, those being very thin [and] suited only for such a climate as Manila." Four days later Dewey and the *Olympia* sailed once more, bidding farewell forever to the Far East where both had gained fame and glory.[2]

Dewey wasn't completely set on his itinerary, wishing to see local conditions at various ports, particularly the quarantine situation. But he was determined to give "his Olympians" an opportunity to discover something of the world as a reward "for good conduct after seventeen months on this station," he wrote his brother. Additionally, desiring personally to return to the scene of earlier happy associations in the Mediterranean, Dewey felt that this track for the *Olympia* would enable the sailors to avoid having to brave much of the "circus racket" that would accompany any debarkation on the West Coast of the United States. So from Singapore, the voyage took the ship to Colombo, Ceylon. They skirted Bombay, where an outbreak of bubonic plague prevented crewmen like Apprentice Longenecher from taking in a tiger hunt, and headed to the Gulf of Aden—reached on a blazing bright 6 July. By this time, the five-foot ten-inch, 190-pound Longenecher had forgotten about tigers, proudly informing his brother that he was taking boxing lessons, sporting a mustache, and "getting fatter every day and can eat enough for two men."[3]

Meanwhile, Lamberton had rendered an encouraging end-of-year report on the *Olympia*, noting her year's tour of service and the consumption of 4,660 tons of coal (at a cost of $57,630.43) since 30 June 1898. "The general condition of the ship is very good and the efficiency is excellent," he observed. Tropical heat had eliminated shipboard drills in summer but they had returned later, although no major target practice had occurred with the main guns of the ship, no torpedoes had been run, and no tactical maneuvers were held excepting those during the capture of Manila. The crew's discipline "has been very good"; thirty-four enlistments, thirty-two discharges, and thirty-three desertions, three men tried by general and forty-one by summary courts-martial, and 660 petty punishments attested

Olympia's Fourth Division entertains while en route home from Manila in 1898.

Officers and ladies dancing the Mazy waltz
aboard the *Olympia* in 1898.

to continuing high spirits among the sailors. Medically, the *Olympia* had suffered three deaths, twenty-three hospital cases, and fourteen cases invalided home. There were, said Lamberton, "one case of smallpox, two cases of dysentery of severe type, two cases of typhoid fever, four cases of consumption of the lungs, four cases of rupture, and one case of appendicitis who was left behind in the General Hospital at Colombo, Ceylon." The ship's doctor also reported an additional 127 cases of "remittent fever of malarial character." In all, however, "the crew has enjoyed good health as a rule."[4]

Suez was the next port of call for the *Olympia* on 12 July, with coaling at Port Said the next day (where the crew cheered the transport *Grant* taking 2,000 U.S. soldiers out to Manila). Then, a longer stay at Alexandria allowed everyone to visit the pyramids outside Cairo. By mid-July, a more relaxed and rested hero of Manila Bay and his flagship were steaming the Adriatic. Dewey was considerably prouder of the ship he now commanded than when last in the region in the 1880s; he was then in charge of the aging wooden sloop *Pensacola*, hardly a match for any of the other nation's flotillas in the region at that time. In excellent spirits and "fairly good" health now that he had left the tropics, Dewey would enjoy the pleasures of Trieste, Naples, Leghorn, and Villefranche, hosting visiting dignitaries while the *Olympia* thundered customary salutes in their honor. He managed one major diplomatic faux pas in the Austrian port by telling a dining acquaintance (who turned out to be an amateur correspondent for the *New York Herald*) that "Our next war will be with Germany." However prophetic such an opinion, Dewey's Germanophobia, developed in the Philippines the previous summer, now caused an uproar in the States and in Europe. Equally controversial were Dewey's statements to a *London Daily News* reporter in Naples, where the admiral espoused self-government for the Filipino insurgents and cessation of violent suppression of the reaction to American rule. "I should like to see autonomy first conceded and then annexation might be talked about," he declared. The press immediately positioned Dewey in opposition to American government policy and policymakers. In truth, the hoopla probably only added to the excitement preceding Dewey's arrival in New York in late September.[5]

Trieste was made memorable for more than Dewey's faux pas, however. Here, the *Olympia* crew buried two of their mates, thirty-eight-year-old Electrician 2d Class Isak Edlamik Rask and twenty-six-year-old Seaman Gustav Alfred Lindholm, both dead of tuberculosis. A funeral group from the ship complete with wreath bearers and band escort took Rask's body from the local hospital two miles to the cemetery on 28 July. A full dirge-playing Austrian military band and soldier escort also went along. Lindholm lingered until 14 September, his ship long since departed. In what was intended as a simple ceremony, another march to the cemetery under Austrian military escort ended in a second burial with full military honors. Thus, in a corner of yet another forgotten foreign field, sailors from the flagship *Olympia* provided a little bit of America for eternity.[6]

From Naples, it was but a day's run to Leghorn where, on 13 August, the *Olympia* received honors from the Italian cruiser *Tripoli*. Dewey, feeling poorly, passed "the quietest week spent at any port in Italy" and, as a result, fully recovered from his indisposition. For the flagship's officers, however, side trips to Florence and Pisa and shore leave for the men provided entertainment. The Italian government was not overwhelmingly pleased at the glorification of America's victory over Spain and had to suffer the protests of that country's ambassador in order to maintain good relations. Dewey and his ship remained aloof from this controversy, duly reported in the *London Daily Mail,* and, "ever intent on the comfort, health and enjoyment of his men," promised them a chance to see France and the famed Riviera. With this in view, they sailed from Leghorn for Villefranche, near Nice, arriving there on 22 August.[7]

Having accepted New York City's invitation for a major reception and parade, Dewey and Lamberton were most anxious that the *Olympia's* crew have a chance to practice their drilling and "evolutions" (impossible aboard ship). French authorities granted permission to land the flagship's battalion "in order for they might be in trim for the parade at New York." The French prefect of the Alpes-Maritimes, as well as American chargé d'affaires at Paris, Henry Vignand met with Dewey while at Villefranche, for he was outranked only by the British commander in chief in the Mediterranean, Adm. Sir John O. Hopkins, K. C. B. In any port where Dewey happens to be, suggested one observer, "unless Hopkins is present, he [Dewey] makes the sun set, and at the time he chooses." These words seem pompous, yet so very indicative of the bumptious young imperial power at that moment. The Americans' triumphal tour from the Far East climaxed at British-held Gibraltar from 4–10 September, where "nowhere in Europe was the reception of the Olympia more heralded or more pronounced."[8]

From Gibraltar, the last part of the voyage was the run across the Atlantic to New York. Getting under way at 10:30 A.M. on a clear and pleasant 10 September, HMS *Devastation* "paraded guard" in salute to Dewey and his crew. More critical at this point was a technical matter. *Olympia's* chief engineer, F. H. Bailey, had informed Lamberton and the admiral at Trieste on 20 July, that the ship's starboard propeller blades were badly bent and the ship needed to be docked in order to make the replacements. This could be done elsewhere in the Mediterranean, but "it will take at least two weeks to renew the blades and three or four days to straighten them should it be found possible." Other technical repairs needed to be done as she had not received a major maintenance overhaul since her original Mare Island outfitting in 1895. Apparently, Lamberton had determined to first get the admiral to his victory celebrations in the States. So, the famous warship accordingly limped across the Atlantic at a fraction of her vaunted speed.[9]

If the *Olympia*'s trip from the Far East thus far had been made at leisurely speeds of from 10 to 12 knots, her trans-Atlantic crossing dipped to about 9.5 knots. Good Welsh coal—Cardiff, Corys Merthyr, and Ferndale—fed her fires, and smooth seas aided the endeavor. According to log entries, disposition of spoiled cans of provisions overboard, the conduct of divine service by Chaplain William H. I. Reaney, battle and other drills, and the taking of bottom soundings were highlights of the uneventful cruise. In the end, Dewey and the *Olympia* made land fall at Barnegat Light on the New Jersey coast at 12:35 A.M. Tuesday, 26 September, turned northward, and entered Lower New York Bay. They returned a 17-gun salute from the army's coastal battery at Sandy Hook, and anchored in thirty fathoms about 7:17 A.M. The *Olympia* was home after nearly five years in the Far East. Moreover, she was two days ahead of schedule. Noted one of Dewey's admiring biographers: "Admiral Dewey took New York and the country by surprise in much the same way in which he surprised the Spaniards."[10]

A NEW YORK WELCOME

Following obligatory communiqués to the Navy Department, plus quarantine inspection, Dewey and his crew were ready to celebrate. The admiral admitted that "we're ahead of time, but my rule is that it's better to be too early than too late." Officially, they had not even arrived yet, he said, so there was no need to affect "in any way the preparations our friends are making to receive us." Expected to stop in Bermuda, he never mentioned the propeller difficulty, merely noting that an expected gale caused the *Olympia* to press ahead directly to New York. Dewey's impatience could be felt in a letter he had written to his son from Gibraltar, noting his itinerary of rapidly going to Washington, then to Vermont, and "after that to get out of everything I can." Unfortunately, his admirers, the public, and the government had other ideas. On the afternoon of the twenty-sixth, not only was Dewey's son George reunited with his father, but countless others were scrambling aboard to greet the conquering hero. They included Rear Adm. William Sampson and other officers of the North Atlantic Squadron, set for the grand naval review in the Hudson River, as well as prominent civilians like Sir Thomas Lipton, owner of the *Shamrock* and challenger for the America's cup, as well as benefactor of all that tea distributed among *Olympia*'s crewmen when stopped at Colombo, Ceylon.[11]

Later that day, the *Olympia's* crew gave Lipton almost as warm a send-off as they might have given Dewey himself. Brandishing the little tins of tea, they rendered cheer upon cheer as Sir Thomas's launch pulled away from the *Olympia's* side. Dewey, hearing the commotion, rushed to the rail, shouting laughingly to the teaman, "There! You see I can't stop them. I can't do anything with them at all!" Indeed, the air was electric with anticipation of the long-planned patriotic reception. Back on 18 May, New York's Municipal Assembly had resolved to commemorate Dewey's victory and had appropriated $150,000 to that effect. The Committee of One Thousand had been formed by Mayor Robert A. Van Wyck to organize the fête and, by the end of June, matters had been put in place once they knew of Dewey's progress back from the Far East. Now, early on the morning of 27 September, the *Olympia* with the admiral on board would slowly steam through the Verrazano Narrows and take her place at the head of the assembled warships off Tompkinsville on Staten Island in preparation for the gala celebration of 29–30 September 1899. At 8:00 A.M., the *Olympia* performed the first of her daily oblations, "Hoisting the Colors." As everyone aboard ship fell into place on deck, the marine band played the "Star-Spangled Banner," and the Stars and Stripes unfolded from the halyards. The flag being up, commented one observer, "the Admiral was officially at home," and the day's visitation once more began. One half hour later, all visitors were cleared from the ship as the journey into Tompkinsville was about to begin.[12]

Under way for New York's inner harbor at 9:00 A.M., the thunderous welcome began in earnest. Every vessel in the vicinity that had a gun or a whistle seemed "to call it into action, each vying with the other in a mighty effort to make the most noise." Warships of the Atlantic Squadron—the *Texas, Brooklyn, Massachusetts, Indiana,* and *New York,* all veterans of the Santiago fight—boomed forth their own salutary tributes to the newcomer. *Olympia's* battery thundered forth its own salvo of thirteen guns in compliment to Sampson and his command. Dropping anchor at 10:20 A.M., Dewey soon set about on his own round of returning the official calls and visits. After going ashore to pay respects at the navy yard, the admiral closed the day's festivities by returning aboard ship and retiring to his cabin.[13]

Dewey was right back at it the next morning. From 10:00 A.M. until early afternoon, the *Olympia* was the scene of comings and goings of dignitaries. They included a committee from Washington, D.C., to clarify that city's

Olympia during celebrations in New York City
upon her return from the Far East in 1899.

upcoming festivities, army representatives, and Governor Theodore Roosevelt, who beamed that it almost seemed like the old days in the Navy Department when he and Dewey had worked to prepare the navy for its new role. The former Assistant Secretary added that, "Since the last time I saw the Admiral he has gone up alongside of Farragut and Nelson," alluding to two fighting sea dogs of old. But most impressive to Dewey, apparently, was when one member of the Washington committee presented him with an admiral's flag that had been Civil War hero David Farragut's pennant years before on the *Hartford* when both sailors had helped capture New Orleans. Dewey was beside himself vowing, "I'll fly it—I'll fly it at the masthead—I'll fly it in the parade—I'll fly it always—and—when I strike my admiral's flag this will be the flag I shall strike!"[14]

Still, Roosevelt remained as always the true crowd pleaser. Once aboard the *Olympia,* he addressed the cheering sailors, proclaiming "I am most proud of the men aboard, from Admiral Dewey down to the least important man in the whole ship's company. We are glad to welcome you back." Roosevelt would later host a reception on board the *New Hampshire* for the brass, but the *Olympia*'s crew may themselves have experienced the most meaningful event of the day. Between 8:00 and 9:00 P.M., the call to general quarters was sounded. The "men behind the guns" who had participated in the Manila Bay victory lined up to receive medals authorized by Congress to honor their deeds. Captain Lamberton took center stage as he told the recipients, "You have been a long time in getting these, men, but they are the sort of thing that will keep, and they mean just as much to-day as they did seventeen months ago." Everyone richly deserved "these tokens" and "the men who commanded you are as proud of you as the country which gives you these medals," he concluded. Some present probably wished that Charles Gridley were still alive to join in. But among the most appreciative of all were the Chinese cooks who, "notwithstanding that their place was among the pots and pans when the serious business of fighting was on hand, left the galley and hustled for Uncle Sam."[15]

It had also been hoped that a 44-inch-high bronze memorial tablet from the people of Olympia and Washington State could be affixed between the two forward 8-inch guns aboard ship prior to its arrival back in the States. Anxious letters had passed between James A. Haight in the state capital and Secretary of the Navy Long in Washington. Alas, this gesture could not be accomplished and had to await the anticipated general overhaul in Boston. Small bronze medals, struck to commemorate the planned tablet, were at least publicly available. On the one side they bore the likeness of the tablet; on the other Paul Winter Morris's likeness of Dewey and the *Olympia*. Meanwhile, Thursday evening in New York Harbor passed with a magnificent illumination fête that defied description. Red fires, bonfires, search lights, electric lights in emblematic figures, words, and groups—all combined to transform night into day. During the display, 1,500 choristers from the People's Choral Union steamed around the flagship singing a repertoire that included "America," "See the Conquering Hero Comes," "Hallelujah Chorus" from "The Messiah," and the "Hymn of Thanksgiving," to which the *Olympia*'s band answered with music of its own. All the while, Dewey stood in the glare of the lights on his flagship's deck, "bowing in acknowledgement of the courtesy of his visitors." The evening ended all too soon, and "lights out" tumbled a weary admiral and crew once more into berths and hammocks.[16]

If anything, Friday 29 September was even more spectacular in its planned program. Dewey again rose early, receiving (and returning the courtesy of), dignitaries like New York Mayor Van Wyck. More pinning of badges and ribbons, more salutary addresses with the admiral—alluding to all those gunnery drills preceding his Philippine victory—admitting of the *Olympia,* "yes, she is a good ship, but it's not so much to the ship as to its armament and trained crew that the result at Manila is due." Then, following the noonday meal, all of the ships of the North Atlantic Squadron, led by Dewey's, steamed from their anchorage at the quarantine station up the Hudson River to Grant's Tomb in a sweeping gesture of American naval power. What a glorious sight it must have been for spectators—city police and fire boats, troop and hospital ships of the War Department, yachts from the New York Yacht Club, including Pierpont Morgan's *Corsair* and Sir Thomas Lipton's *Erin,* as well as large steamboats and countless miscellaneous and unattached vessels—escorting the buff-and-white-clad warships of the navy. Turning about, and anchoring just below Grant's Tomb, the *Olympia* dropped anchor to take full honors of a naval pass-in-review.[17]

What an honor for the *Olympia* to preside over two parallel columns (one of battleships, the other of other fleet elements) and the various non-naval vessels steaming past them down the river. The parade committee's scheme showed the order of passage, "but tugs with their soft-coal smoke crowded against spic-and-span yachts belonging to millionaires, and merchant and excursion vessels crowded these in turn." Vintage photographs and other artwork show a waterway literally teeming with pennant-and-bunting-dressed ships of all descriptions. Salute guns from fleet and shore hammered incessantly as did the steam whistles and other noisemakers. At length, the last boat passed, "the bugles from the war-ships rang out across the waters, the flags came down, the excursion-steamers drifted away, and night closed over all, revealing the ships outlined in light for the evening's illumination." Indeed, the spectacle passed to yet another phase with fireworks sent aloft from all over Manhattan, Brooklyn, out on Long Island, and over on Staten Island's Barron Hill. Lighters passing down both the Hudson and East rivers also contributed fireworks. "Illuminated craft, illuminated piers, illuminated buildings, illuminated bridge; in short, illuminated New York," was the way one commentator put it. From the Brooklyn Bridge alone shone a gigantic electrical display: "Welcome, Dewey."[18]

The three-day extravaganza finally came to a close with Saturday's Dewey parade down New York's Fifth Avenue. Up at dawn and aboard a police

Dewey welcomes
New York State
Gov. Theodore
Roosevelt aboard
Olympia during the
1899 celebrations
in New York City.

patrol boat by 7:30 A.M., the admiral landed at the Battery and was escorted
to City Hall, where he received a loving cup from the mayor at 9:00 sharp.
He escaped hundreds of serenading school children since the congested condition of the street railway system prevented their arrival on time. (They
would be heard from later.) Dewey and Van Wyck left city hall by carriage,
taking their place at the head of the parade. Some 35,000 marchers awaited
their pleasure. Then, at 11:00 A.M., led by Maj. Gen. Charles F. Roe and staff
and followed by John Philip Sousa's famous band blaring forth "Stars and
Stripes Forever," the triumphal procession stepped off. Behind Sousa's musi-
cians strode Lt. Cdr. George D. Calvocoresses's battalion of *Olympia* sailors
just in front of the Dewey–Van Wyck carriage. Behind them came Dewey's
ships' captains of Manila Bay fame in carriage, and farther back were the
Olympia's junior officers in two parallel carriages. If the shore practice at
Villefranche had done any good, surviving photographs of the *Olympia*'s
marchers fail to show it. The crowd did not care—here were America's
heroes, their own American boys, victors in a glorious battle with Spain.[19]

The procession made its way southward from Fifty-ninth Street and Fifth Avenue to Worth Square. The long line of carriages also conveyed Roosevelt and other civilians, such as Sen. Chauncey Depew and various governors, rear admirals Schley and Sampson of Santiago fame, other naval officers and army generals, and, back in the throng, the gray-cloaked cadets from West Point, detachments of both U.S. regular and National Guard soldiers (troops, actually, from fifteen states). Even veterans of the Spanish-American conflict and the Civil War were in attendance. At one point, the 1,600 assembled school choristers had their brief moment of glory when Dewey, catching sight of relatives as he passed the Waldorf Astoria hotel, momentarily stopped the procession to exchange greetings. Much was made then and later about price commanded for positions of vantage for viewing the parade. Not only did seats in the numerous reviewing stands command high prices, but rooms in houses along the route brought $300 to $500 for the afternoon. Speculators offered the owner of one four-story building on Fifth Avenue the sum of $3,000 for the use of his windows.[20]

The parade (captured on early Edison motion picture footage) passed through the famous one hundred-foot-high Dewey Arch. Erected in the admiral's honor and prepared in just six weeks by artists and sculptors from a mixture of wood, excelsior, and plaster of paris overlying a wire frame, it served as a model for a planned permanent edifice to appear later. The structure resembled the famous Arch of Titus in Rome and appropriately recaptured the ancient glamour of Imperial Rome for the heralds of the new American empire. Heroic statues of Union admiral David Farragut, Gridley, and Dewey himself were joined by a group called "the Return," portraying a father and mother welcoming home their sailor son. Above all stood an angelic figure representing Victory. One waggish report criticized her hair, which flowed loosely in a manner later thought stylish but in that era considered suitable only for the boudoir. The reporter thought it was "almost negligee."[21]

Then, at about Thirty-fourth Street, *Olympia*'s sailors stepped to the side of the avenue so that Dewey and the other dignitaries could alight from their carriages and ascend to the reviewing stand that faced the Worth Monument. For the next four to six hours, Dewey stood for the march-past. Finally, about 6:00 P.M., the parade ended. The *Olympia*'s sailors went off to a smoker and vaudeville concert at the Waldorf's grand ballroom. An exhausted Dewey was permitted the luxury of dining quietly ashore with relatives. It is unclear whether or not the admiral ever returned to ship or remained in the city in a house set aside for his use. More certain is the fact that it was yet another night of fireworks—eleven different displays, the most spectacular of which featured a 1,000-square-foot portrait of Dewey, formed of colored rockets.[22]

The celebrations continued the following week in Washington (where Pres. William McKinley presented Dewey with a bejeweled Tiffany sword and belt, commissioned by Congress. That grateful legislative body had appropriated $10,000 for Dewey's sword as well as commemorative medals and badges (among numismatists, the coveted Dewey medal) for his squadron's crews. Then, it was on to Vermont where a cornerstone was laid for Dewey Hall at his alma mater, Norwich University, as well as other commemorations in his hometown, the state capital of Montpelier. Feelings were strong at this time about Dewey making a run for the presidency, and he was well into courting his second wife while riding the high tide of publicity and popularity as he repaired to Washington to assume duties as the top admiral in the Navy Department.[23]

Meanwhile, the country swooned over trinkets, medallions, and other memorabilia sporting the likenesses of Dewey and his famous warship. Milk glass butter dishes shaped like the *Olympia*, as well as water pitchers and tumblers, commemorative plates, and kerchiefs festooned with likenesses of Dewey and his ship—one and inseparable, either side by side or on respective sides of the object—all symbolized America's infatuation with the heroes of Manila Bay. In fact, the country seemed flooded with merchandise labeled "Dewey," with soda foundations dispensing "Dewey nectar" and "Dewey ice cream," as well as Manila phosphate. There were Dewey buttons, marches, gallops, and waltzes, as well as ties, shirt waists, stick pins, paper weights, and both children and towns named and renamed for the admiral. All rather silly, but it was typically American at this boisterous time and place.[24]

The hoopla subsided quickly for both Dewey and the *Olympia*. Just when and where Dewey bade farewell to the "men behind the guns" who had made possible his fame and glory remains unclear. Indeed, the *Olympia's* crew made one more swing past in parade—in Boston, where the ship went in October for the much-needed overhaul. But the admiral and his former flagship departed on separate courses for the duration of their careers. That which had brought the two together in the first place, far across the Pacific, now lay in the hands of other men and other ships. The *Olympia* gained a hard won rest, reporting at the Boston Navy Yard by 10 October preparatory to going out of commission. Dewey's distinctive four-star pennant still flew at the main mast. But her mustachioed, dapper admiral had departed for the hurly-burly swirl of the nation's capital, amidst what one later admirer aptly termed "the Dewey craze." The crew's laundry, hanging from the foremast, signaled the change. A persnickety Dewey would never have permitted that touch.[25]

NEW ROLES AND MISSIONS

The sea breezes of autumn could be felt as the *Olympia* went out of service at the Boston Navy Yard on 8 November 1899. For the next two years, home for the "Queen of the Pacific" would be the venerable facility situated at the confluence of the Charles and Mystic rivers—old Moulton's

Olympia crewmen posing for the camera in 1898.

Point where the British troops had landed preparatory to the battle of Bunker Hill in 1775. Despite having the oldest naval dry dock in the country, Boston could not accommodate much of the New Steel Navy, which required larger facilities, so Dry Dock Number 2 had been started in 1899. It lay unfinished at the time of *Olympia*'s residency. Brick and granite buildings and perhaps 2,000 employees served the needs of the fleet at this facility, commanded from 1899 until August 1901 by Rear Adm. William T. Sampson, hero of Santiago Bay, and his successor Rear Adm. Mortimer L. Johnson. The *Olympia* would be in good care.[26]

Still listed with "schooner" rigging on navy lists, Dewey's flagship was slated for changes to both her outward appearance and interior arrangements. As a Boston Navy Yard spokesman reported to the Navy Department in 1902, "This vessel received a general overhauling, with repairs and changes embodying modern improvements in all respects." For one thing, she would receive new and improved ammunition hoists for her 8-inchers, similar to those destined for the *New York, Indiana, Oregon,* and *Massachusetts,* as the relentless pace of technological modernization continued over the New Navy. Similar upgrading of coal loading and handling gear, installation of thermal insulation, removal of all torpedo tubes, enlargement of the pilot house, installation of a lifting boom on the main mast, and extension of the aft bridge deck along with installation of a signal house were accomplished at this time. Adding icing to the cake—in what the cruiser's modern restoration director, Don Birkholz Jr., has styled this "most extensive refit of her active career"—were the gilt bow and stern decorations commemorating the Manila Bay victory. Yet, as he also notes, the soundness of the *Olympia*'s overall design precluded any major changes to her arrangement and machinery.[27]

The Spanish war had made a battle fleet all the rage. None of the 1890s-era "first-borns" could match newer battleships, monitors, or other class vessels of what would soon be identified generically (if inaccurately) as Teddy Roosevelt's "Great White Fleet." Furthermore, none of these ships would be part of the show-of-force fleet that the president sent around the world in 1907–8. Nonetheless, the *Olympia* well represented the growing American sea power which, by this time, was costing citizens millions of dollars in construction and maintenance. In 1899 alone, the "Queen of the Pacific" racked up $911,026.28 in maintenance costs, including $14,276,30 in repairs for twelve months service in fiscal year 1899. The *Olympia* still cost $278,423.43 to maintain for a mere four and one half months service the following fiscal year. By anyone's standards, she stood near the top in terms of most expensive units in the fleet.[28]

The *Olympia*'s refitting took longer than anticipated. Early estimates suggested as much as fifteen months, or completion by 1 June 1901. As the national press continued to find a source of copy in the famous ship, commentators in December noted repair costs approaching one and a half million dollars. For one thing, tropical insects had literally shredded the exotic Central American interior woodwork in the officer's country. Two packets of damage went to the Navy Department illustrating the worm-eaten wood (almost reduced to chalk in composition), as well as cellulose packing "practically a mass of black mud." Corrugated steel partitions and metal-hinged bunks answered the worm problem. But lessons from the recent Spanish conflict also prompted addition of asbestos sheathing for fire protection and thermal insulation. In fact, any combustible material discovered during the refitting was removed. The hull underwent scaling, repair, and repainting and all the cofferdams were emptied of cacao fiber cellulose and refitted with fireproof cornpith cellulose after the compartments had been thoroughly scaled and painted. Protective air screens and other means of temperature reduction were added in the forward 5-inch magazine. General repairs were scheduled for the magazines, shell rooms, and fixed ammunition rooms. A steel chart house was contemplated, but the existing wooden one was merely enlarged. In April of 1901, the Bureau of Navigation in Washington still explored alterations for the ward room pantry and engineer's log room.[29]

The formal survey report on the vessel was approved on 9 February 1900. In addition to the work mentioned previously, it provided for docking and undocking, closing of torpedo ports, repairing and repainting double bottoms and their fittings, general repairs to bilges, watertight doors, and scuttles, and repairs and improvements to the ammunition rooms, ammunition hoists, and their motors. It cited repairs and renewals to drainage, flushing, fresh-water, and fire systems, as well as repairs and alterations to the ventilating system and dynamo room. Portions of decks needed repairs and renewal, and removing wooden joiner work where rendered necessary by deck renewal and replacing same with metal was called for. Repairs to boats

Olympia at Boston Navy Yard circa
October–November 1899, where she
was decommissioned for overhaul.

and blocks, renewal of boats, and substituting electrical power for steam for
the turning of the turrets and for ventilating blowers completed the
required tasks.[30]

Still not finished by the end of 1901, the Navy Department wrote one
querulous correspondent, Frank L. Vanmess, just before Christmas that the
Olympia would be put back in commission "sometime during the last half
of January." As *Olympia* was still fitted out as a flagship, the New York Navy
Yard had supplied an outfit of table linen and flags, and she had also
received a special auxiliary condenser for use by the dynamo engines
accompanying more electrical power aboard ship. Finally recommissioned
in January, she left the Boston Navy Yard for the North Atlantic station
at 11:00 A.M. on 10 February. The new and improved *Olympia* had lost none
of her "admirable blend of heavy armament, thick protective deck, high
speed, and great endurance" that marked her as "a high point in U.S. protected cruiser design," in the eyes of naval historian John D. Alden. Naval

restorationist Don Birkholz Jr. notes that the absence of major changes to her arrangement and machinery "speaks well of her design" since many of her contemporaries required major alterations "to maintain their utility." But gone were her torpedo tubes and fighting tops, and her anchor hawsepipes were relocated. She also had a slightly new paint scheme, the buff or light straw having been extended to superstructure and turrets as well as masts and funnels. The *Olympia*'s library (assembled by the New York Navy Yard) numbered seven hundred fifty books (three hundred fifty of which were allocated to the crew's use). Two twenty-kilowatt electric motors now turned her turrets.[31]

Most striking, however, were those ornate bow and stern ornaments now indicative of navies everywhere, but particularly pronounced in the turn-of-the century American fleet. Gilded scrollwork with the name "Olympia" for the stern and similar work enclosing a bronze figurehead of an eagle with unspread wings ornamented the bow. Alvan C. Nye of the Hayden Company in New York had made these ornaments from the torpedo ports carried by the vessel at Manila Bay and from additional metal furnished by the manufacturer. Noted sculptor Augustus Saint-Gaudens had rendered the design commemorating the victory at Manila Bay. It almost seemed a throwback to similar embellishment of ships in the heroic age of sail. Ironically, despite the delays the refurbishing did not cost as much as anticipated. End-of-fiscal-year expenditures showed only a total of about $258,000 for repairs to the vessel and her equipage.[32]

Capt. H. W. Lyon now took the helm of the *Olympia*. This nearly forty-year veteran officer took her south to Tompkinsville and Sandy Hook at the entrance to New York Harbor, rendezvousing with Rear Adm. Robley D. "Fighting Bob" Evans (who hoisted his flag aboard ship) and the *San Francisco* and *Cincinnati*. Together, they proceeded to Yorktown, Virginia, before undergoing a two-day Board of Inspection visit and sea trials in late March. Apparently, "sea practice" with the *Olympia*'s guns proved very satisfactory on the thirty-first although both 5- and 8-inch ammunition hoists were not performing very well, noted ordnance officer Lt. C. M. Fahs. Jerrybuilt solutions could not have pleased Lyon at all. On 4 April, Rear Adm. F. J. Higginson—"Higgy, as they called him in the fleet, a bit hard and cranky, yet under his Boston hide a very kind hearted man," according to future Chief of Naval Operations William V. Pratt, who served under him at this time in the *Kearsarge*—transferred his flag from that battleship. Once again, the *Olympia* became a flagship, now of the North Atlantic Squadron.[33]

Then, it was off to Caribbean waters, the area of greatest involvement and concern to the navy. By 1 May, however, the *Olympia* had returned northward in time to welcome its old friend Admiral Dewey and his staff at 2:00 P.M. on 4 May for inspection. Target practice and other drills preceded escort duties later in the month. While flying the flag of the commander in chief of the North Atlantic Squadron in company with the battleships *Kearsarge* and *Alabama*, the *Olympia* helped escort the French battleship *Gaulois* and participating dignitaries for the unveiling of a statue in Washington honoring general and marshall the comte de Rochembeau, commander of French forces in the American Revolution. She then proceeded to the Hudson River and the dedication of the Stony Point battlefield below West Point where, one hundred twenty-three years earlier, American Continentals had wrested that strategic spot from the British. Immediately thereafter, she checked in at the New York Navy Yard and went into dry dock for routine hull maintenance.[34]

A similar revisitation in September led Higginson to complain caustically to the Secretary of the Navy that "The Olympia joined the fleet in April, but has had to spend two months since then at a navy yard, though only just commissioned and having been thoroughly overhauled and repaired." In fact, the *Olympia*'s seemingly repeated visits to repair facilities figured in the secretary of the navy's general lament next year in his 1903 annual report that "The mobility and consequent efficiency of the North Atlantic Fleet particularly, and of naval vessels everywhere to a greater or less degree, has heretofore been impaired by the length of time spent at navy-yards."[35]

Secretary Moody's further observation, that there was "nearly always something about the complicated mechanism of a naval vessel that needs attention, and when at a navy-yard the temptation to take advantage of the opportunity to make and continue repairs is natural," simply reflected the obvious to men like Higginson, Lyon, and other operators of those vessels. Frequent visits to navy yards for repairs and long delays were certainly "objectionable" to both operators and administrators. Minor repairs might place a cruiser or a battleship "in enforced inactivity" for a considerable time, "to the prejudice of the efficiency of the fleet." While the *Olympia's* "enforced inactivity" for fiscal year 1902–3 amounted to fifty-four days (15 percent of the period), she ranked sixth behind other units like the battleships *Alabama* (one hundred thirty-three days or about 36 percent), *Kearsarge* (one hundred four days or about 28 percent), *Indiana* (102 days or about 28 percent), *Massachusetts* (97 days or about 27 percent), and *Texas* (in commission only from 3 November 1902, 48 days or about 20 percent). Still, the secretary, upon the concurrence of the chiefs of both the Navigation and Construction and Repair bureaus, eventually decreed that the North Atlantic Squadron's principal vessels "shall not be required to visit a navy yard for docking or repairs, under ordinary circumstances, more than once a year." Moody wanted it understood that, while applicable especially to the North Atlantic Fleet, the directive applied equally to all vessels of the navy—"a decided step not only in the direction of efficiency, but of economy as well."[36]

At least one of those return visits to Boston, in June 1902, led to refitting *Olympia's* masts for wireless telegraphy. Her original steel rig was changed to "a more archaic form that included fidded or square barred, wooden topmasts and topgallant masts," to permit lowering. The enclosed fighting tops were removed and replaced with open top platforms and the new rig stood ten feet taller than the original. This alteration, suggests Don Birkholz Jr., "may have been prompted by a perceived need to support the wireless antenna with nonmetallic spars." It added ten feet to the height of *Olympia's* masts. In any case, the full accounting of work performed during the navy yard visits suggests a certain "tinkering" that was part of the navy's shore maintenance for what were far more delicate mechanisms and weapons platforms than one normally associates with steel ship technology.[37]

Nevertheless, between these navy yard visits in August 1902 the flagship ably served fleet maneuvers off Massachusetts and Rhode Island, setting out targets for the battleships and transporting naval reserves much as she had done in California before sailing for the Far East five years earlier. She also tested the effectiveness of her new wireless equipment. Perhaps of equal importance, the *Olympia's* contingent of U.S. marines participated as part of the fleet's battalion in various tours ashore at Menemsha Bight, Martha's Vineyard, and Block Island. Here they experienced drilling and instruction in guard duties, extended order, scouting, and entrenching, as well as practical instruction in various modes of attack and defense that formed part of joint army-navy cooperation exercises. "This combination of practical work, followed by theoretical discussion," later reported the Marine Corps commandant, "has enabled the officers of the battalion to derive the fullest possible benefit from the exercises and maneuvers." Obviously, the *Olympia*'s contingent was already adjusting to evolving roles and missions as a landing force, not merely shipboard guards, in the new navy of American empire. At the expiration of the maneuvers, the vessels of the squadron were dispersed to the navy yards to undergo repairs preparatory to the winter's work of the fleet.[38]

Indeed, the roles and missions of both sea services were changing with the new century. Ever present concern about European intrusion into both the Far East and Latin America preoccupied the navy's strategic planning group, the General Board, under Dewey. His own phobia about an ascendant Germany was ever present. So, it behooved the navy to suitably adjust its 1903 force structure of two hundred fifty-two ships fit for service and forty-five more under construction to the new responsibilities bequeathed it by the Spanish war. The strategic plan chosen at the close of the fiscal year (30 June 1902) divided the navy's battleships into two squadrons—one based on the North Atlantic Station, the other upon the Asiatic Station. "It is believed that for the present two squadrons are all that the number of our battleships will permit," admitted the Navigation Bureau chief. In fact, this dictated the use of large cruisers as flagships for the Pacific, European, and South Atlantic squadrons.

Moreover, earlier that spring frequent calls came for naval presence in different quarters of the Caribbean and West Indies "in order properly to discharge our duties of maintaining order by moral influence where disturbed conditions existed, or protecting the interests of our own citizens and those of other countries committed to our care, and of preserving and fulfilling the treaty obligations of the Government." This had led to development of a new battle group. Created on 4 October 1902, to be known as the Caribbean division of the North Atlantic Station, the *Olympia* became its flagship on 20 September with Rear Adm. J. B. Coghlan aboard (incidentally also as second in command of the North Atlantic Station). He would have at his disposal besides the *Olympia* smaller and older vessels such as the protected cruisers *Montgomery* and *Detroit*, plus gunboats *Mari-*

etta and *Machias,* as well as the auxiliary cruiser or repair ship *Panther* and a U.S. marine force aboard a transport. Little more than a show-of-force squadron, it was part of the general rebalancing of the principal fighting force of the navy and reflected strategic priorities of that time.[39]

Arriving back in Boston on 8 September 1902, Captain Lyon had submitted a report to the fleet commander concerning the *Olympia.* Declaring the cruiser to be in "excellent condition and efficiency for all duties called upon her to perform," he still thought that a new pilot house and better stowage of boats would increase efficiency and that the ship would be in better trim and flotation if the conning tower and after bridge house were removed. All military drills prescribed by squadron routine and special orders had been maintained while the ship was acting alone and, as far as possible, while in the fleet, he said. He explained in detail why some hundred and one seamen had deserted the ship since emerging from refitting the previous winter, and suggested that he would "hardly lose another man if those could be sent out of the ship who have given themselves up as stragglers on board other ships, who have pleaded no intent when tried for desertion or have had sentences remitted." Such men were detrimental to the good and welfare of the whole crew since none had improved his conduct from the leniency shown him, and "merely drags down the average." Posting no enlistments to offset those desertions and also enumerating five discharges, eighteen summary courts-martial (but not general courts-martial), Lyon cited four hundred fifty-six petty punishments among the *Olympia's* crew. Yet he termed discipline aboard the flagship "now very good." Similarly, the sanitary condition of the ship remained favorable, with the sick percentage figure standing at only 1.065 for the crew, forty-four having been admitted to hospital and one lost overboard during the reporting year.[40]

The *Olympia* and the rest of the North Atlantic Squadron were now called to the Caribbean, in part because of the combined fleet maneuvers planned by the General Board and Naval War College for early winter. The intention of such exercises, later reported Navigation Bureau chief Henry C. Taylor, was to exercise the fleet in preparation for active campaigns. It was an exercise in "organizing an efficient fleet by amalgamating promptly the various squadrons present into a fleet organization." Further goals included exercising the squadrons in mobility and long distance travel to an appointed rendezvous, and later dispersal, with the same readiness to their respective stations. Taylor, at least, felt that no other exercise or operation could so thoroughly drill a navy in the work "it is required to do," nor in any way so fully inform and instruct "as to the functions of a fleet organization and the relation to it of the squadrons and individual ships." Perhaps more immediate impetus, however, came from the saber rattling among European powers concerning debts owed them by the Venezuelan government.[41]

Increased European naval presence in the region suggested threats to the sanctity of the American Monroe Doctrine and peace in the area. Not that U.S. officials necessarily bridled at punitive collection of such debts. That was accepted policy among imperial powers. But the fear that Germany, Great Britain, even Italy might use debt relief for territorial expansion caused Washington to increase its own naval presence. When European firepower literally destroyed Venezuela's gunboat navy, pressure from Washington eventually led to arbitration. Still, Pres. Theodore Roosevelt ordered Dewey to "go to sea" in command of the warships gathered from North Atlantic, South Atlantic, and European squadrons, which he did on 8 December, about the time of the conclusion of the actual American maneuvers. His presence may have had a salutary effect on European—particularly German—intentions. Later it was discovered that the naval ministry in Berlin had been perfecting war plans against the United States during this period. The paranoia of Dewey, Taylor, and others was not unfounded.[42]

Meanwhile, Lyon and the *Olympia* participated in the very exercise designed to intercept an enemy raiding squadron attempting to descend undetected into Puerto Rican waters that, unbeknownst to the Americans, actually corresponded with one part of German war plans at this time. Under Rear Adm. J. B. Coghlan, the *Olympia* and the Caribbean Squadron arrived at Culebra on 1 November charged with various details necessary to prepare for the arrival of the whole fleet. Considerable hydrographic work was done: range markers were erected, various navigational aides were developed, and logistical chores with sanitary canal, camp grounds for marines, signal stations, and other matters were attended to. Although Higginson's force of battleships (including the *Olympia*) failed to actually catch the intruders in the subsequent war game, the work was "spirited and skillful," Taylor told Secretary Moody. Others like Cdr. Nathan Sargant, Dewey's aide who had been with him at Manila Bay, were not as impressed.

Combined tactical exercises (elementary in character, admitted Taylor) continued until the forces dispersed for Christmas break at Trinidad, the Virgin Islands, and smaller West Indian ports before reassembling on 29 December for more exercises and drills until 5 January, when Dewey hauled down his flag and returned to Washington. Sargent crabbed in a memorandum to the General Board that "the formations, both in line and in column were ragged, distance and guide being badly kept, speed not well regulated and turns unskillfully executed." Yet, suggested Taylor, the general efficiency of the squadrons was good. True, they were all behind in marksmanship, "but not so far behind as they were, and it is going to be a slow process, but the movement is decided and an upward one." The "tone of the officers and men, is excellent," he told the secretary.[43]

Whether or not the hero of Manila Bay's presence successfully intimidated the Germans, Taylor felt that it afforded Dewey a chance to familiarize himself with "our new possessions" in the region as "it seems to us down here that our country is rapidly becoming the big policeman on the corner watching the smaller folks to see that they don't get too noisy at their sports." It had all been a "very powerful concentration" in this corner of the "'American Mediterranean' as Admiral says it is now being called," he iterated. Coal was not plentiful, and Washington had sent down constructors and engineers from the bureaus to determine which ships would eventually need repairs in home navy yards. But in Dewey's mind, suggested Taylor, "the technical success of the mobilization of so large a naval force 1,500 miles from home," especially at the time of European demonstrations against Venezuela, could only add immensely to the country's naval and national prestige. Above all, however, the navigation chief noted that "these maneuvers have already shown that we should put on every station one complete division of vessels as nearly homogeneous as practicable" so that when returned to normal station following maneuvers they "may not have to be broken up and changed about, and many of them be under new Admirals."[44]

In the navy's eyes, assemblage of a fighting force of this size in the 1903 maneuvers forever doomed the concept of heterogeneous cruising squadrons scattered to the four winds across the globe. Traditional "show-the-flag" squadrons lacked requisite fighting power because of their diverse units included in a single "squadron." Both strategy and the exigencies of the real world dictated that basic field organization be changed. From now on, ships would be arranged by class as homogeneous divisions under a particular squadron (fleet). For the moment, however, the *Olympia*, like many of her comrades from the maneuvers, merely continued to cruise Caribbean waters off Trinidad, Guadeloupe, St. Kitts, Puerto Rico, and Honduras. Dewey went back to his somewhat customary German-baiting in the press by pronouncing the efficiency of the German navy "greatly exaggerated" and that the successful maneuvers of the American fleet of fifty-four warships "were an object lesson to the Kaiser." The newspapers had a field day with that one and Roosevelt had to tell Berlin as well as the American public that the admiral's words had not been intended for publication. Seas were certainly calmer where Dewey's old flagship roamed the Spanish Main than they were back on the Potomac, where the admiral still had not grasped the delicacy of world politics.[45]

RIDING THE SPANISH MAIN — AND EUROPE

On 15 March, the *Olympia*, together with the *Marietta*, the *Panther* (carrying the squadron's marines), and the collier *Brutus*, went to Honduras under Navy Department orders and helped restore security to that revolution-plagued area. In April, the navy decided that fleet energies were to be wholly devoted to exercises and drills for improving gunnery—of prime interest after the abysmal showing in the war with Spain. Thus, the *Olympia* accompanied the *Kearsarge, Illinois, Alabama, Indiana, Iowa, Massachusetts, Texas, Atlanta,* and the converted yacht *Scorpion* to Pensacola, Florida. Accuracy of target practice in the Gulf of Mexico proved to be "greater than the Department anticipated," with credit going to Higginson and Lt. Cdr. William S. Sims, the American gunnery expert who helped turn around statistics with devices and techniques patterned after the legendary Royal Navy Capt. Percy Scott. The *Olympia* subsequently accompanied the battleships to Hampton Roads and the Southern drill ground, was reviewed yet again by Admiral Dewey, then docked and coaled at Newport News preparatory to carrying a commission in May to determine and mark the boundaries of the proposed coaling station at Guantanamo Bay.[46]

Captain Lyon dutifully forwarded the *Olympia's* annual report to Higginson on 1 July 1903. He recounted the activities of his command and declared that the ship "has been in excellent condition and efficient for all duties which she has been called upon to perform" during the previous fiscal year. He noted that the flagship had consumed "7,439.3 tons" of coal at a cost of $24,803.02. The crew's health was considered good, with percentage of sick only .879 but including two deaths (one suicide, one the result of violence, a mess attendant knifed by a comrade while at San Juan, Puerto Rico, in March), and thirty sent to hospitals. Lyon suggested that the crew's discipline had been very good, with the men generally respectful, obedient, and cheerful in the performance of their work. The majority of severe punishments were "limited to old offenders, ex-naval prison, and new men who are sea-tramps and utterly unfitted for the service." He suggested that the same might be said of deserters and stragglers, a great many of whom came from the landsmen and engineer's force, new to the service who "have trades or are sure of employment on shore." He cited specifically that there had been three new enlistments against ten discharges, seventy-nine desertions, fifty-six summary courts-martial, eleven general courts-martial, and 769 petty punishments.[47]

Much of Lyon's report focused on the navy's concern with gunnery. He partly contradicted some of the impressions regarding improvement. All military drills prescribed by fleet routine and special orders had been kept up as far as possible, he suggested, with special attention given to "exercising the crew with the Morris tube" (which used a shooting gallery rifle and a miniature target suspended and maneuvered by guy wires just beyond the gun barrel to enable gun pointers to practice without actually firing the ship's guns). Still, stationary target practice at Culebra from 17–20 February 1904 had been marginal, although Lyon did not say so specifically. At a range of 1,400 yards, a target 16×20 feet on a raft "was completely demolished by shots which were not counted as hits." No attempt was made to secure rapidity of fire, and one half the allowance for each gun pointer was fired at this practice session. Sixteen shots from the 8-inch guns had registered but four hits. The 5-inch guns scored only fourteen hits for forty shots; the 6-pounder guns fired one hundred forty shots with only nineteen striking the targets. The 1-inch guns mustered only four hits for forty shots.[48]

Moving target practice was held later at Culebra on 9 and 10 March, with the 8-inch and 5-inch guns firing in traversing one side of an equilateral triangle of 1,600 yards side at a target 16×20 feet on a raft. The 6- and 1-pounders were fired using a similar triangle of 1,000 yards side on a target 8×18 feet. The *Olympia*'s speed was five knots with the remaining half of the allowance for the gun pointers fired in this moving practice. The results were still only mediocre at best. The 8-inch guns fired sixteen shots with no hits; the 5-inch guns delivered forty shots with fourteen hits; the 6-pounder guns registered twenty-five hits for one hundred forty shots, and the 1-pounders managed ten hits for forty shots.

Lyon declared that the behavior of the *Olympia*'s guns and ammunition was satisfactory, although some of the 5-inch and 6-pounder cartridges would not enter the gun chambers so that the breech mechanism could be closed. Apparently the cases had swelled. Then too, shrapnel tests proved on several occasions that fuses detonated prematurely. Although Lyon did not note any problems with powder residue in the gun barrels causing subsequent flash-backs (as troubled other ships in the fleet at this juncture), he did invite attention to the fact that the *Olympia*'s 5-inch battery was still equipped with the "old directing bar mounts and bar sights, as originally fitted out." The Naval Gun Factory in Washington eventually dispatched a 5-inch Mark VIII modification 1 mount for one of the *Olympia*'s guns, to replace a Mark VI mount then in service.

Finally, the end-of-fiscal-year tally for the cost of maintaining ships in commission showed $323,256.46 spent on Dewey's old flagship, most of it for accrued pay of officers, crew, and marines. Again, the cruiser stood as one of the more expensive ships on the navy's list. All of this had little bearing on Captain Lyon or his superiors as the *Olympia* now rejoined the North Atlantic Fleet for the customary joint maneuvers with the army and an annual search problem off New England. Leaving Guantanamo Bay in mid-July for Frenchman Bay, Maine, the flagship was accompanied by the protected cruisers *Nashville* and *Atlanta* and the auxiliary cruisers *Panther*, *Vixen*, and *Potomac*. As Coghlan noted, other vessels came and departed from the squadron normally and, even during the 1904 maneuvers, the *Baltimore*, *Topeka*, and *Scorpion* were temporary additions. It was during this period that the *Olympia* grabbed more headlines in connection with the introduction of new technology to the fleet.[49]

The *Olympia* was now part of an integrated fleet of battleships, cruisers, destroyers, and smaller vessels—even the ancient sailing sloop *Hartford* from Farragut's odyssey in the Civil War. Charged with intercepting an "enemy" making a descent upon the coast of New England between Eastport, Maine, and Cape Cod, maneuver guidelines focused upon establishing a base of operations. Coghlan and his ships engaged in the exercise from 5 through 8 August, with the *Olympia* discovering the hostile squadron twenty-five miles south by east of Mount Desert Rock off the Maine coast. Working her Slaby-Arco German wireless telegraphic equipment, Coghlan alerted the *Kearsarge* some thirty-five miles away. The battleships immediately started in pursuit, gathering other vessels en route, and effected a sunrise sighting and subsequent capture of the intruders about twenty-three miles from the coast. The commander in chief of the North Atlantic Fleet rather peevishly declared that it "was a source of satisfaction" to know that without doubt the "'enemy' would have been captured before the time limit of six hours had expired, even had the ships not been furnished with the 'wireless,' owing to the distribution of the vessels." Nonetheless, as naval historian John Alden has observed, wireless radio "was becoming an integral part of naval operations." This was shown dramatically in the famous world cruise of the U.S. Battle Fleet in 1907–9, when messages between ship and shore stretched over a thousand miles under favorable conditions.[50]

Other things were on the minds of North Atlantic Fleet captains at this point. There was to be a break in the summer training as the recoaled fleet, with the *Olympia* leading the cruiser contingent, left Frenchman Bay and vicinity on 12 August at noon, rushing to get to Oyster Bay, Long Island, by the sixteenth. Not only was a hurricane reportedly coming up the coast, so that it was desirable to make the shelter of Long Island Sound before its arrival, but President Theodore Roosevelt waited in anticipation of a grand naval review. Heavy fog dogged the early part of the voyage for the twenty-four vessels, and the older battleship *Massachusetts* ran on a reef just off Bar Harbor. Both she and her sister battlewagon, *Indiana* (which stopped to assist her), failed to make the review, causing the Navy Department "a matter of deep regret." Nevertheless, the protected cruiser *Chicago* and dispatch boat *Dolphin* (the first ships of the New Steel Navy in the 1880s) substituted in the lineup at Oyster Bay.[51]

It was almost a repeat of Dewey's triumphal reception in New York Harbor, except that *Olympia* no longer occupied center stage. The larger ships anchored in double column with a flotilla of five torpedo destroyers on each flank, thus making four columns of vessels. On the morning of 17 August, the president with his staff, the secretary of the navy, and the admiral of the navy boarded the *Mayflower* and steamed between the column of battle ships and destroyers before turning and passing between the column of cruisers and coterie of smaller vessels. Roosevelt took the honors "due his exalted rank—each ship with rails manned, firing a salute of twenty-one guns as he approached." After reviewing the ships, the *Mayflower* anchored a little in advance of and between the columns of larger vessels and welcomed aboard the flag and commanding officers and foreign naval attachés for a splendid luncheon. Roosevelt in turn visited the flag officers aboard their ships and the *Olympia* once again welcomed aboard her commander in chief. He then reboarded the *Mayflower,* steamed two or three miles ahead, and from her deck reviewed the whole fleet as it passed, each ship giving him a parting salute of twenty-one guns, with rails manned and crew cheering. The day had been a "perfect one for maneuvering," recalled Fleet Commander Barker. The secretary thought so too as he signaled his congratulations from the *Dolphin*.

Barker and his ships again set course for the Maine coast. What followed were the army and navy maneuvers in Casco Bay, with Portland as the focal point. They were "intended more for the benefit of the Army and National Guard than for the Navy," declared the admiral. Yet, every phase of warfare was simulated: a base was seized, forts were bombarded, mines placed, raids made on signal stations, and strongholds attacked by landing parties from 25–29 August. Some twenty-three vessels (excluding colliers and supply vessels) were engaged with "some really brilliant work" being done by landing parties, of which command of the naval brigade was held by Coghlan from the *Olympia*. Certainly Maj. Gen. Adna Chaffee of the army was pleased, writing Barker that "No efforts were spared to thoroughly test the material and personnel of the defenses." When the exercises ended, the ships dispersed. The *Olympia* proceeded to the Norfolk Navy Yard for repairs—having struck bottom in Casco Bay during the maneuvers. Coghlan went south to the Caribbean in the *Mayflower* as his flag vessel.[52]

The *Olympia's* successful manifestation of the cruiser's continuing value had Navigation Bureau chief Henry C. Taylor singing her praises. His 1903 report to the secretary called for more "improved *Olympia*" cruisers. They will be needed in case of war as auxiliaries to the battleships, he observed. In time of peace, they were best suited to carry on the various duties which the nation's interests demanded in the Caribbean and Spanish Main, and upon the east and west coasts of South and Central America. Even European interests "will also be best served by this class of [vessel]." In particular, five Olympia-type cruisers were wanted in the Caribbean Squadron, with two outfitted as flagships. This would leave four seagoing cruisers and two shallower draft for river work available at all times out of a projected additional five-to-three ratio between the two types.[53]

Refloated in November after seventy-five days in dry dock, *Olympia* was in Norfolk from 4 September to 17 December for repairs. These included fixing damages to bottom framing, longitudinals, inner bottom, and sea chests due to the grounding. But at the same time, the workmen fitted new foundations for the ice machine due to its change in location, refitted the cold storage room, remodeled the 5-inch ammunition hoists, refitted 5-inch gunport shutters, renewed flushing system, caulked superstructure deck, overhauled the anchor windlass, and fitted a new and larger main shaft and additional supports. They also made and fitted three new gangway ladders, added ventilation for the firemen's washroom, made and fitted new composition sea chests, and overhauled and repaired all boats. Finally, while in dock the *Olympia* had her bottom cleaned and repainted. Most of this work apparently accounted for her attributed repair costs that year of $66,010.58.[54]

Olympia rejoined Coghlan and the Caribbean Squadron as flagship just before Christmas. Sporting two General Electric generators capable of 2,200 amperes, four Mangin searchlight projectors made by the Sautter-Harle Company, and an Ardois night signal device for the bridge, she was ready for round-the-clock service. She carried the American minister to Colombia and A. M. Beuparé to Colón, Panama, before the new year, as naval presence in the region guaranteed consolidation of the Panamanian revolution in preparation for Roosevelt's plans to construct a trans-isthmian canal. Protecting American interests in this period meant interfering in Latin American affairs, with the navy as convenient vehicle for such endeavors. Relieved there by the South Atlantic Squadron in late March, Coghlan in the *Olympia* convoyed the destroyers *Truxtun* and *Stewart* as far as Key West via Guantanamo before collecting the full Caribbean squadron at Pensacola for more target practice. Arriving on 2 April, she was detached from the Caribbean Squadron command a week later (officially the action dated from 28 March), as Coghlan took command of the European Squadron before being succeeded by Rear Adm. Thomas F. Jewell on 20 April. Record target practice occupied

19–21 April, and then the *Olympia* was sent to New Orleans and the government's floating dock at Algiers for cleaning and painting of the bottom and minor repairs to the underwater body. On 3 May she returned to Pensacola, and two days later proceeded in squadron with the *Baltimore* and *Cleveland* to Guantanamo Bay, a portion of the run being made together with battleships of the North Atlantic Fleet.[55]

Outfitted at Guantanamo, the *Olympia* and her sister ships of the European Squadron proceeded to St. Thomas, Danish West Indies (16 May), coaled and left for Horta, Fayal, Azores, arriving across the Atlantic ten days later. Telegraphic orders, received just as the squadron made ready to go to Lisbon, changed course for Tangier, Moelders, where, on 31 May, Jewell found the South Atlantic Squadron flagship, *Brooklyn*, Rear Adm. French E. Chadwick in command. A Moroccan bandit, Raisuli, had abducted a prominent American citizen living in Tangier, one I. Perdicaris, and his English son-in-law in an effort to win concessions from the Sultan of Morocco. The situation was defused by the American consul general and the British minister, "backed up by the show of such great naval force." The Sultan met Raisuli's demands and the two westerners were released. The *Olympia* was then directed to rejoin the Battle Ship Squadron and spent much of June at Gibraltar coaling and receiving stores. Jewell reported at the end of the month that *Olympia*'s condition was good, with the exception of the "capstan engine," the starboard side of which had been disabled in getting under way at Horta, Fayal, so that only the port anchor could be weighed by this equipment. Morris tube practice had been effected quite regularly but no opportunity had been afforded small arms practice ashore since Jewell assumed command. Four very light cases of measles had developed on board his flagship in June, but had promptly been isolated and cured. Unbeknownst to Jewell, however, the Navy Department would record that his flagship had cost $329,629.21 to maintain in commission over the previous year—the twelfth most expensive ship in a fleet now numbering two hundred sixty-five vessels "fit for service."[56]

In any event, Taylor's successor as chief of navigation, Rear Adm. George A. Converse, echoed the notion of cruiser indispensability both as battleship auxiliaries and local force projection instruments, even for training officers and crews "to expertness in handling ships in company." Converse felt, at least, that the navy had insufficient numbers of this class, since they could not be easily improvised on the outbreak of war and converted vessels could not perform "duty more combative, demanding qualities of offense and defense." Wedded to a battle fleet concept despite the lessons of torpedo-boat warfare shown in the contemporary Russo-Japanese conflict, the diversity of roles and missions ensured the *Olympia's* survival in America's "imperial" navy. She served both as a cruiser and a command ship, thoroughly integrated with navy plans and fleet operations in this period.[57]

The *Olympia* spent the rest of 1904 cruising European waters and visiting various European ports at the head of her squadron. Perhaps she enjoyed less glamorous opportunities as that afforded the fleet's flagship, the *Kearsarge*, which hosted the royal family of Greece in early July or visited Fiume, Hungary, for the first-ever American squadron visit. Yet the cruiser could be found in the Adriatic and protecting American interests at Smyrna, Turkey, during July and August. In September, her squadron steamed north, stopping at Cherbourg, France, Christiania, Norway, and Gravesend, England. Chief Carpenter Frank McDonell of the flagship wrote his sister back in Philadelphia on 26 October that he had used shore leave in the British Isles to go visit family relations in Ireland. Then, it was back to Gibraltar via Genoa, and to Italy preparatory to returning across the Atlantic to the annual winter maneuvers in the Caribbean early in 1905, again attended by the secretary of the navy and Admiral Dewey. The Navy Department now decided to combine the cruisers of the European and Caribbean squadrons into a single division of the North Atlantic Fleet. Senior Capt. H. G. O. Colby of the *Olympia* took charge of this so-called Third Squadron.[58]

On 20 March, the *Olympia* led a flotilla—battleships *Missouri* and *Kentucky* and cruiser *Des Moines*—to Havana for the purpose of "showing our friendly feeling toward the Cubans." The flagship hosted Tomas Estrada Palma's visit and, a week later, obliged the chief executive's request that the inhabitants of Havana might see the vessels by passing in review near Morro Castle, with the *Olympia* firing a national salute to the Cuban flag to the delight of thousands of cheering Cubans. By late March, not only had the combined fleet arrived off Pensacola for annual target practice, but it had a new admiral, as Rear Adm. Robley D. Evans succeeded Barker, who went into retirement. At the end of the month, Rear Adm. R. B. Bradford ran up his pennant aboard *Olympia*, succeeding Colby as squadron commander and, in May, Capt. James D. Adams succeeded Colby in charge of the flagship. The rest of the year was spent primarily "protecting American interests" in the Dominican Republic, with period visits to ports of Monte Cristi, Guantanamo Bay, Kingston, Jamaica, and St. Thomas.[59]

With a generally healthy (two deaths, eleven sent to hospital) and contented crew (twenty enlistments against five discharges, six desertions, four general and twenty summary courts-martial, 1,008 petty punishments, and repairs totaling only $5,315.88), Dewey's old flagship seemed to be in fair condition. But with annual costs of maintaining the ship in service running at $390,309.09 (ranked tenth in the whole navy for 1905) and coaling charges alone running about ten percent of that, the end-of-fiscal-year comments of Admiral Bradford suggested the immediate future for the "Queen of the Pacific." The *Olympia* was approaching the end of the fourth year of her present commission and the end of the second since being repaired and overhauled at a navy yard. Nearly eight months had passed since she had been docked and painted. Bradford thought that she should "soon receive a thorough examination and a number of dockyard repairs." She met the requirements of a modern flagship "in hardly a single respect," he suggested, but by rearranging the quarters below the main deck, "which are now extravagant in the consumption of space," the ship could be made "an efficient unit of a cruiser squadron."[60]

The fifty-seven-year-old Captain Adams (in the navy since 1864) was even more blunt. Writing to Evans from Culebra on the last day of December, the native New Yorker and future rear admiral declared: "The condition of the OLYMPIA is bad: the bottom is very foul and shows evidence of pitting at the water line." The strainers were consequently "badly checked" and impossible to clear until the vessel was dry-docked. The distilling plant piping needed renewal throughout and the temperatures of the magazines had been lowered only by cooler weather at that time of year in the tropics. The ice machines were inefficient and the whole refrigerating system needed repairs beyond the capabilities of shipboard repair. The proud but aging *Olympia* went out of commission at Norfolk Navy Yard on 2 April 1906. Returning to active service over a year later, she would find that technology, mission, and the navy had all passed her by.[61]

6

In Reserve

REPAIRS AND ALTERATIONS

The USS *Olympia* was still the pride of the American fleet. Her photographs adorned such illustrated publications as *The Book of the United States Navy*, published in 1905. But, from 2 April 1906 until 1 June 1907, the cruiser underwent repairs and internal alterations at the Norfolk Navy Yard. Here, her berth deck 6-pounder guns and mounts were removed and the type of 5-inch gun mounts was changed on the gun deck. Alterations to the ventilation system through extension and additional duct work were accomplished as was the conversion of the former aft torpedo room into a blower room. But most of all, changes to showers, staterooms, ward room, and lockers were designed for her next assignment. Outwardly, her appearance changed but little.[1]

The cruiser had amassed $250,026.78 in operating costs for the fiscal year ending 30 June 1906. Still, she fell to twentieth rank among the navy's active ships in that regard, largely because battleships were more costly. But the navy wanted to regularize unit and fleet maintenance, as "the exigencies of the service" too often sent the *Olympia* and her sister ships to navy yards for cleaning and refurbishing. Coal-burning ships were labor-intensive, dirty, and the machinery and equipment sensitive to wear and tear, rust and corrosion. Duty in tropical waters fouled the steel hulls much as they had their oak predecessors. Then too, as the navy's chief constructor, W. L. Capps, said in the Navy Department's 1906 annual report, "The *Iowa, Brooklyn, Olympia, Monterey,* and *Monadnock* have all become ancient in the matter of batteries, and, unless equipped with modern guns, mounts, and sights, can no longer be considered efficient vessels and fit for service."[2]

NAVAL DEVELOPMENTS

There is always a question about aging warships. Not that the "Queen of the Pacific" was necessarily old at ten years of age in 1905. Still, it seemed that the sixteen-year rule had been selectively stretched to twenty in the case of some U.S. ships, as Naval Constructor William G. Groesbeck pointed out in the Naval Institute *Proceedings* for March 1906. He thought she would need a replacement by 1911. Given the heated international naval race and rapidity of technological changes (not just in ship size and design, armor and armament, but also in motive power, speed, communications, and aiming systems), the author suggested that the *Columbia, Minneapolis,* and *Olympia* should all be replaced by two modern ships at the very least. Three years later, comparative tables of American, British, German, French, Russian, and Japanese navies as developed by Cdr. W. H. Beehler in a similar article would underscore the problem. Cruisers like the *Olympia* no longer commanded speed, much less armament superiority, over competitors. In fact, even her sister armored or first-class cruisers were heavier, faster, and better armed. Groesbeck, for one, saw scout cruisers as the logical successor "to the moderate sized, medium-speed, protected cruiser, now more or less antiquated of which we possess a considerable number." From this point on, survival of George Dewey's flagship depended less on her qualities as a cruiser and more on her command ship configuration and historical associations.[3]

The navy was passing her by when the *Olympia* returned to active service after the Norfolk refitting. There had been talk of substituting modern 7-inch guns for her obsolescent 8-inchers. But this was not among the $113,624.30 in "alterations, improvements, and repairs" charged to the ship in fiscal year 1907. Major focus and money was shunted toward new units for the battle fleet—battleships, armored cruisers, and torpedo-boat destroyers. This underscored Secretary of the Navy Charles Bonaparte's earlier thinking that all future naval engagements of any importance "will be between properly organized fleets composed of the necessary classes of ships." He advanced the desirability of organizing the navy's fighting vessels into two fleets for service on the Atlantic and Pacific coasts of the country "in such manner that the whole force may be readily mobilized in cases of emergency." It was all quite Mahanite, considered necessary in the absence of a trans-isthmian canal to rapidly reinforce either coast threatened by enemy battle fleets. By 1907, effective, unified battle fleets had been set up for both oceans with concentrations of battleships and smaller vessels, relegating the various dispersed overseas stations of *Olympia's* formative years to the dust bin of history.[4]

Increasingly more robust construction programs of the navalist presidency of Theodore Roosevelt allowed only for armored cruisers of the *California* and *South Dakota* type (13,000 plus tons displacement and speeds of twenty-two knots) or scout cruisers like the *Chester, Birmingham*, and *Salem* (whippets of twenty-four-knot speed and 3,750 tons displacement). Most discussions concentrated on the merits of center-line and multi-caliber battleships. Ships of the Roosevelt navy were still splendid affairs full of bristling guns, apparatus, and rigging, and still painted the glorious peace scheme of buff and white with glittering bow and stern ornamentation, not to speak of copious amounts of bunting on festive occasions. But the *Olympia* of the old *guerre de course* school of strategy was passé. Of course, at this point, many other units in the 285-ship navy were also.[5]

MIDSHIPMEN'S PRACTICE SQUADRON

Perhaps more instructive of thinking in Washington about the *Olympia* was Bonaparte's significant letter to Roosevelt on 6 July 1906. Whether or not the hidden hand of George Dewey could be seen behind the comments remains unclear. But, explaining why the venerable Civil War screw sloop *Hartford* could not be relegated to the Connecticut Naval Militia or the New York Nautical School because she was destined as a training ship for the United States Naval Academy, Bonaparte suggested a similar assignment for the *Olympia*. "The purpose being to assemble these historic ships at Annapolis where the associations attached to them would be of material and practical value and where they are needed in the work of instructing the midshipmen," he explained. Whether or not the eager young midshipmen could truly appreciate learning aboard naval memorials as compared with the latest battle wagons of the fleet was irrelevant to their seniors in the picturesque state, war, and navy building next to the White House in Washington.[6]

Olympia underwent repairs at the Norfolk Navy Yard in the spring of 1907 in preparation for her duties at Annapolis. Midshipmen's needs differed from those of the normal crew, so a majority of the alterations to the ship involved modification of spaces previously allocated to junior, senior, and warrant officers. In addition, all 6-pounder guns and mounts on the berth deck were removed at this time and alterations were made to the ventilation system, with more ducting and conversion of the former aft torpedo room to a blower room. With that she joined the monitors *Arkansas*, *Florida*, and *Nevada* of the Naval Academy Practice Squadron for the summer cruise of 1907.[7]

Olympia anchored off Greenbury Point Light on 3 June, when she replaced the cruiser *Newark* as flagship for domestic cruiser purposes (the international cruise was eliminated that year) while other cruisers—*Minneapolis*, *Denver*, *Cleveland*, and *Des Moines*—returned to fleet duties in the rotation. Only First and Third classmen would participate (a total of 380 midshipmen to be shared by the four vessels). Sixty-eight First classmen and one hundred eighty Third classmen went aboard the "Queen of the Pacific." Plans earlier in the year had focused on such matters as recruitment of mess stewards for the flagship—two stewards, three cooks, two pantrymen, two bakers, one barber, and thirty-six mess attendants—absent both departmental and academy funding, providing a mining package for training purposes, what clothing each middie would carry, and the general fitting of the vessel as a practice ship. Time was tight. The navy wanted the flotilla to get to Hampton Roads soon after graduation so as "to land a battalion of all available midshipmen" to parade on "Virginia Day" as well as to receive President Roosevelt's shipboard review in conjunction with the tercentenary of the Jamestown landing. Final arrangements in April and May raised the requisite crew from other ships and officers from those attached to the academy. Capt. T. B. Howard, an 1873 academy graduate and thirty-eight-year naval veteran, took command.[8]

Problems persisted even after the Navy Department sent orders to the

Olympia circa 1902–8 with radio installed.

Olympia's commanding officer on 16 May to get under way "as soon as the vessel under your command is in readiness to leave the Navy Yard." "There are no navy code flags on board this ship, none in store at the Yard, [and] the only means of communication between this ship and others of the Naval Service being the International code," the temporary skipper of the flagship, Lt. Cdr. Louis M. Nulton, notified the yard's commandant on 26 May. They were dispatched hastily to the academy the next day, to await the ship's arrival six days later. Having left Norfolk at 10:30 A.M. on 20 May with a complement of one hundred seventy-five plus two hundred twenty-eight men for the monitors, Nulton wired the academy of his arrival off Annapolis at 8:48 P.M. on 3 June. But consternation accompanied that arrival. The *Olympia*'s steam launch plowed into a sloop, the *Hornet*, lying at Parlett & Parlett's wharf, staving in the stern, carrying away the traveler talfel, and knocking timbers from the deck. The sloop's owner and master, John Matthews, immediately claimed his ship was leaking badly and demanded repairs from the navy. Since the *Olympia* was due to sail soon, a substitute repair gang from the USS *Hartford* was sent to repair the *Hornet*. But Matthews continued to demand compensation for lost work days, much to the annoyance of the academy superintendent.[9]

Problems with the steam launch's boiler did not deter prompt departure of the Practice Squadron on 8 June. Other boats carried the heavily-laden middies from the academy docks to the waiting ships. Addition of the 41-member Naval Academy Band at 6:00 P.M. the previous evening aggravated crowded conditions aboard ship. But the bandsmen were important for the parades scheduled for 10 and 12 June at Jamestown. Absence of march music could prove fatal to properly dressed ranks in the parades. The middies took everything with them from whites and blues to oilskins, work clothes, a dozen pairs each of socks, cuffs, collars, and handkerchiefs, plus toiletries and personal items, even pillow cases, stationery, and pajamas. All of this caused much grousing among the midshipmen and even the ship's officers when it came to overcrowding. As a polite passage in the next year's academy yearbook, *Lucky Bag*, noted, they had had experience with crowded quarters and small locker spaces aboard the monitors on previous cruises. "The Olympia, however was new to all," reported the editor. "So many of us had been assigned to that ship that we had felt certain there wouldn't be room to turn around."[10]

The young midshipmen could conceivably adjust in time. But the ship's surgeon pointed out on 12 June that such limited space was "detrimental both to their health and comfort." He protested the allowable amount of cubic air space for each man aboard ship and worried about communicable disease. He sought a reduction of forty-four midshipmen from the *Olympia* to alleviate the situation. Nulton (the ship's executive officer now that Howard had assumed command) went even further, suggesting that "This congestion produces difficulty from four points of view, sanitation, discipline, discomfort and financial loss to the midshipmen." It seems that the middies were to be placed near the galley where they would have to dress, study, and live amidst preparation of raw meats and vegetables and the accompanying dumping of slops and ashes. Moreover, installation of their lockers narrowed the passage ways to something like two feet from serving places to mess tables and seriously inhibited the thirty servers at meal time. Discipline and discomfort derived from inadequacy of storage space, and overflow of personal effects atop the lockers and in clothing bags stowed in the hold. Thievery became rampant, possibly originating with the crew, thereby necessitating guard watches day and night for the academy boys. Wet weather promised further problems. Planned return of the dress jackets to Annapolis after the Jamestown festivities promised little relief to the congestion.[11]

Howard sent word of all this to Rear Adm. James Sands at the academy, who approved transfer of forty-four Third classmen to the USS *Severn* (the school's own practice ship) before the *Olympia* departed Newport News for the main part of the cruise on 19 June. Howard should select the "forty-four," said Sands. Disappointing to those young men, they at least would participate at the exposition, although reading the somewhat tongue-in-cheek account of that experience in a subsequent *Lucky Bag* might cause one to think that it was anything but enjoyable. This distinctive feature of the first part of the summer had been raised above all other considerations in order "to make a creditable showing" at the festivities, claimed the editors. Weeks of conscientious preparation, especially for a special contingent known as the "Provisional Battalion" (and facetiously among the middies as "Teddy Bears" in tribute to President Roosevelt's fetish, or "Goats" alluding to the academy mascot), had proved nettlesome. First classmen had escaped the dragnet for participants initially only to find themselves eventually conscripted and "facing the prospect of a first-class cruise with something to do."

Ultimately, on the Sunday following embarkation at the academy and various preparatory exercises such as "swinging ship," "man overboard," and "abandoning ship," the *Olympia* steamed down the Bay and into Hampton Roads. Passing the imposing Fortress Monroe, everyone "saw the whole of the U.S. Atlantic fleet together with several foreign ships as they lay at their anchorage in long line of graceful formation." Slowly passing Rear Adm. Robley D. "Fighting Bob" Evans's flagship, the battleship *Connecticut*, they fired a salute in his honor and anchored at the end of the line almost opposite the Jamestown Exposition. There, the middies found themselves participants in what "was heralded on the billboards" as "the most noble naval pageant of recent years."[12]

The midshipmen waxed eloquently about the ensuing naval review—that "imposing and magnificent congregation of one of the finest, most powerful, and homogeneous fighting ships afloat." From monster ironclads, spotlessly white and gleaming in the sunshine with black guns protruding everywhere, down to those graceful and swift race horses of the sea, the little torpedo boats, everything vied for the middies' gaze. It was "a sight grand enough to inspire patriotism and pride of country in the heart of all true Americans." The foreign warships were especially fascinating, with "signals flashing from mast to mast, steam launches darting hither and thither, everything moving like one huge clock, wound up and watched over by a master hand." Presence of the old relic monitor *Canonicus* reminded them that "one ship of her type decided the supremacy of a people in the throes of civil war."[13]

On Monday morning at colors, the *Olympia*'s officers, crew, and midshipmen dressed ship, manned the rail, piped saluting gun crews to quarters, and fired off a national salute as Roosevelt, on the bridge of the *Mayflower*, steamed past the fleet. All of the ships were fully dressed and majestically decorated with bunting. Following the review, the middies disembarked, "and after waiting countless hours in the broiling hot sun, finally swung into line in step with all of the sixteen spigetti bands who were 'in sweet Vociferation out vociferating even sound itself.'" Marching back from the review, "leg-weary and dusty throated," they passed hateful glances at a barker hawking "nice cool beer" from his stand. The march-past over, the middies' thoughts turned to liberty, as the exposition afforded "amusement for a time" with its international pavilions. Somehow, they—like the *Olympia*'s regular officers and crews generally over the years—found more enticing the fraternization over "tea" aboard foreign warships and other diversions of a social and terpsichorean nature. Not a few of the young sailors required comrades and marines to help them back aboard the flagship after doings ashore. At night, "each ship was outlined entirely by myriads of brilliant electric lights, making this one of the most magnificent displays ever witnessed," wrote one of the *Arkansas* middies.[14]

Howard simply reported to Sands about the President's Review and parades on Georgia and Virginia days but made no mention of frivolity. It was not until the excitement of the Jamestown parade was over, noted the middies, "that we had the opportunity of really settling down to the regular routine of the cruise." After refueling at the Newport News shipyard (while the First classmen toured "one of the foremost shipbuilding plants in the world"), the flagship returned to Annapolis on 19 July, transferred the unlucky "forty-four" to the *Severn*, and rejoined the rest of the squadron that had been simply cruising in the lower bay. Together, they left for New York on 22 June and the planned appearance of the monitors as well as academy boat crews at a gala race scheduled at Poughkeepsie.

The pace for the whole summer cruise was now set—8–11.5 knots speed on New River and Pocohontas coal. At first, the squadron ran into dense fog the whole way up the Atlantic coast, moving at reduced speed, while "navigation . . . was done by the lead, keeping outside the track of ships, until the deep hole off New York was found," reported Howard. The midshipmen "were fairly comfortable below decks" despite the cold, damp weather, he quickly added, knowing of the superintendent's concern. Arriving on 25 June, and anchoring in the North River off 135th Street (some of the middies thought it was 154th Street), the young sailors once more became transfixed by the bustle of a major harbor as well as the shoreside attractions like the Statue of Liberty, Grant's Tomb, and the skyscrapers of lower Broadway.[15]

Here, Howard received a wireless invitation from the superintendent of the Military Academy at West Point to bring the squadron up the Hudson. But Howard declined, claiming that the *Olympia* needed to take on stores and be ready to continue her cruise after the Poughkeepsie races. Meanwhile, her middies enthusiastically scrambled off to liberty in "little old Manhattan Isle" before taking a special train upriver to the boat race. Their comrades in the monitors, however, made the trip by water. Cornell and Columbia crews proved too much for the middies in the eight-oared shells over the four-mile course. "We didn't win," admitted the *Lucky Bag* of the contest, "but we had the satisfaction of seeing our crew finish third after a plucky race." Then, all too soon, they abandoned the "Gaieties of Gotham" and—despite delays in getting stores from the Brooklyn Navy Yard—made for summer cruise headquarters at New London, Connecticut, where they arrived on the twenty-eighth. The squadron passed the Fourth of July there, enjoying hijinks ashore that included milking cows, a circus, and various athletic events like obstacle and potato-races, boxing, pie-eating contests, and spending money for fireworks. The *Arkansas* travelers meanwhile also enjoyed diving for money in a large salt water tub set up on the deck of their craft.[16]

Various periods at New London allowed the *Olympia* to engage in training exercises, boat, and other drills over in Gardiner's Bay, Long Island,

while the monitors overhauled engines and boilers. The young middies, of
course, had other things on their mind. Apparently, "the summer colonies"
at Pequot and Eastern Point "surpassed even their customary hospitality,"
the "hops" and "multitude of fair ones" as well as other diversions (including the solemn intonations about "Temperance and Prohibition" from one
comrade as they were conveyed ashore) proved more memorable than the
business side of the cruise. Still, despite the impossibility that "prolonged
stay in the Thames would have become monotonous," Howard, at least,
was pleased to get them away from New London dives. The dearth of sufficient uniforms meant that the middies went ashore in "white working
dress, [are] driven to the worst parts of any city, and generally, being young
boys, they return to the ship under the influence of liquor," he told superi-

View forward in *Olympia*'s sick bay. Note the bathtub
with shower curtain. Photograph taken at Boston Navy
Yard on 14 October 1899.

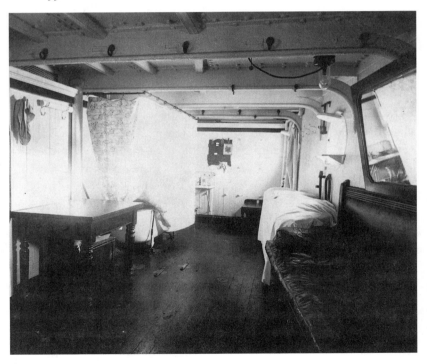

ors. Pointing to the need for better outfitting (so "that they may wear a 'dress' uniform at General Muster on board ship"), "the trifling expense is much more than returned by the comfort resulting from men wearing proper clothes on shore and on special occasions on board ship; to say nothing of the injury to health in this cool, damp climate," reported Howard. The skipper seemed to have two different issues in mind.[17]

Picturesque Newport, Rhode Island, was another brief stop on the summer itinerary, "although very few availed themselves of the opportunity of visiting this famous place," claimed *The Lucky Bag* editors later. More memorable were periodic stints "hustling on board 250 tons of the black diamonds" at the Naval Coaling Station at Bradford, about eight miles up Narragansett Bay. In early August, the flotilla went further north to the Tercentennial of American Shipping celebration at Bath, Maine. Once again, shoreside activities demanded the services of the Provisional Battalion. So, aboard the cadet officers "scraped the seaweed and verdigris off their swords," and the rest of the *Olympia* "youngsters broke the rifles out of the forehold and shook dice for odd leggings, and there was a contest to discover who could lose his white cap the quickest." Finally, all hands went ashore with "happy, smiling faces to march in the parade to the appropriate tune of 'Onward Christian Soldiers'." Despite later complaints about the "long hard tramp through the muddy streets" and ships being overrun with visitors, "we really spent a very enjoyable time in Bath," was the general conclusion.[18]

Boat races, the Grand Water Carnival, the excellent dinners at the New Meadows Inn, the delightful hops that the celebration committee gave the middies, and the "very generous hospitality extended by the Sagadahoc and the Elks Clubs—these were pleasure that will long remain in our memory." Howard and his officers garnered the praise and thanks of U.S. Customs Service official H. S. Crosby for adding to the success of Bath's celebration. The superintendent of the academy sent Howard his own congratulations on 14 August, gratified "that you had such a pleasant visit to Bath" and quite sure "that the people there would lay themselves out to make you have a good time." "I have no doubt the presence of the ships made many friends for the Navy," Rear Adm. James Sands added. It was unquestionably the better part of wisdom to let the midshipmen parade, he told Howard. "That was one of the things you went there for."[19]

Departing the Maine city, the *Olympia* took on an additional chore. Miss Jessica McDonald had donated a seventeen-foot Boston "Knockabout" to the academy as a gift in memory of her late brother, Assistant Naval Constructor J. E. McDonald. The flagship was charged with carrying it back to Annapolis. Unfortunately, the gift probably added to the already crowded space aboard ship, although the ever adaptable middies had by now learned some tricks of comfort in this regard. The admiral's cabin ("including the bath-tub") and the old ward room afforded "ample space in which to eat, smoke and sleep," recorded the *Lucky Bag* while "a great discovery was the veranda, a pleasant stage for our evening jubilations." So the middies made Dewey's old space aboard *Olympia* their home afloat. "Think of swinging your hammock in a place so full of historic association," noted one First classman later, "of hanging your blues in the china closet and packing away whites in the buffet." A card game of "twenty-one" ran for many afternoons until "that was ragged one day and card playing ceased." After supper, the cabin filled with music and lusty singing from young throats.[20]

More First-class quarters were down in the old junior officer's ward room on the berth deck. This was that "large airy room extending clear across the ship, [where] on each side were comfortable, leather-upholstered transom lockers; and one had to come early and sit tight if he wanted to hold down his place." Book learning was put aside, although "once in a while a little navigation and seamanship" training kicked in and "the dynamo detail had quite a comprehensive spiel to write up on electricity." Basically, after eight months of classroom instruction at the academy, all hands were glad to dispense with books for awhile. Eventually, differences of opinion between the middies and the *Olympia*'s exec had been resolved in a meeting of the minds ("we aired our grievances and he told us a few of his troubles, [and] we were able to come to an understanding and everything had run smoothly from then on"). Even the sardine can living conditions did not fester as much as the cruise progressed.

Still, the summer dragged on and there had been no opportunity for even a change of clothing since leaving Annapolis. The tardiness of the USS *Standish* (sent north with such replacements) caused "a great deal of inconvenience among the midshipmen," Howard wrote the superintendent late in July. So it was when they left the Maine coast, claimed the *Lucky*

View aft in *Olympia*'s starboard galley. Photograph taken
at Boston Navy Yard on 14 October 1899.

Bag, that "it was with the feeling that the end of the cruise was in sight,
and that we were at last starting south for Annapolis."

Not quite, as it turned out, for they stopped again at Newport for several
days, and "went through with the same old program of coaling ship and visiting the torpedo Station (Cook's personally conducted tours)." Indeed, the
continuing round of prescribed drills and tests may have bored the tiring midshipmen, but they enabled Howard to write the secretary of the navy on 2
August how "the midshipmen were instructed in obtaining tactical data for
the *Olympia*." He cited statistics derived from speed runs, turning and stopping time drills given various engine revolutions, and other ship-handling
data secured during the return voyage. There was "a decided feeling of unrest
and suppressed excitement," for First-class leave beckoned so that "even great
events at a time like that cannot but be treated as mere episodes."[21]

Finally, the Practice Squadron made one last visit to "dear old New London," where the middies all took their cruise exams. Orders were issued concerning dirty laundry and policing up belongings for their impending return home to the academy. Then they made for the capes. It was fair weather all the way down, past Cape Henlopen, Delaware, to Cape Henry, Virginia. "We had no excuse for failing to keep the day's work in Nav[igation]" said the *Lucky Bag*. But, in spite "of all our gun deck sights, and notwithstanding the fact that we logged the trip only by the deck clocks," few of the middies had collected data past Delaware Bay when "we dropped our hooks off the mouth of the Potomac" on 25 August.

Then the squadron went upriver as far as Indian Head, Maryland. There, the monitors cruise participants, at least, received their rewards for the summer's work by "a veritable foretaste of leave," an overnight liberty in the Nation's Capital, before the whole flotilla again anchored off Annapolis at the end of the month. Here, all hands assembled "at the veranda abaft the admiral's cabin" on the *Olympia* to sing cruise songs, reminisce about their experiences, and render raucous poetry as well as tributes to shipmates under master of ceremonies Midshipman "Janus" Saufley. Sardonically, they recalled that on the flagship "bright work and study call were sounded together while retreat from study hour and fatigue call were blown at the same hour." R. R. "Skimmer" Welshimer of the "Grand Old Commonwealth of Illinois" waxed eloquently about the "vast and all absorbing topics of temperance of pro-hibition," while more songs wafted across the Severn "until taps called us home." All hands joined in three cheers for Captain Howard, the officers and the *Olympia* as well as "George Dewey, Manila Bay, Rah, Rah, Rah, O-lym-pi-a," and so ended the summer cruise of 1907.[22]

During this time, Howard, the academy, and Navy Department officials had been more concerned about the post-cruise deployment for the squadron. The superintendent wrote Washington on 31 July that the monitors could easily come into Annapolis harbor and remain there as before. Each had a commanding officer and several warrant officers detached from the academy's staff. But the *Olympia*'s situation was different. She was too large to safely and comfortably moor in the harbor and insufficient water alongside the wharf meant costly and considerable dredging. He recommended sending the flagship back to Norfolk with enough officers to take her there and remain in reserve until readied for the next year's practice cruise. Howard's "special and temporary" duty as skipper would end and he could rotate back to fleet duties elsewhere. The other officers should return to the academy and serve there again until the next cruise. However, the Navy Department replied on 12 August that all the vessels would be placed in reserve at the Naval Academy, as "the final disposition of the OLYMPIA would be taken up at a later date." Sands was clearly displeased since "there is not enough room for the ship to swing in the harbor" and "to care for a ship of that kind in the stream when the ice makes, etc., is always a nuisance." Still, he told Howard on 14 August, "orders must be obeyed, and we will do the best we can."[23]

As Howard wrapped up the cruise, he reported to the superintendent on the "efficient, economical and satisfactory" performance of the midshipmen's commissary aboard the Olympia that summer. The two hundred forty bodies was the largest number of midshipmen "ever sent in one ship," and the happy result was due to the paymaster's department of the practice ship—Midshipman R. R. Welshimer, (whose "executive and business ability is of the highest order") and M. E. Fletcher, the head steward, assisted by the thirty-eight cooks and mess attendants who were "very attentive and well behaved." More worrisome to Howard and his officers, however, were the prospective docking arrangements when they got back to Annapolis.[24]

Howard thought that the Olympia's mooring in the Severn would require "a sufficient number of people to perform boat service" between ship and shore independent of the monitor crews, who would be employed in the care and operation of material in daily use for the midshipmen and the usual work incident to station ships. There would have to be a chief electrician and crew to operate the turrets, maintain the wireless plant (as an element of instruction or as a reserve station should the academy's main wireless break down), ventilate the ship, and render the dynamo plant an additional source of instruction for the midshipmen. Gunner's mates of one per turret and two for the 5-inch and 6-pounder batteries, as well as for proper preservation of magazines and electrical ammunition hoists would also be necessary. Warrant officers should include a chief boatswain, a chief carpenter, and at least one such officer for the engine room. Necessary commissioned personnel, observed Nulton, should include the commanding officer plus an executive officer (in general charge outside of the engine rooms), an officer in charge of the engineer department, and one available for general service for rotation in duty on board. The ship's complement should also include messmen, quartermasters, lamplighter, and steam launch crew, in addition to those thought necessary "to properly care for the ship."[25]

Howard's consequent estimate of a 138-man complement reflected Nulton's own comment that "The demands upon a ship in reserve at Annapolis as part of the material of that institution are considerably greater than under ordinary circumstances [for station ships]." But Washington's rejoinder was that the number was more than "we will be able to find available" given pressing personnel needs elsewhere in the ever-expanding fleet. Even senior admiral Dewey himself looked in on the *Olympia*'s particular case. He concluded that "the maximum number for her would be 50 and he hoped you could reduce it even below that." The superintendent's frustration at the slowness of departmental resolution of the issue was mitigated by admission to Howard that putting the ships in reserve at the Naval Academy was a "sort of special thing." Describing the delicate maneuvers that would be required to moor her "between buoys 1 and 3, her stern being fast to No.3," he anticipated that *Olympia*'s dynamos would be kept running and "the ammunition will be left in her, unless otherwise instructed by the Department." And so the "Queen of the Pacific" passed into reserve status at Annapolis on 30 August 1907. Nulton had relieved Howard the previous day. The crew dispersed to other ships and stations leaving fifty-one chiefs and sailors to turn in medical equipment and chronometers, shut down the wireless office, and batten down for the autumn and winter. Ironically, as late as December the *Olympia* still had the ammunition stowed aboard that was left over from the '07 cruise.[26]

Comments concerning the *Olympia*'s initial year at the academy mentioned seventeen deserters as well as a total of $141,994.20 for maintenance. There was talk of replacing her 8-inch turret power hoist and rammer arrangements with hand-worked equipment. Yet the Naval Academy Board of Visitors enthusiastically reported on her service to the Practice Squadron and the "excellent arrangements" anticipated for taking care of six hundred midshipmen aboard the *Olympia*, *Chicago*, *Arkansas*, and *Nevada* in the next summer's training exercises. There would be no Jamestown exposition this time around, as Lt. Cdr. D. E. Dismukes brought her up in May from a winter refitting at Norfolk. Nevertheless, the *Olympia* would again lead the flotilla, departing Hampton Roads on 22 June and returning to the academy at the end of August.[27]

The '08 practice cruise was déja vû all over again for the *Olympia*. Winter planning anticipated thirty to fifty messmen for handling the ship's crew plus the one hundred sixty First, Second, and Third classmen allocated to the ship. This year, however she would preside over a flotilla comprising the monitors *Arkansas* and *Nevada* but joined by the aging cruiser *Chicago* and the venerable wooden screw sloop *Hartford*, upon whose decks Adm. David Farragut had paced during the Civil War. Cdr. William Shepherd Benson, USNA '79, currently commandant of midshipmen (and destined to be the navy's first chief of naval operations), took command of the flotilla. The *Olympia* was declared ready for sea on 13 May with all her stores, ammunition, and coal aboard. She had been freshly painted both inside and out, Chief Boatswain S. W. Gardner told academy superintendent Capt. Charles J. Badger on that date. Meanwhile, Badger's people busily filled out detail rosters and published regulations for the shipbound middies.[28]

The ports of call proved familiar once the flotilla got under way. New London, Newport, Boston, Portsmouth, and Bath as well as visits to the Fore River, Massachusetts, shipyard and the Torpedo Station in Rhode Island prompted little notice in the *Lucky Bag* this time. But the almost continuous social calendar from Fort Monroe to Bath and back certainly received every middie's attention. High spots included cotillions and devastating the hearts of the fair ones at the annual Harvard/Yale crew race. Yearbook photography, however, devoted more shots to coaling ship than any other shipboard regimen—hated as that activity always was. A large fog bank off Long Island almost caused the squadron's demise as lost ships nearly plowed into one another. Middie Tommy Jones qualified as "Admiral of the justly famous Prune Navy of the Olympia by consuming 103 prunes at one sitting"—no mention being made of the consequences. Then, Captain Benson became embroiled in a dispute with New London town fathers, who attempted to close a dining and dancing pavilion at Ocean Beach to sailors from the Practice Squadron. Benson promised that he would request a change of station to Newport, thereby omitting the Connecticut seaport from future fleet visits. The politicians prevailed in the end. Still, Badger praised Benson for his stand in the affair.[29]

View aft in wardroom country. Note the 8-inch turret support structure in the center. Photograph taken at Boston Navy Yard on 14 October 1899.

By comparison, Bath, Maine, again rolled out the red carpet with its annual Old Home Week and Merchants Carnival. Future vice admiral Olaf M. Hustvedt remembered years later that the summer of 1908 was the first one "when motorboats began to proliferate in the ports like New London and Bath." Local belles caused the middies to nearly forget their cruise discomforts and even the anticipated home leave once they returned to Annapolis. The run back down the coast was ideal, although it may have seemed rather anachronistic to see the fully-sailed *Hartford* "frolicking along ahead of the other ships." The monitors could not keep pace and dropped far enough behind "to allow us to do some very pretty searchlight signaling" at night, recalled the middies. Back at the academy by the end of August, everyone reminisced about no longer having to live out of a clothes bag or that "rainbow feeling in the morning after turning out of Uncle Sam's palatial swinging bedrooms." Gone too were the evening gatherings on the *Olympia*'s "back porch" or in the old port sponson of the

Chicago. Norfolk to Bath "will always be cherished in our memories," declared the *Lucky Bag* editors.[30]

Then the young sailors went off on leave, leaving ship complements to place the vessels into reserve once more. Lt. F. D. Kraus, senior engineer officer aboard the *Olympia*, reported problems with the starboard ice machine, the need for a new piston for the starboard cylinder of the anchor engine, and a new plate for the forward inboard wing manhole of boiler A. All this would once more require an off-season visit to Norfolk, but it would be November before the ship's reserve crew could take her south. Everyone expected a two-month stay at the navy yard, although Badger was anxious to have two of his ships (the *Severn* was also at Norfolk) back at Annapolis by 1 March 1909 "in order that the spring drill programme may be commenced on that date."[31]

While Dewey's old flagship continued in her role of academy training ship, the navy fully engaged the international naval race. Her total force as of the end of June 1909 included two hundred ninety-two vessels fit for service (as well as those under construction, authorized, or even unfit for service but still on the rolls, adding seventy more). By November of that year, Washington clerks could rank the U.S. Navy as third in the world (behind Great Britain and Germany) in terms of sea strength, tonnage, and numbers authorized and building. Roosevelt had sent the battleships (preceded by a torpedo flotilla of destroyers and officially designated the Battle Fleet of the United States) off on a world-circling cruise at the end of 1907 and this so-called "Great White Fleet" had only just returned in February 1909. Thousands of people from the Caribbean and South America to the Far East and Suez had thrilled at this display of American naval prowess. Of course, as in any era, appearances and figures were quite deceptive, however much they conditioned attitudes and perceptions around the globe.[32]

Technological obsolescence relegated warships like the *Olympia* (together with the *Chicago* and *Newark*) to "Cruisers, Second Class" status. Of the $186,686.87 lavished on keeping the *Olympia* in commission during Fiscal Year 1908, eighteen days had to be spent in dry dock and about $25,000 expended on repairs for her eighty-nine actual days in service. Her average complement of one hundred one crewmen tallied a rather high rate of sick call admissions for disease and injury per thousand men, but low totals in actual lost sick days. Only twelve men ever went to hospitals and there were no deaths aboard the aging ship. Her absence rate was down, with four of six deserters actually returned to ship that year. The Bureau of Construction and Repair rated "good" her machinery, and plans now had her 8-inch turrets and guns being replaced with "7-inch guns on pedestal mounts fitted with shields," with these mounts to be designed and manufactured by Bethlehem Steel and tested at the navy's Indian Head, Maryland, proving ground. Granted, nothing ever came of those plans circulating in the Navy Department.[33]

Back at Annapolis by early March 1909, the "Queen of the Pacific" embarked on what was billed as the customary coastal cruise, with the tugboat *Tonopah* added to the flotilla that year. If no one had complained about crowded conditions in 1908, they certainly had cause to do so now. Commanded by Capt. C. A. Grove, some one hundred eighty-five First, Second, and Third classmen scrambled aboard the *Olympia* carrying their usual allotment of gear and clothing. In fact, the middies affectionately styled the summer activity "the old Crab Cruise—better known as 'Charlie Grove's yachting trip.'" Preparations included shoes "going into Admiral Dewey's sideboard, Bull and Cube, where once reposed the classic silver service, everything in orderly confusion," recounted the *Lucky Bag*. At 10:20 A.M. on Monday 7 June, the signal "Get underway in succession" was hoisted. And the squadron steamed away from the academy and out into Chesapeake Bay— *Olympia*, *Chicago*, *Tonopah*, and *Hartford* in full array. "Swinging the ship" (to adjust the compass by measuring compass deviation), as well as fire quarters, abandon ship, general quarters, man overboard, and other proficiency drills, took place off Solomon's Island at the mouth of the Patuxent River on the morning of 9 June. The squadron then proceeded on its way.[34]

Maine ports of call once again drew the greatest notice by practice cruise participants. Portland and Bath welcomed the young sailors warmly, but not so Bar Harbor, where "our reception was as chilly as the weather." Bath gave a grand reception and ball with a dance card of waltzes, two steps, and schottisches that kept the middies and their partners whirling about and completely forgetting the onerous drills and details of shipboard. Those assigned to the old *Hartford* seemed to take particular delight in this last cruise of the Old Navy where the "Black Maria" with steam and sail made nearly twelve knots and with the *Tonopah* "under forced draft dropping behind and wildly signaling for us to 'douse sail' or 'stop our engines.'" As usual, a tired but trained body of young men returned to Annapolis at the end of August.

If the passages in the yearbook seemed more constrained about this particular cruise, they recounted just as much socializing as previous summers. Perhaps the pattern had become somewhat tedious for the impressionable young lads. By the following year, the *Olympia* would be replaced by battleships with the Practice Squadron and a changed itinerary. Yet the *Iowa* and *Massachusetts* were also of the *Olympia*'s vintage and, almost wistfully, *Lucky Bag* editors would suggest that "We found the ships very broad, each of twice the tonnage, several times the fighting ability, and any number of times the inconvenience, from our point of view, of our old friend, the Olympia." Apparently, protected cruisers of the '90s were no more cramped in space than their sister battle wagons of the age.[35]

These practice cruises occasionally drew attention in professional naval circles. Lt. Paul Foley thought that the larger and newer armored cruisers *North Carolina* and *Montana* were better suited physically to handle the two academy battalions than the aging craft assigned the duty. He pointed out in a 1910 article in the Naval Institute *Proceedings* that turrets and turret control, intermediate batteries, and boilers of battleships of the vintage squadrons "are neither modern nor uniform," and that engines, piping system, and electric installation were not uniform. Their interior arrangement and fittings are not those illustrated in the textbooks used by the midshipmen, he scored. In short, he suggested, "they represent throughout an older school of naval architecture."[36]

Furthermore, money could be saved by having the middies perform all the crew's duties, thus training these apprentice officers in precisely the hard work they might expect of their future commands. Moreover, the practice ships should be kept close to the battleship fleet "so that the students can keep in touch with the atmosphere of the fleet," he concluded. The impression that the squadron cruises resembled more a yachting excursion than serious training exercises hardly rippled across the regimen in Annapolis, however. Praiseworthy as reformer suggestions might be, the question of best use of ships in the fleet hardly meant assigning the most modern, first line vessels to training academy midshipmen. The *Olympia* might be succeeded by larger or different craft, but not necessarily the most recent additions to the fleet.

AGE CONSIDERATIONS

Photographs show the *Olympia* in her prime at this time. Crisply painted in buff and white with her hull and stern ornaments brightly burnished, it was little wonder the navy liked to show her off along the Northeast coast of the country. Secretary of the Navy George Meyer publicly cited statistics that compared the *Olympia* quite favorably with sister ships completed prior to 1902 in terms of cost of hull and machinery and total repairs down to 30 June 1910. The thirteenth most costly in terms of the fifty-three ships completed in that time frame, seven other protected cruisers had proved more expensive than the aging cruiser.

Yet, the navy's chief noted that "experience has shown that ships become obsolete within twenty years and that during only half that period are they eligible for the first line." Both the Navy Department and the academy wanted to discontinue her use as a practice ship, merely retaining her at Annapolis "as an object lesson to the midshipmen, and for the purpose of Steam Engineering drills." By now she needed repairs. Her inner bottom required attention, her steam launches needed replacing, her hand and hydraulic steering gear, ice machine, and plumbing needed overhauling, and her lockers required removal from the admiral's cabin so it could be restored to its original look and purpose. The large midshipmen's lavatory needed removal and other machinery and structural work was also in order.[37]

In commission just one hundred and six days of the following fiscal year (July 1909–June 1910), the *Olympia* still chalked up $107,654.00 in cost. Her on-board complement drew down from an average one hundred forty officers and men to a mere sixty-four at the end of the year. Nevertheless, the ship still retained usefulness for the service even in reserve. Concerned about insufficient depth of water in front of Mare Island Navy Yard, California, she was mentioned among the fifty-three vessels of the fleet (including fellow cruisers *Charleston*, *Columbia*, *Milwaukee*, *Minneapolis*, and *St. Louis*) that could not get over the bar and into the yard at low tide. Moreover, the surgeon general quoted the observations of the *Olympia*'s medical officer from the previous summer's practice cruise concerning some of the middies nearsightedness and inability to read signals at a distance of only four hundred yards without the aid of glasses as a reason to develop a new, improved, and relocated dispensary ashore at Annapolis.[38]

View aft from starboard corner in captain's cabin. Note
the ornate bar at left and the library built in around
the overhead. Photograph taken at Boston Navy Yard
on 14 October 1899.

Acting Secretary of the Navy Beirman Winthrop had told the superintendent on 27 August 1909, "Upon completion of the cruise of the Naval
Academy Practice Squadron, you will please place the vessels of that
squadron in reserve at Annapolis, Maryland." Simply put, *Olympia* was to
go into reserve as a static training vessel, which she did the next day. She
would stay there for nearly two and a half years, gently riding the tide on
the Severn, an object lesson and sort of floating classroom in steam engineering for the middies. Extensive correspondence about needed repairs
and transfer ashore of her complete equipment and outfit passed between
Annapolis and Washington for much of 1910. In October, *Olympia* sent
four of her 1-pounder guns to the Washington Navy Yard gun factory for

reasons as yet unclear. On 20 November, Cdr. Archibald Scales reported a fire in the first steamer, number 708, while moored to the boom of the vessel. Life aboard the cruiser had become quite prosaic; perhaps this was more than symptomatic of the end of an era.[39]

IN LIMBO AT CHARLESTON

In the words of naval historian John D. Alden, the Great White Fleet's return to the United States in 1909 "marked the end of an era." The magnificent battleships of that fleet were overhauled, their gilt bow and stern ornamentation were removed, and old fashioned military masts and fighting tops were replaced with cage masts and fire control platforms. Other structural changes occurred and all of them received a new coat of paint—dull, battleship gray. "The tide of U.S. imperialism had nearly reached high slack," said Alden, as there were already "stirrings of withdrawal from the responsibilities and burdens of empire." Technological breakthroughs were rendering fleets obsolete in nearly every way—oil driving out coal for fuel, turbines replacing reciprocating engines, electricity taking over even more functions aboard ship, and wireless and scientific fire-control systems introducing still more science to the fleet. All-big-gun battleships and submarines and the first reverberations of aeronautics provided new dimensions to the strategic implications of seapower.[40]

Meanwhile, from 1912 until the very eve of American involvement in World War I, the *Olympia* transferred her reserve status to Charleston, South Carolina. Already in this capacity during her post station duty at Annapolis under Commander Scales's command following the 1909 midshipmen's cruise, she left "Crabtown" on 2 March 1912. A February survey and inspection had ascertained the material condition and necessary repairs for the vessel. She arrived four days later at the Charleston navy yard. Here she assumed rather ignominious duty as barracks ship for the men of the reserve torpedo or destroyer division stationed there. Still categorized as a Cruiser, Second Class, she was anything but the proud flagship that led Dewey's battle line at Manila Bay, or the pride of the buff and white fleet for a time thereafter. Later, on 2 January 1915, she returned to commission briefly under Cdr. Frank B. Upham, USNA '95, both to test her continued utility and efficiency as well as to "protect American interests."[41]

"Showing the flag" and "protecting American Interests" (as the official phrase of the day had it) were fine. But "the difficulty attending this duty," decided one officer, "lies partly in its vagueness and partly in the lack of instructions." At any rate, from 5 April to 15 May the *Olympia* stood in at Progresso, Mexico, just when Mexican-American relations were more than a little frayed. Then, it was back to Savannah, Georgia, and May-week festivities before re-entering reserve at Charleston on 9 June 1915. In sum, the *Olympia* represented a potentially convenient force projector for a battleship navy attempting to operate under former President Roosevelt's enjoinder to successor William Howard Taft never to divide the battle fleet.[42]

Reserve status made sense in a budget conscious navy. In 1911, a manning force of only sixty-three men, estimated repairs under $4,000, and an annual maintenance cost of but $57,500.67 ranked Scales's *Olympia* only slightly above the least expensive of forty-one active ships on the navy list. Secretary Meyer emphasized scrutiny of expenditures, and stated bluntly that money spent to improve and update old ships "is often a wasteful expenditure, and, as a rule, not justified by any corresponding gain in fighting efficiency." "The military value of the work" was the benchmark applied to anything but the most modern dreadnought battleships and armored cruisers. When the secretary clearly stated in his annual report that no addition to the number of slow protected cruisers was advisable, since scout cruisers "can do all the duty of which these vessels are capable," then warships like the *Olympia* seemed superfluous. Why not scrap them? Was it pure sentimentality because Dewey was senior admiral and Manila Bay had been his Trafalgar?[43]

The operable term was "readiness" and the Navy Department couched its meaning in "service at all times of at least 17 battleships," taken in connection with a reserve fleet organization. A building program, calling for at least two battleships per year plus other supporting craft, was operable (hammered out in costly political battles between the White House and Capitol Hill). Ironically, the number "17" was precisely that of the number of protected cruisers on hand in 1911. An answer, then, lay in the concept of a reserve fleet, with the *Olympia* as a ship-in-being holding greater value for the moment than one merely on the drawing boards or construction ways.[44]

Numbers and readiness undergird naval ministries everywhere in this period. Fleet development prices were skyrocketing. "Owing to the cost of modern warfare, wars will be of short duration," declared Meyer. Numbers up front would be a determinant. Grouped around older battleships and armored cruisers, an Atlantic Reserve Fleet (and, subsequently, one for the Pacific as well) were deemed necessary. Sufficiently large crews (despite severe shortage for the operating fleet) aboard these reserve vessels would prevent undue deterioration. The vessels could be taken to sea in rotation for short periods each year as a test of their condition and to keep the crews proficient. "The department regards this innovation as one of the most important improvements in process of accomplishment, since it will insure the readiness for war of practically every vessel of military value," Meyer noted. Gone were the days when as many as ten battleships at a time, not to mention vessels of other classes, were under extensive repairs and

View aft in admiral's stateroom showing bunk and bureau. Note the wooden decking over the steel structure. Photograph taken at Boston Navy Yard on 14 October 1899.

unavailable for combat. No ship would be disabled for major overhaul at a navy yard for a period longer than three months.[45]

A reserve fleet would be a "cadre navy." It would provide the sinews of reinforcement for wartime mobilization. "The fleet that is in all respects prepared and can quickly obtain a first decided advantage over the enemy is the one that will win," said Meyer. "Half preparedness is as bad, if not worse, than no preparation at all, since the former condition would likely hurry disaster," he added. Thus, the *Olympia* had a bona fide role to play after all. She would succor reserve elements of a balanced fleet—the torpedo squadron—that would reinforce the Atlantic fleet battle wagons in event of crisis. The cruiser that had helped shape the transition from traditional *guerre de course* naval strategy to Mahanite battle line confrontation via Manila Bay now found herself part of a larger defense scheme that would find expression after 1916 in the popular political phrase "Preparedness."[46]

On 12 May 1912, an Atlantic Reserve Fleet was established at the Philadelphia Navy Yard under Rear Adm. Austin M. Knight as commander in chief. Later that month, a similar organization for the Pacific came into being at the Puget Sound, Washington, yard. The *Olympia* and sister cruisers *Baltimore*, *Tacoma*, *Des Moines*, *Chicago*, and *Machias* became organizationally part of a flotilla of battleships, armored cruisers, scouts, colliers, destroyers, torpedo boats, and submarines. By 1 July, the "Queen of the Pacific" and the *Baltimore* had set up housekeeping at Charleston, where they were to squire destroyers *Macdonough* and *Worden*, torpedo boats *Craven*, *Dahlgren*, *De Long*, *Shubrick*, *Stockton*, *Thornton*, *Tingey*, and *Wilkes*, as well as the submarines A-1, B-1, B-2, and B-3.[47]

"We provide a navy as we provide insurance," Roosevelt had declared upon completion of the annual Atlantic fleet mobilization in New York in 1912. Such insurance guarded "against a possible loss or a danger which we hate to anticipate, but which under present conditions we should be foolish not to treat as possible." The *Olympia* had not been at that mobilization event, but it was against such philosophy that her continued service had to be considered. The $47,714.91 that it cost the navy to keep her in commission that year also had to be weighed against what Secretary Meyer saw as, perhaps, an equally commendable reason for preserving and maintaining "unserviceable vessels" like wooden ships *Constellation*, *Portsmouth*, and *Hartford*. They would be "a constant inspiration to the

Navy and to the country at large to live up to their noble traditions," he announced in his 1912 annual report. Really only the *Constellation* was in bad condition, and "the *Olympia* should be maintained in serviceable state for her present use for many years to come, and thus be preserved as a famous relic of the War with Spain." The *Olympia* could play a realistic role with the reserve fleet, as well as serve as inspiration to the country and the service.[48]

Economy continued to drive official thinking even after the new, Democratic Party administration of Woodrow Wilson took office in 1913. With additional dreadnought battleships promising to cost nearly three times that of the older pre-dreadnought craft, Secretary of the Navy Josephus Daniels called for an international conference to discuss arms reductions, government fabrication plants for armor, guns, and powder to reduce costs and introduce competition with private contractors, and elimination of obsolete battleships of the *Olympia*'s vintage. The *Massachusetts, Indiana, Oregon,* and *Iowa* "no longer contribute to the fighting strength of the Navy," he declared in his first annual report, although it was conceivable that "they might be able to render some slight service as coast-defense vessels in time of war." No mention was made of their contemporary, the *Olympia*, possibly because her reserve role cost the taxpayer under $10,000 that year. Daniels, at least, felt that the reserve fleets were fulfilling "the principle upon which they were inaugurated" as all available ships not required for active service had been assembled, "frequently short cruises have been made," and satisfactory progress attained toward keeping all vessels "in the highest condition of efficiency and material upkeep" permitted by their reduced complements.[49]

The first general war in Europe in a century broke out in 1914. The Navy Department continued to preach the need for a government armor plant, a large capital shipbuilding program, better trained and educated naval personnel, and technological breakthroughs like radio and aviation. Daniels prohibited alcoholic consumption both at sea and ashore, and noted prophetically "the passing of coal and the advent of oil" as fuel—something he said would "mark an era in our naval development almost comparable with the change from black powder to smokeless powder for our guns." The struggle to build up the purely distinctive fighting ships of the navy—like battleships, destroyers, and submarines—had neglected cruising and scout-

View aft from opposite the after funnel hatch of starboard berth deck. Photograph taken at Boston Navy
Yard on 14 October 1899.

ing elements of the fleet, with none provided for since 1904, he observed.
Little of this directly affected the *Olympia* lying in ordinary at Charleston
with Lt. James W. Hayward in command. Such status still cost an astonishing $104,368.56 that year largely due to $32,768.25 in repairs to hull,
machinery, and equipage.[50]

Nonetheless, Daniels could point to a certain economy of scale for the
ten cruisers in reserve, as they called for only twenty officers and seven hundred thirty enlisted men for their "nucleus crews." By the end of the year,
the *Olympia* was ready for her post repair run. In addition to the European
war now spreading worldwide, Mexican-American relations had deteriorated. Since the *Olympia* was both available and had a track record for Latin
American preventive diplomacy, she once more cruised tropical waters. She
visited various trouble spots like Port au Prince, Haiti, and Progresso on the
Yucatan peninsula, where she relieved the *Tacoma*. She was buffeted by the

same hurricane going to Mexico that "gave New Orleans the severest storm they ever had," recalled *Olympia* crewman Frank D. Lederer, who was thrown down the fireroom ladder, incurring severe injuries to neck and spine. By 25 May she was back at Charleston and once more taken out of commission.[51]

The navy's General Board, as well as Daniels, now talked about making the American fleet "equal to the most powerful maintained by any other nation of the world." This would incur a multiyear, multimillion-dollar construction program with strong emphasis on a "command of the sea"–type force centered upon dreadnought battleships, battle cruisers, and fleet submarines with some increases in scouting cruisers, destroyers, and coastal defense submarines. Wilson concurred and Congress eventually voted authority for constructing one hundred forty-six ships in addition to sixteen battleships and battle cruisers. The *Olympia*'s speed and command ship configuration kept her in navy calculations at this time. This was perhaps fortunate, since taxpayers had lavished some $1,064,086.50 in repairs and changes over her cumulative term of service to 30 June 1916—on top of the initial investment of $2,484,027.54 two decades earlier. If only $9,998.24 were paid out for repairs in 1915, the figure jumped to $79,891.32 for repairs and alterations including equipage the next year. Total maintenance and operation for 1915 tallied $80,056.70, despite the fact she had not been in commission a single day![52]

Sometime late in 1916, *Olympia* was refitted at the Charleston yard. Work was done on her superstructure deck and boat stowage, on the main, protective, berth, and platform decks, on the inboard profile, on expansion of shell plating, on berthing and messing arrangements, and on her double bottom and hold. Her armament configuration changed significantly. Eight-inch guns, turrets, barbettes, and the 5-inch .40 caliber guns were removed, being replaced by twelve 4-inch .40 caliber pieces. Riveted steel barbettes of $1/2$-inch thickness were installed where the original armored barbettes had been, and circular platforms were constructed to support single 4-inch guns at those locations fore and aft. As nearly 300,000 pounds of weight were thus removed from the *Olympia*, these changes were very significant. She now lost her principal historic meaning, her legacy of inspiration, the value of what she had accomplished at Manila Bay. It had not been her configuration or her speed that had won that day, but rather her heavier guns, despite pitiful marksmanship. In sum, by 1916, the *Olympia* as "colonial battleship" was no more.[53]

What was hot with the navy at this time were the larger guns, speed, and protective platforms of a capital fleet. The navy board's drive for battleship parity—organizational reform represented by onset of a chief of naval operations and a naval consulting board under inventor Thomas A. Edison—as well as the work of "preparedness" drove the day. Congress created a Council of National Defense at the highest levels of government "for the coordination of industry and resources for the national security and welfare." The United States was preparing for eventuality—although Wilson and his party were reelected in 1916 on a platform of keeping the nation out of the bloody and costly Great War then raging in Europe. At the time, what policymakers intended was deterrent parity, not involvement in conflict. In their enthusiasm, however, the 1916 program left the fleet unbalanced. As one historian has declared, "Doctrine had blinkered naval planning, blinding it to dimensions of sea warfare other than fleet engagement."[54]

When the General Board declared that the navy "ultimately should be equal to the most powerful maintained by any other nation of the world," it was a far cry from the political climate when *Olympia* had joined the fleet. Admirals even spoke of a "fleet train" rather than leased or purchased supply vessels like those Dewey took with him to Manila Bay. Savants deliberated about "what should be the relations between the battle fleet and the reserve fleet" and how to procure men and material. What the future held for the nation, its navy, and the *Olympia* remained unclear.[55]

7

Interventionism and the First World War

On 16 January 1917, the *Olympia* lost a dear friend and patron. Admiral of the Navy George Dewey died in his eightieth year. Back from the Philippines and their victory together at Manila Bay, Dewey and his flagship had parted company. He went on to serve as the navy's senior admiral and president of the General Board, providing a potent force behind fleet development. He also served as policy adviser to secretaries and presidents and pointedly stressed civilian control of the military as part of the American system. At times, as he aged, he was perceived as "an obstacle to progress by more radical and impatient officers," noted one historian later, but more often than not he truly supported their goals and purposes. Moreover, he had kept an eye out for the fate of his former flagship. Several times he gently pressed to keep the aging warship in meaningful service. Now he was gone, Pres. Woodrow Wilson summarized "the qualities that place him with the immortals" as "his practical directness, his courage without self-consciousness, his efficient capacity in matters of administration, the readiness to fight without asking any questions or hesitating about any detail."[1]

Dewey's former shipmates from the *Olympia* would have nodded in agreement with the president's assessment. But those yet living passed to other chores. Only navy chaplain J. B. Frazier, who had served aboard the cruiser at Manila, was present to read brief services before the admiral's body left his K Street home in Washington and again at his burial across the river in Arlington National Cemetery. There, Dewey took his place near the graves of Benjamin Lamberton, Charles Gridley's successor as captain of the *Olympia,* and Joseph B. Coghlan of the *Raleigh.* The admiral's old ship, meanwhile, languished at the Charleston, South Carolina, navy yard. Still, warships and warriors exist for war. To deter war, to fight wars when they occur, and to enforce the postwar peace—that is the role for the military in society. The *Olympia* had gained fame in war; she would snatch her final moments of glory as a result of war. Neither she nor the United States Navy were necessarily prepared for the lot thrown to them by American entry into European conflict. But both accepted what fate determined and performed with distinction in unaccustomed roles in that conflict.[2]

THE OLYMPIA, THE NAVY, AND THE GREAT WAR

When President Wilson took the nation into World War I later that spring, George Dewey's prophecy came true. His Germanophobia, stemming from events long past in Manila Bay, now proved all too prescient. And Dewey's navy found itself confronted by what historian Peter Halpern has called "war without Mahan." The godfather of seapower, battleships and battlefleets too was overtaken by events. The Battle of Jutland between British Grand and German High Seas fleets two years before had settled battlefleet confrontation. Now, both navies lay inert—dangerous as forces in being but little more than deterrents to renewal of such costly naval battles. Instead, the German government had turned to that other mode of warfare—*guerre de course*—but with a twist. Undersea craft, developed to a higher art than previously, enabled the Germans to attack the lifeblood of empire for the Anglo-French allies. Unfortunately, neutral shipping—such as that of the Americans—often intruded with dire results. Whatever the geostrategic agenda and political reasoning in Washington, it was the resumption of unrestricted submarine warfare that caused Wilson to drive from the White House to Capitol Hill on that rainy evening in early April and ask Congress for a declaration of war.[3]

Ironically, *guerre de course* was precisely why ships like the USS *Olympia* had been constructed some two decades earlier. But now the role of the

American navy in such affairs would be defensive, not offensive. Anti-sub patrols, mine barrages, and convoy escort duty dictated the operations tempo. The *Olympia* would do her bit in this cause—and much more. Neither she nor the navy was ready, despite the optimistic pronouncement of Cdr. Joseph K. Taussig, leader of the first contingent of American destroyers to arrive in England. When asked by the British flotilla commander as to when he would be prepared to assume combat duties, he replied, "we are ready now." True, in the general sense, the navy had spent all those peaceful prewar years as well as the three years of neutrality in quiet but steady "preparedness." But, imbued with Mahan's gospel, the post-1916 expansion program pointed to large capital construction programs, not wartime deployment.

In October of that year, the navy's General Board had observed of the European war: "Nothing apparently has occurred to modify in the essentials the broad principles laid down and the conclusions reached by the board in former years . . . the battleship remains, as heretofore, the principal reliance—the backbone—of the sea power of the nation." But now, a half-year later, mobilization of more balanced forces, acquisition of manpower, training and disposition of those forces as demanded by major war—not a brief excursion against Spain—called for massive measures and quick results.[4]

Yet, in quickly discerning that "the nature of the necessary naval operations to date has emphasized the necessity for vessels of greatest value against the submarine," as Daniels wrote in his 1917 annual report, dispatch of that first small destroyer flotilla was prophetic. "Preparation for impending and actual war" governed that first year of American participation. Again, as Daniels emphasized, "Among the numerous lines in which the Navy has expanded since the war began, none is more marked than that of the coast patrol and the operation of the naval districts." Cooperation with the Allies and force projection (both naval and land, given the army's expeditionary force that was to be sent to battle in France) would all come in due course. For the moment, in the spring of 1917, however, base and home waters protection as well as forging the instrument of war took precedence. And here the *Olympia* answered the call to service once again.

At first, the Germans tried to maintain the fiction that they were not even at war with the United States. U-boat captains were directed to avoid attacking American warships for the moment. While it was only on 22 May that the German admiralty authorized attacks on American shipping in the blockade zone around Great Britain, it had no immediate intention of carrying the war to the American coast. This isn't to say that extending the war zone westward to North American waters wasn't always on German minds. The Americans could not be sure. Lacking a war plan other than for purely coastal and hemispheric defense, the American navy reacted in customary fashion, as Chief of Naval Operations Adm. William Benson later recalled. Badgered to dispatch more anti-submarine craft to help in Europe yet buffeted by the grand strategic consideration that German victory might leave the United States exposed to possible threats both in the Atlantic and from Japan in the Pacific, the navy kept to the large battle-fleet scheme. As Benson observed, "My first thought at the beginning, during and always, was to see that first our coasts and our vessels and our own interests were safeguarded."[5]

FLAGSHIP OF COASTAL PATROL

The *Olympia* was en route to the Norfolk Navy Yard from St. Thomas, Virgin Islands, when the United States declared war on 6 April. A week later she began work as Rear Adm. Henry B. Wilson's flagship of the Atlantic Patrol Force on antisubmarine duty. As fate would have it, while going from Tompkinsville, New York, to Gardner's Bay, Long Island, for target practice, she ran onto an uncharted rock in the fog south of the Cereberus Shoal buoy in Block Island channel late on 25 June. One chief machinist's mate died from being struck on the head by a falling hatch. With ripped hull, her port engine and fire rooms flooded, the "aftership listed 10 degrees." The crew tried desperately to use blankets to plug the holes while the pumps worked overtime to stem the inflow of sea water. As reported by the *Army and Navy Register* on 30 June, "Ship was then in shoal water for observation and is now resting easily in 4½ fathoms on edge of shoal." Refloated on 7 July, she anchored safely in a sheltered position, since it was feared that a sudden storm might further damage the old warship. Secretary of the Navy Josephus Daniels reported that everyone was convinced that "she could be quickly repaired and returned to duty." But, as it developed, she would spend nearly eight months in a Brooklyn navy yard dry dock.[6]

Newly arrived electrician Lloyd Thomas O'Kelly observed in what he styled his "Diary-letter" to folks back home in Iowa that the ship had been "stove up" in the bow and was in pretty bad shape. She had a work crew on her all the way from the quarter deck to the bow, and in his opinion they practically rebuilt the ship. During the *Olympia*'s release from the shoal, her twelve 4-inch guns were removed to "lighten ship and free her from the rock," recalled another crewman, Gunner's Mate 2d Class Chester V. Jackson. Later, at Brooklyn, these guns were replaced with ten modern 5-inch .51 caliber pieces intended for the uncompleted battleship *Tennessee*. All the magazines and fore and aft 4-inch gun platforms were changed correspondingly to accommodate the larger caliber pieces. In fact, the 5-inch .51 caliber pieces and their mounts were so much heavier and more powerful that navy yard gangs had to install massive support columns and girders under the main deck at the four gun positions inside the superstructure. The casemate gun ports were enlarged by cutting away the armor plate around the ports and the midships casemates were sealed and not used again.[7]

USS *Olympia* as Reserve Torpedo Group Barracks Ship at Charleston Navy Yard. Note that she retains her 8-inch guns at this time. The masts visible on *Olympia*'s far side belonged to USS *Hartford*. Photograph taken 4 January 1914.

Additional 6-pounder guns were removed at this time. A device called an "oscillator" or "submarine signaling device" was installed in the hull bottom, and a radio office replaced the signal office. By this time too, the ornamental bow and stern devices had been removed and, as ship restorationist Don Birkholz Jr. put it, "Olympia had acquired the more prosaic character common to later warships." But, for crew members like O'Kelly, none of this meant as much as the opportunity to see New York City's bright lights afforded by the Brooklyn Navy Yard layover. Visiting the Metropolitan Opera and listening to "Tosca" sung by Geraldine Farrar and the Irish tenor John McCormick made more of an impression. So too did the Museum of Natural History and the sights and sounds of urban life unfamiliar to a midwestern farm boy. Typically, this serviceman was put off by what he saw as profiteering businessmen in an atmosphere "crooked, indecent, obnoxious and corrupt."[8]

On 6 September, Capt. Waldo Evans turned over command to Lt. George P. Brown, the executive officer. In mid-October, he was succeeded by Capt. Bion B. Bierer, a Kansas native who had entered the navy as a cadet in 1887. He would be an interesting character to watch as the Olympia embarked on its new missions. Finally, at 10:00 A.M. on 6 February 1918, she sailed under secret orders to convoy and patrol duty off Halifax, Nova Scotia. Arriving three days later, having steamed through an ice field all the way, she again had the misfortune of incurring a hole in the bow just below the waterline. Fortunately, three hundred 100-pound bags of flour stowed in the forward hold got soaked with salt water, swelled up, and plugged the hole. "We just closed the waterproof hatch to that compartment and went on into Nova Scotia and into dry dock to get the hole patched up," noted O'Kelly, who for one time in his naval career relished being a fireman on this trip because it kept him warm and dry. Still, about half the crew had never been to sea before and that half got seasick. Everyone was pretty content to stay aboard ship during the three-day patch-up stay at Halifax. It was a "blistering cold time of the year up there and very few men wanted to take liberty and go ashore," remembered O'Kelly.[9]

Two weeks later, however, the cruiser was back at Tompkinsville, having escorted British merchant vessels to New York. She consequently spent most of March on convoy duty. One particular twenty-ship convoy crossing proved stormier than normal with waves breaking over the weather decks and cascading down the hatches to slosh deep through the coal car-ried in "jury-rig wooden bins throughout most of the berth deck," remem-bered Chester Jackson. The capacity of *Olympia's* bunkers had been inad-equate for such duty so that this experience meant that "deckhands manning the ash buckets looked as if they had been dipped in ink, besides taking a beating from the roll and pitch of the ship." All hands were pro-foundly glad when somewhere west of Ireland, they turned the convoy over to Allied destroyers, and on the twenty-third, set a course for Hampton Roads, where they arrived on 4 April. Jackson noted, as usual, they "imme-diately coaled ship." To date, there had been no opportunity to even test-fire the new battery of 5-inchers so, three days later, the *Olympia* steamed up to Tangiers Sound for practice. On the fifth day—and right in the mid-dle of a run—according to Jackson, "we broke off and proceeded out to sea" and south to Charleston. By mid-month, she was back in a Charleston dry dock with a variety of workmen preparing her for service in northern waters. Thus far, *Olympia's* contribution to the Allied cause had been rather minimal.[10]

INTERVENTIONISM IN NORTHERN RUSSIA

The quixotic intervention of the Allies into the revolutionary Russia of 1918 as yet defies understanding. While the *Olympia* underwent repairs in Brooklyn and later at Charleston, events in Europe determined her future. A democratic revolution had ended the Tsarist monarchy in February 1917. The subsequent provisional government declared a republic in September, establishing a constituent assembly and free elections. Then, all had been thwarted by the October Bolshevik revolt and eventual signing of a sepa-rate peace treaty with Germany at Brest-Litovsk in March 1918. Allied governments and the United States may have cared rather less who might be momentarily ruling Russia at this point. They did care about the loss of an ally in the war with the Central Powers. The possible freeing of German troops for insertion on the Western Front, plus the fear that tons of war materiel that had been shipped to Russia would now fall into German hands, led Anglo-French leaders to prod the Americans to intervene, if only to protect that material. Other forces were at work too—the plight of anti-Bolshevik contingents of the Russian army like the Czech Legion and White Russians, fears of German utilization of northern Russian ports for submarine bases, the whole question of overthrowing bolshevism in general, and even thwarting Japanese expansionism into the collapsed Russian empire in the Far East. But, if London and Paris were fretful, Washington officials remained tepid if not outright opposed to any interventionism. There had been enough of that for the Wilson administration—twice in Mexico, then in Haiti and the Dominican republic, not to mention the dispatch of the American Expeditionary Force to France. British and French officials persisted and even American diplomats in turbulent Russia pressed for action. Finally, Wilson authorized dispatch of a warship to Murmansk, the most threatened point. The *Olympia* would be that warship. In the words of one historian: "In this casual manner, the United States initiated its intervention in the Russian Revolution and Civil War."[11]

Interventionism, or as often euphemistically phrased as "protecting American interests," was hardly unfamiliar to Dewey's old warship either. But here it was more a case of her availability than anything else. Wilson bowed to British pressure to send a warship to augment Allied naval forces at Murmansk, but only "if it can be done without sacrificing more important objects" (such as sending doughboys to France). Moreover, he also told his naval secretary that such a warship "of sufficient force to command respect" could be sent only "without taking any vessel from the overseas convoy business." Apparently, the navy overlooked the fact that Dewey's old flagship was in the convoy business or that its over-age condition hardly commanded respect. More likely, its command ship configuration offered a certain attraction.[12]

Dry-docked once more to alter interior spaces for better accommodating her new mission, *Olympia*'s two weeks at Charleston proved to be an eye-opener for the ship's many new crewmen, like Lloyd O'Kelly. Now serving in the ship's dynamo room as an electrician, he wrote home that the navy yard there did not hold as many ships as its New York counterpart; only fifteen had been present at the time. But the weather and the lush foliage and flower gardens of early April in South Carolina contrasted with the bleak North Atlantic and cityscape at Halifax. The sight of illiterate dockhands lolling about when they should be in the military service irritated this crew member. True, there were dances ashore, although O'Kelly dodged attending on the grounds that he did not trust himself with all the good-looking southern girls. He was most aware of the "enormous amount of supplies" taken aboard and the rumors that their destination was Russia, South America, or even Australia. "Russia was both predominant and preferred," he told his family.[13]

Soon enough the supplies had been stowed and, at 8:30 A.M. on 28 April, a tug pulled the *Olympia* away from the navy yard dock. "We beat it down the river and out on to the broad expanse of blue, sparkling ocean under full speed," O'Kelly recounted. The weather was perfect, the sky was clear, the sun was shining as only a southern sun can shine, and "the ocean is glassy in its smoothness," he jotted in his journal. They sailed from Charleston "with our destination a well-kept secret," added Jackson, a Gunner's Mate 2d Class. O'Kelly had already recorded in his diary that the ship's exec had read them a bulletin sent from Washington stating that all mail would be censored under penalty of general court-martial and "18 mo. in the Pen at least." "So my girls if you don't want your Sailor boy to do that 18 mo. never write other than New York City c/o P.M.," he penned. Further, they should not let "every mutt in the neighborhood" read his mail and "never put any of my stuff in the papers." Rumors aside, the *Olympia's* ultimate destination was not going to be disclosed to just anyone.[14]

Captain Bierer, brought out of long standing retirement for Atlantic convoy duty, took his cruiser into the Gulf Stream about seventy-five to eighty miles out of Charleston. "Rolling" instead of "pitching" as before, they steamed for the British Isles at speeds of twelve to twenty-one knots. O'Kelly and his mates playfully teased the rookie seamen about seasickness and prescribed candy and other sweets as antidotes knowing full well that was the worst of remedies. They listened to the ship's band—"it's a bum band but is better than nothing," said the Iowan—on the first afternoon out of port. "Monkey," "fire," "abandon ship," and other drills kept the crew busy together with four-hour shifts as coal passers. Jackson found himself in charge of a machine gun squad as part of the crew began training as a "landing party." "The ship had two of those ancient .30 cal. Colt solid barrel weapons," he recalled, and "a heavier and more awkward device to carry would be hard to imagine."[15]

Flying fish, seaweed, sailing schooners, and other ships off on the distant horizon also helped break the monotony. The 5-inch guns were continuously manned and ready and the crew slept fully clothed every night. Bad weather blew in on 2 May and continued intermittently for a fortnight. It did not deter the popular six-foot chaplain of the *Olympia* from holding Sunday services although some of the crew's spirits flagged with the constant bucking of the ship in rough seas. By 12 May, they were so far north that there were only about four hours of darkness. About 5:00 A.M. the next morning, two British torpedo boats appeared and escorted the cruiser around the north coast of Scotland into Pentland Firth and through mine nets to the Royal Navy's great fleet anchorage at Scapa Flow. Bierer and his ship anchored among the British vessels off Kirkwall in the Orkney Islands. The *Olympia* was the only American warship in port at the time.[16]

The week-long stay at Scapa Flow permitted cleaning, coaling, and inspection of the ship. It was just long enough too for O'Kelly to comment upon the high prices charged the sailors for ginger snaps and soap, the quaintness of Kirkwall's twelfth-century church, peat fuel, and other cultural comparisons with home—including comely-ankled local girls. Jackson was more interested in the exchange visits with British men-o'-war and a Sunday football game ashore as well as "the necessary Field Day" after coaling. But he too remarked about the cold and windy weather, the stark landscape of the Orkneys, as well as the residents' simple life "isolated from the rife and strife of a double dealing, doublecrossing, sinful world."

Bierer and his officers, meanwhile, prepared for the next stage of their mission. On the eve of departure, they received two sets of guests: British Maj. Gen. Frederick C. Poole, his country's military representative in north Russia, and his staff as well as the French civil mission to Russia. Poole's people took over the admiral's cabin and stateroom while the captain's quarters went to the French. Jackson remembered that he and Poole's chief of staff—"an extremely tall colonel from a Highland regiment"—"swapped yarns almost every day while I shined my bright-work" (since four of the sailor's assigned five guns were located in the two cabins). O'Kelly was impressed that these were not the "swivel chair" kind of army officers "but men who have been in the trenches," citing one of them as having "a big scar across his face—just a reminder of an exploded shrapnel from the hands of a Hun." Then, at 3:30 or 4:30 A.M. on Monday 20 May, the *Olympia* shipped out of Kirkwall shepherded by British destroyers.[17]

Bierer hardly enjoyed the same clarity of mission and independence of action afforded Dewey two decades earlier. While Wilson committed himself to sending a warship to Murmansk, and allowing its commander to "cooperate there," he did set ground rules. He implored both secretaries of state and navy to caution Bierer "not to be drawn in further than the present action there without first seeking and obtaining instructions by cable from home." But, as transmitted through naval channels, including Rear Adm. William S. Sims, commanding U.S. naval forces in Europe, the injunction against involvement "seems to have become lost, somewhere, in the shuffle," to quote veteran diplomat and noted Sovietologist George Kennan.[18]

Then too, the Allies presented their own set of problems. From the start, the British senior naval officer in Murmansk, Rear Adm. Thomas W. Kemp, had pressed for operational command and control over the American warship just as he exercised over a French cruiser sent north. "There can be only one Allied head here," Kemp quite justly told London, and "I consider this step indispensable for both military and political reasons." There was also the matter of Sims's involvement and how he handed off instructions to the *Olympia*'s captain. Thus, Bierer would operate under difficulties not faced by Dewey in the Philippines. But if Bierer was not Dewey, many of his subsequent actions showed a similar combative spirit.[19]

Sims may have compounded Bierer's problems. He simply gave the cruiser captain a copy of a telegram that he had sent to the navy department on 13 April (never shared with State officials before 22 June). It simply said that Kemp was "to take any steps which he may consider necessary and desirable with the forces at his disposal to protect and further the Allied interests generally, and to assist in recovering the Allied stores at Archangel." Furthermore, Kemp was not "to commit himself to land military operations away from the port" but (subject to this restriction) "may utilize the crew of the ships for the purpose of stiffening the local resistance against Germans if it be found practicable." The same instructions were issued to the French senior officer and by implication, now Bierer too.

Since Kemp would command all Allied ships at Murmansk, their captains were directed "to cooperate to the fullest capacity." Thus, it would seem that the situation was ready-made for dilemma. On both hands, aside from cooperating in protecting and furthering Allied interests, recovering the Archangel stores, and "stiffening the local resistance to the Germans," the American naval captain would naturally be subject to orders reflecting whims, agenda, and interpretations of the senior British official—Kemp, and subsequently with the latter's successor, Frederick Poole, coming aboard the *Olympia*. Still, he was subject to the wishes of the home government in Washington.[20]

Of course, little of this could be foreseen as the *Olympia* left the Orkneys. Off the Shetland islands, the Royal Navy's Fourth Battle Squadron saluted the *Olympia*'s passing. Crossing the Arctic circle on 21 May, she rounded North Cape and stood off the Murman coast by noon on the twenty-fourth. Sailing the Barents Sea unescorted, she was rife with rumors that two German submarines lay in wait. When quarters sounded at 3:30 P.M. that day, the crew loaded and stood by their guns until the ship anchored for the sunlit night in Kola Inlet. O'Kelly noted in his diary how the everlasting strain was getting on the crew's nerves and how it would be better if something happened "because I don't think there is a coward on this ship unless it is I, but it's the unknown, the invisible danger that gets our goats." He surmised they would get through if they kept their nerve. A British trawler took the cruiser through the mine fields, and they resumed passage at 6:00 A.M. running full speed and sighting land "or rather several large hills covered with snow" about two hours later. Yet, the Russian mainland was not reached before early afternoon. The crew of the *Olympia* watched seals and seagulls riding great cakes of ice melting off the hills as they began to ascend the deep Kola River and navigate its crooked course between high rocky shores on either side.[21]

The inauspicious town of Murmansk was hardly inspiring, even compared with Kirkhall. Her year-round harbor facilities (compliments of the Atlantic Gulf Stream) meant that in 1917 alone some two million tons of supplies had been unloaded here despite the submarine threat. What had been a tiny fishing village before the war (the larger town of Kola further upstream) had become a wartime shamble of unpainted, mostly single-story structures. Sort of "like the old Alaska mining towns one reads about," O'Kelly surmised. It was also the terminus of a railroad extending north from Saint Petersburg (Petrograd), and local Soviet authorities had been initially receptive to the Allies appearance (as had the central regime of Leon Trotsky in Moscow) although more so when the Americans hove into view. It was rumored that a German force was advancing through Finland to cut the rail line and take the port. So two hundred Royal Marines,

Kemp's flagship *Glory*, and the French cruiser *Amiral Aube* lent their presence until the *Olympia*'s arrival. A Russian battleship (*Chesma*) and a cruiser (*Askold*, which had escaped disaster in the Russo-Japanese War) were now under control of Bolshevik mutineers, and lent an unstable air to the place.[22]

The *Olympia* crew thrived on rumors—that their stay in north Russia might be up to a year, that American soldiers were on the way, and that if the Russians sold out to the Germans, the sailors expected to blow the Russian ships out of the river and send a party ashore to take over the town and all the provisions and ammunition there. "Just give the old 'Olympia' a chance and we will make her old name ring out in history once more," declared O'Kelly. But, for the most part, life aboard ship was quite prosaic. They coaled ship and then had a field day to clean up. Contingents of British and French sailors paid a visit on Sunday, 2 June, and the Americans won a boxing match among the Allies. Jackson took a whale boat crew and rowed around the harbor on the last day of 30 May, just for exercise.

The whole crew now went on "war rations"—a quarter pound of meat per week, no milk, limited quantities of coffee, sugar, and tea but plenty of bran bread. O'Kelly spent a great deal of time learning and practicing electricity studies, when he wasn't penning poetry or reading Creasy's *Fifteen Decisive Battles of the World*. Pretty soon, to keep them busy, all the *Olympia* crew members broke out paint brushes to repaint the vessel from top to bottom in addition to their normal housekeeping duties. Some of the crew went off to operate with Russian crews aboard a decaying destroyer but shore liberty was out. Same old chow, same old sights from the ship, same old hectoring officers, thought O'Kelly, although he soon found himself engaged almost day and night running a movie projector for his bored shipmates. It would be late June before a supply boat with mail and better rations arrived.[23]

Then came a break when, on the evening of 8 June, the ship sent ashore a landing force of 110 men (a fourth of her complement) to police the city of Murmansk—a move viewed in some circles as a "momentous day" for America since "it marked the point of no return in our war with Russia" and in Moscow's eyes "indelibly lumped" the United States with Britain and France "as aggressors against a struggling new Russian republic then facing a universally hostile world." That was certainly the furthest thing from the minds of the *Olympia* crew members at the time: They were still too much enamored with the adventure. As O'Kelly noted, it was the wish of everyone on the ship that they would go somewhere, do something besides "loaf" around Murmansk.[24]

Certainly American ambassador David Francis was pleased with the *Olympia* crew's landing. He had hinted in a message to Bierer that while he did not presume to command the navy captain in such matters, "I should want American marines to land, provided the French, British and Italian troops were landed." He later learned from assistant secretary of the navy, Franklin D. Roosevelt, that Bierer was instructed to obey the ambassador's orders. Still, this first landing was almost stillborn. Lt. Henry Floyd's command of two infantry companies, including the machine gun section (together with cooks, signalmen, and a pharmacist's mate), found that the Royal Marines had not evacuated their barracks so as to proceed upriver to Kola as planned. So initially, the *Olympia*'s crew had to return to ship for the night, leaving their gear on the jetty under guard. The next morning, however, they secured one end of the log barracks and began their drills all the next week and "went over the positions that we would man in case of an attack." Much of their time was spent setting up a two-hundred-foot firing range, digging a defensive emplacement, and explaining to locals the advertisements for cars and clothing in the newspapers they eventually received in mail from home. Absent its marine contingent since the Block Island mishap, the *Olympia*'s bluejackets had to handle all shore or landing force duties.[25]

By early July, Allied shore parties had stabilized the Murmansk situation. Buildings were searched and arms caches had been seized after Russian sailors rioted with some loss of life on the eleventh. Many of these arms included brand-new Lewis machine guns and Russian-pattern rifles manufactured in the United States. Accordingly, "we stopped worrying about ejectors breaking in our old Springfields," noted Jackson. Otherwise, the mosquitoes were more of a problem than either mutinous Russian crews or Bolshevik sympathizers. O'Kelly now counted twenty-six different kinds of "uniforms" present at Murmansk—French, English, Russian, Persian, Japanese, Chinese, and American of various services, as well as Finn, Lapp, Slav, even Bulgarian prisoners. An "aviation ship with 3 hydroplanes on her" plus observation balloons also attracted his attention.[26]

Olympia landing party at Murmansk in July 1918.

Some of the *Olympia*'s crew were disappointed that America's Independence Day drew no fireworks, salutes, or big dinner—just the same two little slices of bread, the one spoon of stew, and one cup of coffee, noted
O'Kelly. But British and French warships flew the Stars and Stripes in honor
of the day and Russian sailors gave a party and served sandwiches and tea.
Jackson also noted that the *Olympia*'s band gave a concert for the whole
town, while a team from the landing force played a second team from the
ship in a game of baseball. Boxing matches with the Allied crews and the
continuous curiosity about the Russian people garnered attention. Still, the
Americans remained dependent upon English potatoes and flour as well
as in-country provisions of cod, salmon, and haddock. British ships brought
in the mail, but the *Olympia*'s own American supply ship was nowhere in
sight. O'Kelly observed that he got off the ship only twice since 20 April
and when he did, it was to visit the tiny Y.M.C.A. facility or simply walk
up to the snow line outside town and back. This constituted entertainment
ashore.[27]

Still, the *Olympia*'s close-knit shipboard society offered its lighter
moments. Electrician O. S. "Ote" Fairbanks, who had a family back in
Brooklyn, was also the official ship photographer. He was required to sub-

mit all pictures to Bierer before printing any for sale to the crew. Sometimes he did and sometimes just the opposite, for if a picture did not meet the captain's approval Ote was supposed to destroy the film in Bierer's presence. If, however, Ote got a "very delectable picture," which he was sure would not meet Bierer's approval, he would print four or five dozen before showing the original to the captain. In this way he always had a popular supply of pictures on hand—all done with government equipment and film. Apparently, Ote made lots of side money on such ventures and his buddy O'Kelly helped print them on occasion.[28]

By August, the brisk comings and goings of Allied troop transports and the repetitive showing of "ancient" movies had a new twist. Hundreds of French, British, and other refugees now streamed out of the revolution-torn hinterland seeking asylum. The British transport *Porto*, which had carried Royal Marines to Murmansk, in turn transported refugees back to England. Prior to sailing, Jackson's landing party was sent to help the marines screen the lot for weapons. It became a mob scene as the refugees rushed to the ship, one woman getting aboard in time to deliver a baby. Jackson's group contained a skinny little Irishman from Boston named Murphy who had met an American among these refugees, a representative for an American farm machinery firm. Caught up in the war and revolution, he and his wife had lived for months in a railroad car which had finally ended up on the jetty in Murmansk. They had very little food for the voyage so Murphy slipped through an ostensible 12-inch porthole in the *Porto* and requisitioned several loaves of bread from the ship's bakery for the couple. They awarded him the Pullman car for his trouble. Jackson's gang spent one night in it. But, when the *Porto* sailed the next day, they all returned to the log barracks.[29]

Those members of the *Olympia* crew still aboard ship battled three hours of rifle drill every day—and boredom. The shore party had all the activity, it seemed. Jackson's working party of forty or fifty seamen unloaded the British supply ships and this "offered the opportunity to accidentally drop and break an occasional box of canned goods." Getting "the loot" away from the dock was no problem since their mess combined with that of the Royal Marines, and the English cooks supplied the Americans food in covered metal containers called "dixies." Here lay the means for taking the pilfered cans back to the *Olympia* and when the Royal Marine officer tried to inspect the dixies, Jackson (backed up by Lieutenant Floyd) balked. This device worked for awhile, but eventually Floyd himself took over daily inspection. "Thus ended our supply of jam, sugar, and lime juice," ruefully admitted Jackson.[30]

Actually, while continually grousing about their "limey" compatriots, the *Olympia* crewmen learned much from their veteran allies. They discovered how to match the Royal Marine formality of changing the guard each morning. They found out their comrades were survivors of the bloody Zeebrugge raid and that each British soldier wore a wide flannel cloth wrapped around his midriff which kept him both warm and provided a place to stow spare cap and collar devices. O'Kelly often commented about the hygiene and customs of the other Allied contingents and the Russians, but more in absence of other news. On 5 August, however, he recorded that the *Olympia*'s crew was all split up with the 100 men in the Murmansk landing party, 50 more helping man a Russian destroyer, leaving only 150 men on the cruiser. The rest—"50 men, the band, and the skipper—are in Archangel," he jotted.[31]

By this time too, a new wrinkle had developed in the "intervention." Once again, it involved men from the *Olympia*. The ice-bound port of Archangel, founded by the Dutch in 1584, offered thirteen miles of dockside as well as railroad links with the trans-Siberian railroad in the Russian interior. It was now reopened to oceanic traffic. No German threat to Murmansk had appeared from Finland, yet the Allied Supreme War Council, the British home government, Poole, Francis, and others urged expanding the Allied intervention to include taking this second north Russian port and even moving hundreds of miles southward on the rail line to link up with and free the so-called Czech Legion (an assortment of ex-prisoners of war from the Austro-Hungarian armies and elsewhere who had taken the anti-Bolshevik side). The Wilson government continued to agonize over the whole affair holding to its original instructions. But, by early July, Allied pressure and new information led Washington to increase the intervention not only in north Russia but also in Siberia. Dispatch of partially trained and inexperienced doughboys of the 339th Infantry from Minnesota and Wisconsin resulted from such decisions.[32]

The unpredictability of Moscow's Trotskyites also contributed to the confusion. The Bolsheviks had changed their opinion of the Allied moves and now threatened a full-scale confrontation. What resulted was a sort of pop-top expeditionary force of some dozen vessels under Poole (with Bierer in accompaniment aboard the general's yacht, HMS *Sylvator*) that set off from Murmansk at the end of July. The force numbered only 1,300 troops, but included fifty *Olympia* sailors of the 1st Company (fitted out with British steel pot helmets, said Jackson, plus Russian Moisin rifles) and the flagship's band ("to be used ashore in recruiting Russians, Poles, etc., for the Slavo-Allied forces," according to Bierer).

Boarding the SS *Stephens*, the Americans were joined by Serbian, French, and British contingents as well as a "Russian Legion" of ex-Tsarist soldiers and sailors trained, equipped, and uniformed by the British. Dewey's old flagship remained at Murmansk; her twenty-six-foot draft making her a poor candidate for the shallow approaches to Archangel, well up the Dvina River. Poole got his force ashore on 2 August, under an engineered coup arrangement that ousted the local Bolshevik leadership. They discovered a wildly enthusiastic populace and receptive new local government, according to Bierer. Then with Olympians in the lead, they pursued the Bolsheviks into the swamps south of the city. The next day bluejackets "in search of adventure after several months of boredom in Murmansk," according to one author, and "in no mood to be cheated of a chance at combat," found an old wood-burning locomotive in the railroad yards at Bakaritza, across the Dvina river from Archangel. Hitching up a couple of flatcars, they began a furious pursuit of the retreating "Reds" until stymied by stiffening resistance some thirty miles down the rail line to Vologda. Nevertheless, Ens. Donald M. Hicks's party brought in fifty-four Bolshevik soldiers who had surrendered at Tundra.[33]

Soon, the *Olympia*'s Archangel contingent became involved not only with activities on the railroad but also with a river operation to Kotlas and a Russian-Allied Naval Brigade at Solombala. The *Olympia*'s band was busy "attracting recruits" with its music at Archangel while Hicks, commanding the Dvina River party, encountered stiff Bolshevik opposition despite sending back glowing reports of warm receptions in small hinterland towns and villages. Opposed by one group under a local leader named Popov, the Allied force ran into heavy fire from an armored car, machine guns, and British-made 18-pounder artillery. By now just about all the sailors manned machine guns. "The fight lasted about five hours and kept us fairly busy," admitted Hicks. One of the *Olympia*'s seamen—appropriately named George Dewey Persche—was wounded.[34]

This was merely the start of a series of seemingly endless firefights between the Allied forces and the Bolshevik bands of the region. Prisoners were taken; villages captured and given up. *Olympia* crew members even temporarily reinforced a British garrison that had occupied Onega, on a bay of the White Sea, seventy miles east of Archangel. Like the rest of the intervention force, the Americans fanned out deeply into mother Russia. Persche's wounding was "the first American blood to be shed on Russian soil for the cause of democracy," according to his hospital report, and Poole thought Hicks's action so exemplary that he put him in for his country's Distinguished Service Cross. But it did defy Wilsonian logic and wishes, and the merry-go-round of intrigue and suspense soon bogged down in the trackless north Russian forests. Other scouting expeditions only partially let up with the arrival of the 339th infantry in September.[35]

The rump *Olympia* crew back in Murmansk finally welcomed their own supply ship on 9 August, while all summer British steamers carried the Asian flu among their crews. The *Olympia* crew also managed to repair and partially man the Russian destroyers *Kapitan Yourasovski* and *Beschumni*, both dirty coal burners and lice-ridden, causing Jackson to recall during a visit to the retired ship years later that one should take a look at the bath-tub in the sick-bay. "It was in this tub, filled with sheep-dip that we soaked loose the 'wee beasties' when we finally returned to the ship," he recalled. Then on 14 September, the last of *Olympia*'s landing force and band returned from Archangel, having been ashore fourteen weeks, setting a new record for such "undeclared war" activity.[36]

As affairs dragged on, even American officials—from Sims in London to Bierer at Archangel—began to express reservations. Sims argued for a force sufficient "to whatever tasks are undertaken in that country." Bierer, like Bolshevik leaders Lenin and Trotsky, finally concluded that both the British and the French were seeking to place the region as well as the adjacent waters "under their control or domination." Saving enormous Anglo-French investments in Russia rather than saving the Czechs, establishing an eastern front, or protecting the tons of military supplies—most of which had already slipped into the hands of the Bolsheviks—seems to have taken precedence. The crusade had clearly shifted to an anti-Bolshevik tone.[37]

On 24 October, Rear Adm. Newton A. McCully and his staff plus thirty-six men arrived in the French cruiser *Gueydon*. At 4:00 P.M. that day, he hoisted his flag in the *Olympia* as Commander U.S. Naval Forces, Northern Russia. An 1887 graduate of the Naval Academy, gifted assistant naval attaché in Russia during the Russo-Japanese War, and naval attaché as world war gave way to revolution, McCully traveled with orders from Sims that continued an American policy "as vague, contradictory, and unrealistic" as when the *Olympia* had appeared six months before. Highlighted in the guidance were the words "in the interests of the Russian people" and "no ulterior military or political motives inimical to Russian sovereignty." McCully better understood the Russian language, culture, and land than Francis, Poole, or many others. Still, he was under the orders of the senior naval officer of the co-belligerent powers in north Russia, Admiral Kemp.[38]

McCully read his orders to the crew of his new flagship then departed for protocol visits to British, French, and Russian commanders at Murmansk. Typically, he came away thinking the British as uncommunicative, arrogant, and condescending, while he found the French and Russians "very frank." He then quickly toured the city, judging the populace sullen and unfriendly, suffering from hunger since receiving only about two hundred tons of food since the Allies took charge. McCully then prepared to leave for Archangel. On 26 October at 1:30 P.M., the *Olympia* weighed anchor and pulled away from Murmansk—O'Kelly jotting in his diary, "I hope forever."[39]

Arriving at the mouth of the Dvina on 28 October, fog prevented the cruiser from crossing the mud bar and going on to Archangel. McCully, however, proceeded upriver on a tugboat to meet with Francis, Poole, and others. Once the flagship had closed on the city the next day, liberty was given to the crew. The Orthodox churches that had escaped Bolshevik wrath, cobblestone streets, and friendly people impressed crewmen like Chester Jackson, but one visit ashore was enough for Tom O'Kelly. He was more taken by a brightly lit American Red Cross ship that tied up just behind the *Olympia*. Major excitement occurred when crews of the cruiser and the British battleship *Glory* found themselves battling a nasty fire in the hold of the flax-laden ship *Ascutiny*. Bierer and his officers had to convene an investigatory board on the matter.

McCully's discussions with Allied officials confirmed what he considered Britain's imperial designs in Russia. By mid-October, Poole was recalled to England and replaced by an eminently more neutral Maj. Gen. Edmund Ironside. Soon, Ambassador Francis's prostate condition made it necessary for him to leave Russia also. McCully volunteered the *Olympia* for such purpose, as well as to transport American wounded and invalids to hospitals in Great Britain. On 6 November, Francis was carried aboard the cruiser by eight bluejackets. Departure itself was then delayed by a sudden visit from two hundred unfriendly red guards into Archangel, according to O'Kelly. The next day the *Olympia* pulled down river and out in the White Sea awaiting sufficient tide to cross the "blooming mud bar." By the eighth she was on her way back to Murmansk.[40]

Anchoring again at Murmansk at 8:23 A.M. on 11 November, the crew coaled and cleaned the ship and took on mail as well as a large number of doughboys who were suffering variously from frostbite, rheumatism, consumption, and even "shell shock." News of the armistice ending World War I apparently occasioned little comment, according to Jackson, but rumors had it that the *Olympia* would soon be headed home to the United States. Then, at 7:00 A.M. on 13 November, the American cruiser left Murmansk. Some *Olympia* crew remained behind—several officers and small parties aiding McCully and the naval attaché at Archangel, those sailors still helping man Russian warships, and Ensign Hicks and his party with the Allied naval brigade. The ship ran into a severe storm with forty-six-mile-per-hour winds about six hours out, and all hands were profoundly sick. Stormy, rough sailing attended passage all the way to the British Isles. But, by the seventeenth, British destroyers had come out to escort the ship, now making eighteen knots under a beautiful moon and slightly warmer temperatures. They arrived in time to see sixty ships of the German Grand Fleet steam into Scapa Flow under Allied tutelage. Not stopping in the Orkneys, the *Olympia* sped on to Invergorden, Scotland, mooring there just after noon on 18 November.[41]

After transferring Francis and the invalid soldiers to a fast transport leaving for America, the *Olympia*'s crew received liberty, thanks to McCully's earlier directive to Bierer. Again, Invergorden was a small place with high prices, cramped stores, and poorly lit streets. Most of the people seemed to be in uniform, even the women who worked for the government, observed O'Kelly. Then, this experience too was past as at 8:00 A.M. on Thursday 21 November the ship weighed anchor and headed due east at sixteen knots.

Originally, the *Olympia* was to return to Russia and in fact, McCully was planning on it. Instead, at 5:00 P.M., she turned south and set course first for Harwich and then on to Portsmouth. All along the way, said O'Kelly, they spotted sunken ships which had been torpedoed and at one point cheered the sight of twenty German submarines going into English ports under Allied colors. At 10:00 A.M. on 24 November they arrived in Portsmouth. The north Russia adventure was truly over.[42]

TROUBLESHOOTING THE ADRIATIC

The *Olympia* spent the month of December 1918 in dry dock at Portsmouth. The repairs were routine but the lull permitted extensive, rotating furlough parties for the crew. Those who remained aboard ship, like O'Kelly, worked at installing new equipment such as a radio arc set for longer distance transmission. They suffered the wretched English fog and rain of winter and took in shore liberty that highlighted exploitative prices and pugnacious returning British servicemen offset by very grateful and friendly civilians. In-theater censorship of the mails was lifted on 5 December, and rumor had the ship going back to Russia, much to everyone's consternation. A warm Christmas turkey dinner and Y.M.C.A. gifts made amends to brighten the holiday as did mail call and a new rumor that Gibraltar was the ship's next stop. Indeed, the very next day the cruiser left Portsmouth, passed the arcane nineteenth-century forts now sporting modern long-range seacoast guns, and out past the Isle of Wight. Then the ship turned southeastward. Off Brest she passed a large convoy of American troops going home ("lucky devils," O'Kelly jotted in his diary) and three British battleships. The *Olympia*'s pace was a leisurely eight knots and she made Gibraltar anchorage at 8:00 A.M. on the last day of the year.[43]

Once again, shore leave was in order. The sights and sounds of this British colony affixed to the blue-gray rock fascinated the young Americans, now including a good complement of replacement officers. On 5 January, the ship left Gibraltar only to turn around almost immediately in order to pick up the new admiral, paint the whole ship, and accomplish fix-up chores, as when O'Kelly and mates put an armature in the number 3 blower and set up a starting panel for the ship's printing press. At 3:50 P.M., the flag of Rear Adm. A. P. Niblack was hoisted on the ship and, five minutes later, he embarked as a passenger for the cruise to Venice, Italy. Smooth seas and distant glimpses of Spain and Africa were early features of the 1,150-mile run to Malta. Here, liberty for crew and coaling by natives took place and then off to the Adriatic, which was reached on 20 January. An American destroyer came out from Venice to convoy the flagship through the mines but the *Olympia* lost course and had to anchor for several hours.

The cruiser finally pulled into Venice at 9:00 A.M. on Tuesday 21 January. As the *Olympia* crew settled into a restful month's stay, Niblack assumed command of the U.S. Naval Forces Operating in the Eastern Mediterranean and Captain Bierer was succeeded as *Olympia*'s skipper by Capt. David F. Boyd Jr., USNA '97. The crew battled the flu (losing the admiral's steward and three or four seamen to its ravages), compulsory drills, inspections, and Bluejacket's Manual examinations. Large quantities of mail caught up with the ship, and the U.S. Navy supply ship *Celtic* transferred two months resupply of stores. At 10:00 A.M. on 21 February, the cruiser left for Spalato, Austria. Niblack remained behind, later taking passage on the destroyer USS *Maury* for Pola.[44]

Once more, the speed was leisurely at eight knots over smooth seas. Despite an accompaniment of twelve Italian, British, French, and American destroyers, the problem was floating mines. One nightwatch sailor exploded two with a rifle at a distance of five hundred yards. About five miles out of Venice, the ship passed Italian barges mounting 20-inch guns that had been used to bombard Trieste. The *Olympia* reached Spalato on George Washington's birthday. The city, soon given the name "Split" by the Americans, had been selected as the naval base for the zone patrolled and protected by American forces under the terms of the Austrian armistice. Six submarine chasers, destroyers, and station ships were eventually augmented not only by the *Olympia* but six other destroyers, and the navy set up a supply and communication base here for the region. Improvement of medical and sanitary conditions accompanied the U.S. Navy's peacekeeping role in the region. Diphtheria was especially rampant, striking even the flagship during her stay at "Split."[45]

The *Olympia* at first found herself in the very thick of the Austro-Italian dispute over who would eventually secure this part of the Adriatic coast in the peace settlement. Probably the most impressive thing about the place was the high hills covered with vineyards that dropped to the sea, the initial animosity of the populace toward the Americans (ever tempered by the universal children's begging for cigarettes and candy), and the mayhem ashore between the feuding Austrians and Italians. *Olympia* Lt. Cdr. S. Field became chief officer of the Inter-Allied Patrol ashore, while twelve armed sailors under Lt. Henry F. Floyd deployed as part of that police force. The Allied naval force in the harbor included two American-manned Austrian warships. But incidents were rife, the threat of mob action ever present, curfews enforced, and every night the *Olympia*'s searchlights scanned the city for unrest. Eventually, things quieted down and liberty parties even attended Yugoslav dances on the north side of the city. O'Kelly decided that American sailors were popular with the ladies because they had money to spend whereas the local males did not. Rumors had the *Olympia* returning to Brindisi and then Southampton before going back to the Adriatic. On 16 March, the flagship (for Niblack had returned) packed up and left Spalato for Brindisi. The admiral and Field stayed behind.[46]

The ship went no farther than Brindisi for coaling. The *Olympia*'s true mission now was cruising the Dalmatian coast, helping the Inter-Allied Patrol maintain tranquility in the Balkans in the wake of the collapsed Austro-Hungarian empire. While her crew made the most of every stop for sight-seeing, Brindisi offered only a typically southern Italian cityscape, a self-important railway station, a seaplane base, and a reputation for its inhabitants' felicity with knives in narrow, dark alleys. Back at Spalato six days later, the Olympia welcomed a new admiral—Rear Adm. Philip Andrews, who "started right off with an inspection and he sure is raising cain," opined O'Kelly. More pleasing were a "smoker," boxing matches aboard ship, and field day ashore during which the flagship sailors bested competitors from the destroyers *Maury* and *Stribling* and the American-manned *Radetzki* and *Grivia*. But Andrews was the subject of all conversation. A hard-driving thirty-seven year career officer, he even banned the wearing of patched dungarees as work clothes. The crew of the *Olympia*, in particular, were only too happy to see him transfer his flag to the *Stribling* (if only temporarily) on 5 April.[47]

Morale slumped with Andrews's presence as thirty-seven dishonorable discharges plus eleven general courts-martial cases resulted. But, later in April, since the *Olympia* seemed destined to stay at Spalato for the foreseeable future, the crew rigged up a canvas corner over the aft gun deck and fo'c'sle, decorated the ship with flowers and tried to make

Rear Adm. Phillip
Andrews, USN,
aboard the *Olympia*.

her more livable in drab battle gray. One photograph taken during the
Spalato tour shows a rather dingy warship, the Signal House (on aft
bridge) as a radio shack, while additional yards on the rig suggested supports for a web of antenna wires. But the clean duck awnings fore and aft
stood out from all the *Olympia*'s drabness. New men arrived and others
(especially wartime reservists) departed. Furlough parties went off to
Rome, Belgrade, Sarajevo, Drobrovna, and under the Y.M.C.A. to view
the wartime Piave fighting front. Still, men like a very homesick O'Kelly

looked to transfer or just go home and leave the service. Unfortunately, orders arrived in May prohibiting release of any more men in European waters, so O'Kelly and others were stuck. Minstrel shows, rowing parties, and other entertainment afforded temporary release. In July, it was back to shuttle diplomacy by steaming to Fiume, Croatia, and Andrews had transferred his flag to the USS *Pittsburg*. On 21 July, the cruiser returned to Spalato where the inhabitants had finally grown attached to the fun-loving Americans who delighted in walking about town and chatting with the residents. Suddenly, on 18 August, Andrews issued orders sending the *Olympia* to Constantinople.[48]

Reaching the Golden Horn by 23 August, the *Olympia* crew were fascinated by Turkish sights—but not just the Mosques: the bazaars, veiled women, the Sultan's Palace, markets, and a good city streetcar system. Rather, as they passed through the Dardanelles, they viewed the forts that had been badly battered by the Allies in 1914 and 1915. Gallipoli that had so long defied Allied capture struck a responsive cord, as did the long line of sunken ships in the passage and the hillsides clad white with Turkish army tents. But the time passed too quickly and by 26 August, the *Olympia* entered the Black Sea and the next day appeared at Batum, Russia—a dirty, wine-flowing city lacking in civilization but possessing, apparently, a superb bathing beach. The distant Caucasus mountains afforded more beauty and, from Batum, the American vessel cruised along the Turkish coast, putting in at Trebizond, Herasunt, and Unich (where American refugees were taken aboard for passage to Samsun). Sinub, Ineboli, and Sungal were further stops before the return to Constantinople by 8 September.

O'Kelly got his wish on the twelfth and, with others, transferred aboard the destroyer USS *Lamb*, slated for home and discharge. "Am I a happy man O'Boy, ain't it a grand and glorious feeling," he jotted in his diary. On 13 September, his old ship—"the tub" he derisively called her—departed for Smyrna, Turkey, arriving the next day. The *Lamb* was not far behind, but now there would be no more coaling ship for O'Kelly and mates, for the destroyer was an oil burner. In the end, O'Kelly may have had the last laugh. It was probably he—given to poetry during his moments of home-sickness and boredom—who left the quaint World War I sailor's lament on a dirty piece of paper discovered behind a cabinet in the electrical store room in the *Olympia*'s dynamo room area in May 1983.

O'Kelly's poem aptly reflected an *Olympia* crewman's lament:

Darling I'm coming back
Silver threads among the black

Now that peace in Europe nears
I'll be home in seven years

I'll drop in on you some night
With my whiskers long and white

Yes this war is over dear
And we're coming home I hear

Home again with you once more
Say by nineteen twenty-four

Once I thought by now I'd be
Sailing back across the sea

Back to where I sit and pine
But I'll still hear taps at nine

You can hear the gang all curse
War is hell but peace is worse

When the next war comes around
In the front ranks I'll be found

I'll rush in pell mell
Yes I will like hell like hell[49]

The old "Queen of the Pacific" returned to Spalato on 19 September. Now, the Italian senior naval officer present informed U.S. naval authorities of a renegade Italian contingent that had captured a Serbian garrison at Trau, and specifically asked Boyd that "the raiders be turned back." So, the cruiser moved there a week later, disembarking a small landing force reminiscent of the Murmansk and Archangel operations. The excursion was brief, the Italians apparently induced to return to their own zone of activities. So the landing force returned to ship and the American vessel steamed back to Spalato the same evening. As the secretary of the navy later reported, "That no serious result happened is due to the prompt and efficient action of American forces." Had they not done so, he continued, "there would almost inevitably have been bloodshed, which would perhaps have resulted in a state of actual war between Italy and Jugo-Slavia, owing to the intensity of feeling existing over the Dalmatian question."[50]

The *Olympia* resumed its peacekeeping mission at "Split" on the seventh, remaining a month before sailing for Valetta, Malta, en route home to America. Dry-docking at Malta was captured in a sailor's snapshot showing the *Olympia*'s bottom being cleaned with weather cloths on bridge and pilothouse and scarring from anchor rub clearly visible in the photograph. This task completed, the ship sailed for Gibraltar on 1 November, arriving there and then departing four days later. She reached her old home port of Charleston, South Carolina, just before Thanksgiving. Here she remained until Valentine's Day 1920.[51]

In the interim, Boyd stepped down as skipper in mid-December, succeeded temporarily by Lt. Cdr. C. N. Platt. Then, on 6 January, a forty-two-year-old Illinois sailor, Capt. Henry L. Wyman, took over as the *Olympia* returned to the Adriatic in late winter. From April 1920 until May 1921, the cruiser served as flagship of the U.S. Naval Forces in the Adriatic, with Admiral Andrews aboard once more. Spalato and Venice

Olympia circa 1919 after being rearmed with
.51 caliber 5-inch rapid-fire guns.

were her principal ports of call as she shuttled back and forth, but she also stopped in at Pola, Ragusa, Malta, and Naples. In December, she was hastily dispatched to the Black Sea to assist hundreds of thousands of refugees fleeing the Crimea after the Bolshevik victory over their opponents, the so-called "Whites" led by Gen. Baron Peter Wrangel, but stopped midway since the operation had already been effected. She more successfully carried out a similar mercy mission at Ragusa, Dalmatia, where some 2,500 refugees lacked food and shelter and suffered an outbreak of smallpox and typhus. The crew provided fuel for cooking stoves, soap and towels, clothing, and food while the ship's medical officer cared for the sick and inaugurated sanitary measures. Wyman received touching testimonials from the refugees at Christmas and promptly hung them in his cabin aboard ship.[52]

In November, the flagship assisted in delivering the ex-Austrian battleships *Radetzki* and *Zrinyi* to Italian authorities, having manned and held them in trust since the armistice. But the high point of this tour for the crew perhaps came at Christmas 1920. The holiday festival at Venice, Italy, on 25 December, was the biggest day for American naval forces since they had been in the Adriatic. Celebrations began at Spalato on Christmas Eve when a committee representing the various women's organizations of the base supervised distribution of 2,000 Christmas boxes containing shoes, stockings, chocolate, and toys to a proportion of the children in all the Dalmatian towns. Rear Admiral Andrews had made an appeal through the Junior Red Cross at home on behalf of these children. Added to these packages were 1,000 more gathered through the generosity of American naval personnel. Each contained one-half pound of chocolate, a toy, some fruit and nuts, and a card giving each child the good wishes of America.[53]

A similar number of boxes and greetings were distributed on board the *Olympia* on Christmas afternoon among the children of Venice. Some 980 blind, crippled, orphaned, or otherwise indigent children were located in the thirteen charitable institutions of the city. Hundreds were too little or infirm to come to the ship, so their packages were sent to their institutions. But the remaining six or seven hundred scrambled aboard the cruiser, guests of the crew, and were taken by hand to see the different trees and decorations as well as nooks and crannies of the famous warship. Ninety little sailor boys from the Italian schoolship *Scilla* were also presented with gloves and candy.

Removal of the Casket of the Unknown Soldier from *Olympia* at Washington Navy Yard on 9 November 1921. Among the dignitaries at right are the secretary of war, the secretary of the navy, the army chief of staff, and the chief of naval operations.

It was a glorious moment, capturing typical American humanitarianism in a war-torn region. As contemporary photographs attested, smiling youngsters, a grinning Santa Claus, and closely supervising swabbies were much in evidence. But, all was not just for the Italian children. The *Olympia*'s crew had received the congratulations of Andrews and Wyman that morning, Christmas packages of their own were distributed, and the best-decorated portions of the ship received prizes. Divine services were conducted, and later in the day, the Y.M.C.A. held a dance for the ship and her fellow destroyers of the flotilla, followed Christmas night by a Knights of Columbus reception and concert. It was an appropriate way for the

American warship to finish her several years abroad. She sailed back to America, arriving at the Philadelphia Navy Yard on 25 May 1921 and the following month became flagship for Rear Adm. Edward Simpson, commanding the Train of the Atlantic Fleet.

During Simpson's tenure, Dewey's old workhorse witnessed the famous experimental aerial bombing of ex-German ships by army aviator Billy Mitchell's air squadron. The cruiser *Frankfort* and battleship *Osterfriesland* had been among the warships allocated to the United States at the end of the war and were required to be sunk by the agreement with the other powers associated with the winning side. The experiment took place at the Southern Drill Grounds fifty miles off Cape Charles Light in late July. Of course, as the secretary of the navy stressed in his annual report, "the conditions for hitting were made very easy, and it is not possible to draw sound conclusions from them as to the accuracy in bombing that might be expected under war conditions." Still, army aviation enthusiasts drew the opposite conclusion and used the tests extensively in their airpower propaganda. By month's end, Rear Adm. L. H. Chandler replaced Simpson as train commander and in September the *Olympia* moved to the Norfolk Navy Yard dry dock for servicing.[54]

The wartime period had been a busy one for the *Olympia*. Total maintenance and operating costs for fiscal year 1917 totaled $300,619.40, a sum that tripled the next year ($930,010.86 before slipping back to $555,503.59 in fiscal year 1919 but leaping to a whopping $1,179,800.66 for fiscal year 1921) thanks to her wide-ranging operational duties. Proud of its contribution to the war effort, the navy's immediate postwar annual reports emphasized escorting more than 2,500,000 troops to France and back and the safe shipment of billions of tons of materiel to Europe. The *Olympia* had contributed to that escort effort. It had not been her only, or in fact her major, contribution in the period, however.[55]

The *Olympia*'s principal service had been as part of America's first crusade in Europe. She had also served on the front lines in north Russia. She was part of what Secretary Daniels in 1920 called an "American Navy a force for peace." Of course, he was referring to a very traditional role "from its inception," and particularly in the world war, as helping save "the liberties of mankind." But the next year he further cited that the navy was engaged "continuously in useful and humanitarian enterprises in all maritime waters." Its various fleets on all seas were engaged in very important duties and "constitute peaceful instruments for bringing about, by personal international contact, a better understanding of American aims and ideals," he concluded. Certainly that had been the *Olympia's* role in the Adriatic following the armistice. Whether or not the same could be said for her north Russia mission may have seemed questionable—although probably not to Bierer and his crew at the time.[56]

The secretary called attention to Rear Adm. Philip Andrews, "in the historic *Olympia* and a detachment of destroyers," as concluding a most memorable tour of duty in the Adriatic. They had engaged in "aiding all nationals alike in that much-harried region and signally relieving the sufferings of the Russian refugees from the Crimea." Because of the complete breakdown in ordinary means of communication throughout the Near East, he noted, ships like the *Olympia* had functioned as "radio traffic ships" and operated on regular schedules for carrying officials and stores of agencies like the Food Administration "for the immediate sustenance of the impoverished inhabitants." "By means of a high-power radio set in the United States, it is possible to receive communications in the force commander's office in London, on board the *Olympia* in the Adriatic, and at [Rear] Admiral [Mark] Bristol's headquarters in Constantinople," Daniels suggested. Perhaps such postwar "peace" efforts were simply more definable than "guarding American interests" in the cauldron of revolutionary Russia.[57]

The *Olympia* had departed those Arctic waters before the north Russian adventure soured for all the participants. But she had been there at an early stage, when intervention had seemed both advisable and necessary. Defeating the Germans and quite possibly nipping the "Bolos" (as the Bolsheviks were derisively called) in their revolution seemed honorable goals to many people. The cause turned inglorious for others—a diplomatic and military tragicomedy to later scholars like Benjamin D. Rhodes. Still, the *Olympia's* service was part of a chapter quite related to ideological if not physical imperialism. It was a chapter in "interventionism" and thus so very typical of what would come to be called the American century.[58]

8

Final Honors and a Last Hurrah

Memories and impressions of the Great War to save democracy conditioned the America that awaited *Olympia's* return in 1921. But anticipation of the benefits of peace and "normalcy" did also. The victorious, visionary administration of Woodrow Wilson had temporarily set aside its massive 1916 "Navy Second to None" building program in order to win the war. In 1919 it returned to that goal, only to see it washed away the next year by the same Republican Party election sweep that swamped acceptance of the Versailles treaty and League of Nations by an isolationist Congress.

Public opinion shifted against naval expansionism. The new administration of Pres. Warren G. Harding subsequently sought naval reductions, not additions. Proposals advanced by Secretary of State Charles Evans Hughes at the Washington Naval Conference in 1921–22 pointed toward disarmament, shocking the great powers of the time. But the resultant, reduced American "treaty navy" proved more powerful, more modern than ever. Yet the watchwords of economy merged with modernization, efficiency, and stabilization. It was in this climate that Dewey's old flagship served her final assignments.[1]

Not that economy and efficiency were anything new. Wilson's own naval secretary, Josephus Daniels, had trumpeted that party line before the war. Now his successor, Edwin Denby, embraced it. Proclaiming a sort of combination of Wilsonian and Hardingesque (Hughesian) naval policy (a "first" for the navy and Congress in American history), Denby melded the concept of "navy second to none" in conformity with the capital ship ratios established by the treaty for limitation of naval armaments. "This policy should be accomplished as soon as consistent with our economic situation," while still adhering to the basic premise that "The Navy of the United States should be maintained in sufficient strength to support its policies and its commerce, and to guard its continental and overseas possessions."[2]

Indeed, the dimensions of the navy had changed. Cruisers, for instance, were now heavier, bigger, and closer to battlewagons rather than sleek greyhounds of the sea as in the *Olympia*'s prime. Aviation, new communication systems, organizational reform, and manpower quality and quantity for a peacetime fleet also vied with operational readiness and proficiency training for diminishing dollars. Aging warships of the New Steel Navy, if still on the navy lists, were prime candidates for the scrap heap. The *Olympia* had a role to play, perhaps partly because of her flagship configuration, but more so because of her publicity profile.

GUARDIAN OF THE "UNKNOWN SOLDIER"

Sometime on the morning of 24 October 1921, Sgt. Edward F. Younger of Headquarters Company, Third Battalion, Fiftieth Infantry, American Forces in Germany, with a spray of white roses in hand, moved slowly around four caskets at the city hall in Charlons-sur-Marne, some ninety miles east of Paris. His task was to select one. Like the others, it contained the remains of an American soldier, killed in fighting three or four years earlier on the Western Front. But the casket he chose would be immortalized as America's Unknown Soldier. The same day, the USS *Olympia* slid to rest at the Pier d'Escale in Le Havre on the English Channel coast. Still clad in dingy wartime battle dress, she remained America's most famous warship yet on active duty. And she had been selected to bear the body of the "Unknown" home to the United States. In a sense, this new honor would close her prominence as herald of empire.[3]

The genesis for honoring unknown fallen from the Great War lay with Europe. France and Great Britain began the practice on 11 November 1920. Italy and others soon followed. At first, the United States government felt that it could identify all of its dead, but by 4 March 1921 Congress had authorized the return of an unknown American soldier killed in France and his re-burial with appropriate ceremonies in a tomb at the Memorial Amphitheater in Arlington National Cemetery. The process of selection of the body proceeded therefrom, culminating in a solemn but elaborate process before French and American officials at Chalons-sur-Marne. After speeches of friendship and remembrance, intricate preparations ensuring the secrecy of the body, funeral dirges, and a moving procession through the city, the box containing the casket was put aboard a special funeral train and taken to Paris overnight. It was all eminently French and emblematic of friendship and appreciation for American participation in the conflict. The event also reflected a nation which itself had lost 1.3 million dead in defense of *le Patrie*.[4]

In September, the *Olympia* had been chosen for the trans-Atlantic mission. After a three-day maintenance dry-docking at Norfolk and other preparations in Hampton Roads, she got under way for France on the twenty-eighth. Fog held her up briefly but, by 3 October and still commanded by Capt. H. L. Wyman, she was under way once more and arrived at Plymouth on England's south coast on 14 October. She made Le Havre ten days later. The senior naval officer aboard was Rear Adm. Lloyd H. Chandler, commander of the United States Atlantic Fleet Train into whose charge would be committed the Unknown Soldier's body. Upon docking at Le Havre he issued specific instructions of the flagship's participation in embarking "the Body of the Unknown Dead American Soldier," scheduled for the morrow.

The special train left Paris at midmorning on 15 October and reached Le Havre about 1:00 P.M. As at Chalons-sur-Marne, elaborate ceremonies attended passage to the dock including French and American military escorts, little school children showering the passing caisson with its casket, and a wreath-delivery at city hall. Waiting at the dock itself were honor guards and M. Maginot, the minister of pensions (later famous for the ill-fated frontier fortress line on the German border bearing his name). He would present the Croix de chevalier de la Legion d'honneur to the

Unknown Soldier. Chandler and Wyman had the officers and crew of the *Olympia* standing at quarters in dress blues, with flat caps for the sailors, dress for the marine contingent, and full dress for the ship's officers. They were certainly more spectacularly garbed than the cruiser. At 3:00 P.M., the solemn procession came to rest beside the ship, Maginot rendered honors, and the transition was made from army to navy responsibility.

The *Olympia*'s band played French and American national airs and Chopin's "Funeral March" as six sailors and two marines relieved the army body bearers. The flagship's marine honor guard presented arms and the casket was carried up the aft gangway, passing through eight side boys with the boatswain piping the Unknown's body aboard. Chandler took charge of the remains amidst tributes of flowers, some brought aboard by three hundred French school children. The casket was then tucked just beneath the stern 5-inch gun, under an awning fashioned from two large American flags. At 3:28 P.M., the *Olympia* pulled away from the Le Havre dock.[5]

Six to eight French warships and the American destroyer *Reuben James* (destined to be the first American warship sunk in World War II) served as escort. The flotilla received a 17-gun salute as it cleared the harbor and the French ships provided a second as they dropped astern when the procession left French territorial waters about 4:50 P.M. Rough seas prompted removal of the casket to the elevated after signal bridge and the inability to pass it below decks "with dignity" (i.e., without upending it) meant that the body of the Unknown had to remain topside through a very stormy passage. At one point nearing the Azores, conditions became so bad that the skipper supposedly asked the ship's chaplain and off-watch to gather and pray that "the Unknown Soldier, high above them on the aft weather deck, would safely be returned to his homeland." Divine intervention notwithstanding, the flagship and her charge reached the Virginia Capes on 7 November and, escorted by the destroyer *Bernadou*, anchored at the mouth of the Potomac River in Chesapeake Bay at day's end.[6]

Getting under way again at 8:00 P.M. on 8 November, passage upriver was slow and for some reason the cruiser scraped bottom several times during her passage. At 2:00 A.M., she anchored at Indian Head and at 12:38 the next rainy afternoon, 9 November 1921, the *Olympia* steamed past thundering garrison salutes at Fort Washington and the Washington Barracks on the final leg of her journey. The battleship *North Dakota*, lying off Piney Point, had dipped her ensign in respect and everywhere on the river 21-gun salutes (normally accorded only a chief of state) attended *Olympia*'s passing. Of course, she herself rendered prescribed honors when abreast of former president George Washington's Mount Vernon home. Finally, she tied up at the Washington Navy Yard at 3:01 P.M. and about an hour later, completed her responsibility of delivering the Unknown Soldier to American soil. Under watchful eyes of high officials including secretaries of war and navy, Chief of Naval Operations Adm. Robert Coontz, Maj. Gen. John Lejeune, commandant of the U.S. Marine Corps, and the Unknown's former expeditionary force commander, now Army Chief of Staff Gen. John J. Pershing, the once-again smartly attired and drilled Chandler and his flagship crew finished their duties.

The *Olympia*'s band played a dirge, the ship's minute guns boomed out twenty-one final salutes, and as the casket went through the railings, the boatswain piped the Unknown Soldier ashore befitting a full admiral. A bare-headed Chandler and his staff, disregarding the rain, followed the casket until the naval procession cleared ship, halted, and the band rendered four flourishes and the national anthem before resuming the funeral march to the point of exchange with the army's body bearers. Then the mounted escort and caisson moved slowly away as the Third Cavalry's mounted band played "Onward Christian Soldiers." Off into the city by 4:08 P.M., the cortege went up to Capitol Hill where the body would lie in state until the full panoply of honors and tributes had been paid by President Harding and his wife, dignitaries, and the military.[7]

Final interment at Arlington, near an amphitheater completed the previous year, would take place on the third anniversary of the signing of the armistice that had concluded the "war to end all wars." While the *Olympia*'s association with the Unknown Soldier was over by the evening of 9 November, ceremonies thereafter inspired a public and official response as only the nation's capital could mount for its heroes. Associated Press correspondent Kirke L. Simpson would gain a Pulitzer Prize covering the event and, perhaps, best caught its tone when he penned: "Under the wide and starry skies of his own homeland, America's unknown dead from France sleeps tonight, a soldier home from the wars. Alone, he lies in the narrow cell of stone that guards his body; but his soul has entered into the spirit that is America."[8]

It was prose worthy of the era of Dewey, the Spanish War, the *Olympia*, and empire building, nearly a quarter-century earlier. But it also belied the war weariness that had overtaken America after her crusade in Europe, as well as the souring political fight for treaty ratification and the slide into Harding "normalcy" of peacetime. It was something too of a requiem for the *Olympia*, as soon the hints that she would be de-commissioned and committed to history would become reality. But, for that moment in November of 1921, the honors as she passed up the Potomac must have seemed a repeat of the halcyon welcome at New York two decades before when she returned from her greatest moment of victory. As in 1900, she once more had served the nation and its people, less now in adolescent triumph and more with recognition of the tragedies and responsibilities associated with war and global maturity.[9]

FINAL DUTIES AND RETIREMENT

Leaving Washington on 15 November, the *Olympia* moored the next night at the navy yard where the Delaware and Schuykill rivers join in south Philadelphia. Pier 5 would be her temporary home, as on 12 December Chandler hauled down his flag turning over the duties of Commander Atlantic Fleet Train first to Capt. T. L. Johnson and subsequently to Capt. Louis R. de Steiguer. Wyman left the ship on 7 January, succeeded by Capt. W. C. Asserson, a forty-seven-year-old Virginian with twenty-nine years of naval service. The cruiser moved out of her berth and upriver that same month to participate in ceremonies beginning construction of a Delaware River bridge linking Philadelphia and Camden, New Jersey. Her 17-gun mid-river salute may have been impressive, but the crowd was probably more taken with a seaplane dropping a ribbon-wound wire across the water symbolizing this new link for the region. The wind, however, carried the ribbon across the ship and the crew got most of it as souvenirs. Then it was back to the navy yard for outfitting before departing to the Caribbean and Atlantic Fleet winter maneuvers on 11 January. In April she was back in Philadelphia for three more days of dry dock, and then, on 22 May, the *Olympia* left for reunion with the Naval Academy and one last Practice Training Squadron cruise with the young middies. De Steiguer, meanwhile, had left the ship, thereby ending the cruiser's proud days as a flagship.[10]

There was no regular Naval Academy practice squadron for the summer cruise that year. The midshipmen of the First, Second, and Third classes, together with those turned back into the class of 1926, were assigned to Atlantic Fleet battleships *Florida, Delaware,* and *North Dakota* as well as the *Olympia.* The cruiser now occupied the lowly place accorded those monitors with which she had sailed earlier at the academy. Midshipman Schyler Neilson Pyne, who went along on Dewey's old war horse and later rose to rear admiral's rank, wondered afterward why she was included, "but it made an interesting cruise." The vessel certainly rolled and pitched in the rough waters of the Caribbean and the North Atlantic, he noted, for that year the cruise went to Halifax as well as Panama and the West Indies in the period 5 June to 30 August.[11]

In fact, the editors of the 1925 *Lucky Bag* noted that they had been about two days at sea and "looking over the stern we could see the *Olympia* steaming along with her decks swept by every wave." She was rightfully termed the "Submarine," decided the slightly disrespectful middies. Everyone realized later that this was her last cruise before completing a glorious career and, "as a fitting conclusion, she was used . . . as a training ship for the 'Young Admirals.'" And the experience was vigorous with little of the old focus on cotillions and socializing ashore that had accompanied the coastal New England cruises.

Introduction to the Panama Canal and the ever-obnoxious chore of coaling the *Olympia* were memorable, as was the unique visit by the ship to Port Castries, St. Lucia. The highlight, however, came with the hospitality extended by the people of Halifax. Here at last, socials, parties, and dances blossomed although the expended energy did not hamper the cruiser from going to the aid of HMS *Raleigh* which ran aground off Belle Isle, Newfoundland, during their visit. An appropriate finish to the cruise came with short-range battle practice at the Southern Drill Grounds before a return to Crabtown at the end of August. The *Olympia* then returned to Philadelphia, arriving 1 September. Three months later, true to predictions, she was decommissioned at the Philadelphia Navy Yard.[12]

Sadly, yet another grand old lady of the fleet had outlived her usefulness. Still, she had served well past most of her contemporaries. Secretary of the Navy Denby said it succinctly in his 1923 annual report, when he suggested how fleet train vessels had much improved in operating condition and how two routine freighters had converted to train flagships, thus relieving the old fighting ships *Olympia* and *Connecticut* of such duties. These command ships were designed not only to carry the flag officer and his staff, but were also useful for towing target rafts and photographing the fall of shot. Here, truly, was a logistical ship for a logistical mission. But how sad too that it reflected a complete abrogation of the illusion of Horatio Nelson, David Farragut, and George Dewey on the bridge of fighting flagships. Times had changed, as caught so well by Denby's final comment: "It will be seen these ships fill a long felt want at low operating cost and reduced crews being far more economical in every way than the *Olympia* and *Connecticut*."[13]

Economy and cost reductions govern every navy in peacetime. The United States Navy of the 1920s placed a considerable number of ships out of commission and sold others "which are of obsolete type or of such character that they will probably not again be useful for naval purposes." The aged *Olympia* fit such parameters. No longer battleworthy, she was a coal-burner in an oil-burning navy. She cost taxpayers $1,179,800.66 in maintenance and operating costs in fiscal year 1921. She was the most expensive of any second or third class cruiser still in commission, although not so by a long shot in terms of maintenance and property investment figures gathered by the Navy Department. Still, her historical significance probably delayed her retirement and most certainly would prevent her scrapping in the years ahead.[14]

THE PRESERVATION SAGA

In a letter written from the Naval Academy on 8 November 1922, Midshipman T. R. Dotzler responded to an article in that day's *New York Times* regarding the naval exposition at the Grand Central Palace. It contained the astonishing news that "Admiral Dewey's flagship of Manila Bay fame is now at the bottom of the sea as a result of a collision during the great war, but her replica is on exhibit at the marine show." Not so, said the young midshipman—after all, he had been a firsthand witness to her continued existence during the previous summer's practice cruise. While the Navy Department had discontinued her use in the service, he continued, "the ship will be kept by our government as long as it will float, or as long as Mrs. Dewey lives, to fulfill a dying wish of the great hero of Manila Bay." Therein would lie two continuing themes over the next eighty-eight years. The old ship would be in continuing threat of demise as the navy needed newer vessels to meet requirements, but the *Olympia*'s survival would always turn on its association with Adm. George Dewey and that heroic day in Manila Bay.[15]

The ship remained at the Philadelphia Navy Yard reserve basin after decommissioning. The Navy Department shipped the bronze figurehead and stern ornaments to the Naval Academy as inspirational tools in 1920, with the junior officers' mess clock also going there three years later by private donation. *Our Navy* reported in its mid-October 1925 issue that the *Olympia* certainly was going to be refitted and reconditioned to appear as of old during the next year's six-month-long sesquicentennial in the city. And she did appear so, although still clad in her gray uniform. Even then, the navy was maneuvering to sell off the *Olympia* as it "had no authority to preserve the ship as a historic shrine" unless measures for her preservation were passed by Congress. Washington politicians blocked scrapping or sale as American Legionnaires were up in arms and vowed to fight disposal. Finally, Secretary of the Navy Charles Francis Adams directed that she be preserved for historical reasons. By 1929, rumor had it "that a movement is under way at Washington to have the vessel towed up the Potomac and bedded in concrete in the river just off the capital city as a perpetual monument."

There were still *Olympia* veterans about and the Dewey Congressional Medal Men's Association was headquartered in Philadelphia. In fact, on 3 May 1931, thirty survivors of the battle of Manila Bay met on the deck of the *Olympia*. Vice Adm. William L. Rodgers presided over these ceremonies at the yard, attended by a crowd of ten thousand people. Navy planes in battle formation roared across the sky as these holders of the Dewey medal assembled on the ship's afterdeck. Rodgers told the veterans that "Everything possible will be done to preserve the *Olympia* as a historical shrine at Washington along with the *Constitution* and Admiral Farragut's *Hartford*." By 30 June 1931, the navy had reclassified her as a naval relic and painted "IX-40" on her bow. The admiral's son, George Goodwin Dewey, regularly told those survivors that "I shall always feel that the annual expression of love and devotion to the memory of my father by those who served under his command is the truest and most fitting of all tributes in his memory." And that admiral's widow went even further, maintaining a virtual museum to his memory at their Washington home, proudly displaying mementos of his life and career, and keeping the *Olympia*'s old salty parrot uttering "Hello, George" instead of a more ribald conversation with visitors.[16]

Becoming eccentric—even to the point of having the admiral's body exhumed from Arlington and deposited at the Washington Episcopal Cathedral of Saints Peter and Paul—Mildred Dewey lived until 21 February 1931. The tragic auction of the furnishings of the thirty-five-room Dewey house on K Street by the C. G. Sloan auction house after her death rivaled the controversy years earlier when Dewey had given her ownership of the house bequeathed to him by the American people. At least some of the admiral's mementos from the *Olympia* days were retrieved by his son and sent to the Chicago Historical Society. Of equal importance, however, yet another guardian of the *Olympia*'s fate—Mildred McLean Hazen Dewey—had passed from the scene.[17]

For a span of six or seven years, however, it appeared that a major reprieve would be given to the retired warship. Starting in the late 1920s, Congressman John J. Cochran of Missouri pushed legislation that would have taken the *Olympia* to Washington, excavated a channel to Haines Point, then encased her permanently in concrete whereby the Office of Public Buildings and Public Parks would have maintained the vessel. He estimated that $25,000 would have been required for cleaning, painting and towing the ship to Washington and a force of from ten to twelve men necessary for cleaning and acting as watchmen. The Navy Department (based on comments by the Bureau of the Budget) responded "that the expenditure contemplated by this legislation would not be in accord with the financial program" of President Hoover. With the onset of the Great Depression after 1930, this certainly was a valid point.[18]

Cochran was persistent. As he told it, "about three years ago several thousand young ladies from the west were sight-seeing in Washington." They included some from his home state and, as they were about to leave, they told him about their wonderful visit but admitted "they did not have an opportunity to see a battleship or cruiser." Cochran had then read something about the *Olympia* and how it would be a very good idea to bring that ship to Washington. There was nothing of that kind around the city and the navy yard held only tugs and destroyers. So he had introduced his original bill. It found favor with the navy, which had just done a survey on the vessel concluding that the cruiser had "few serious defects," good general value which justified the expense of repair work to place her in condition for service, and that the National Capital Park and Planning Commission favored Cochran's scheme. He did admit that the navy had told him the ship was of an obsolete type but, by reason of speed, gun power, and fairly good condition, could be of considerable value as a cruiser and would be required in the early stages of war until newer ones could be built. But, as Cochran stated bluntly, "I want to bring this ship, the *Olympia* to Washington where the people can see for all time to come Admiral Dewey's flagship in the Battle of Manila Bay."[19]

Committee hearings in February and March 1930 brought out how Cochran's colleagues felt about the *Olympia* issue. Most were favorable. George P. Darrow of Connecticut reported, however, that he had heard the Naval Academy might want the old ship for practice purposes (a notion quickly squelched by naval officers present as the ship lacked accommodations for the purpose). Congressman William Coyle of Pennsylvania injected that the navy should have the care and expense of the vessel, not public works people, and thought it would take $50,000 a year to keep the warship in order. But, again, a navy representative suggested that similar experience with the old battleship *Oregon* (maintained at Portland in that state), produced figures of only $15,000 per annum allocated by the state and supplemented by $4,000 in visitor revenue. Perhaps the greatest challenge (outside navy opposition) came from Congressman John F. Miller from Washington, who stated forthrightly that his state had a long-standing interest and concern in securing the *Olympia* for display there. Cochran laughingly told him that, as a compromise, they would give the ship's silver service to the capital of Miller's state.[20]

Indeed, on March 13, the committee met to consider Congressman Albert Johnson's bill to require the secretary of the navy to deliver the silver service set and bronze tablet from the cruiser to Olympia, Washington. The committee wondered where the silver service was and, after stumbling about, navy representatives at the hearing admitted it was currently in use aboard the USS *Saratoga*. This disclosure immediately provoked opposition from Congressman Fred Vinson of Kentucky that silver services should follow the ship representing the local community that gave it. "The people have a local pride in it, and after the ship goes out of use it ought to be sent back to the State capital or to the city for which it is named," he observed. The City of Olympia wanted it, and they should have it; the bronze tablet, however, having no connection with the people of Washington state should remain aboard. And so it was determined by the group.[21]

Two years later, Cochran still battled for the cause. The navy still opposed memorialization of the *Olympia,* citing a projected figure of $100,000 necessary for the undertaking and anxious that she be demilitarized "in order that she may not be counted as cruiser tonnage under the terms of the London treaty for the limitation and reduction of naval armament." Cochran claimed the latest estimate of the cost of restoration and demilitarization would only be about $63,100. Undoubtedly, the deepening economic depression and the onset of a new administration and new programs—including rearmament of the navy—caused Cochran's solution to a rusting, vandalized war relic in the Philadelphia Navy Yard to die aborning. As each year passed with no congressional action, the navy raised the figures for towing, demilitarization, and restoration with the sum in 1934 computed at $65,000 and annual maintenance at $20,000. The following year, Secretary of the Navy Claude A. Swanson hammered the final nail in the coffin for congressional action with figures of $84,000 and $25,000 respectively. As a naval official wrote a member of the Olympia Chamber of Congress on 9 August 1944: "Since then the matter has rested and probably will continue to do so until after the war. Then you might be able to interest Congress in legislation for her preservation."[22]

First the Depression/New Deal years and then the Second World War impinged on the *Olympia*'s retirement. Sister ships from her era went off to the scrap heap and her equally famous sister from the Union Iron Works ended her days as an ammunition hulk at Guam (thanks to the Oregon governor's patriotism). However, Pres. Franklin D. Roosevelt, an old navy buff himself and Wilson's assistant secretary of the navy in the tradition of his cousin Theodore, had but reluctantly agreed to disposal of the *Oregon.* Now he drew the line on the *Olympia.* Writing to his own secretary of the navy, Frank Knox, on 26 October 1942, he noted that "It is my understanding that the Department will take immediate action toward the preservation of the USS *Olympia* as a naval relic of the Spanish-American War period." Thus, the old cruiser—unmanned, unguarded, and maintained poorly over the intervening years—gained her greatest reprieve.[23]

At one point the navy considered bringing the *Olympia* out of retirement for convoy duty once more. In April 1945 she was dry-docked for the first time in almost twenty-three years. But, by 1954, Congress was ready to authorize disposition of all the navy's historic ships except the *Constitution*. Others, like the *Olympia*, the *Constellation* (eventually spawning great controversy over its authenticity), and Farragut's *Hartford* would be scrapped unless taken by some private museum or patriotic group at no expense to the government. The navy announced that it sought some group with about $650,000 "in ready cash to restore and make a public memorial of the warship Olympia." She was in such poor condition that the public had not been allowed aboard since before the war. Suddenly, some of Philadelphia's historic-minded citizens stepped forward to take her, restore her to 1898 condition, and add her to the city's landmarks as a tourist attraction. The Committee to Save the Olympia, led by Temple University modern languages professor Henry D. Learned, attorney Francis D. Pastorius, and real estate promoter Alan Corson Jr., led the way. They faced an estimated $250,000 restoration job even before the navy would transfer title. It would be nip and tuck for nearly two years, with little aid coming from the navy except periodic consultations about progress with the funding. Finally, Asik K. Brener, Russian-born president of the Keystone Dry Dock and Ship Repair Company, took the "public-spirited action" of underwriting $168,000 in repair costs.[24]

"No scrap heap for the historic cruiser Olympia," was the *Philadelphia Daily News* headline on 25 March 1957. With the navy finally giving its blessing in May and the city promising a mooring space at a proposed new small boat marina, Pastorius and what was now styled the Cruiser Olympia Association plus various veterans groups breathed easier. A marine and naval museum was promised aboard ship and artifacts solicited across the country. But, most of all, a public subscription was mounted to eventually include selling souvenir bronze coins, ostensibly fashioned from the propellers of the old ship (a scheme okayed by the navy in June 1958). Finally, on 11 September 1957, at a ceremony at the Navy Department in Washington, Secretary of the Navy Thomas S. Gates Jr. presented the ship's title to the association (although retaining the right for repossession and scrapping if the preservation/restoration effort foundered).

Accordingly, on 19 September, assisted by two tugboats and loyal volunteers—who scrambled down ladders into the dark holds of the ship to hand set the rudder amidships—the ship left pier 5. To the sounds of a navy band playing "Anchors Aweigh," and with the Philadelphia Service Office of the Insurance Company of North America providing liability protection, the distinctive silhouette of the *Olympia* moved into the Delaware River and upstream to a Norris Street pier where she would be refurbished. Navy

Olympia under restoration at the Keystone Ship Repair Company, formerly Cramp Shipyard, in Philadelphia in August 1958. At the time of the photograph, most of the structural work had been completed, but she still needed repainting.

seamen spent the cruise dipping the 45-star ensign and Union Jack to the enthusiastic salutes of all passersby on the river. The headline of the *Philadelphia Daily News* now beamed "Hail Olympians!"[25]

The calendar suggested that it had been fifty-nine years, four months, and nineteen days since Dewey and his ship had grabbed world headlines with the Manila Bay victory. Retired Capt. Edmund Crenshaw Jr. took over supervision of the restoration project for the association, even spotting and saving a 5-inch gun going up river to the scrap yard aboard an old coast guard patrol boat. Other concerned citizens included Arthur T. Lou, a Chinese-American merchant whose father (Lou Hee) was aboard the *Boston* at Manila Bay. Lou personally promoted the ship's restoration on cross-country business trips.

Even the niece of Juan de Concha, commanding officer of the Spanish cruiser *Don Juan de Austria*, vanquished and captured by Dewey and the *Olympia* at Manila, made headlines when she received a personal tour of the ship from Crenshaw in 1958. When a slight fire broke out below decks on 18 July, local headlines playfully screamed "Olympia Gets Up Smoke." The ship was everybody's darling in Philadelphia, although the navy continued to blunt requests for a return of some sort of ordnance aboard the old warship. It said that it was not authorized to expend $9,000 to dismantle and transfer guns from the battleship *Colorado* undergoing scrapping at Bremerton, Washington, and raising the scoffing ire of Bryn Mawr history professor Arthur B. Dudden that at least Dewey and Vernon Gridley had guns to fire in 1898.[26]

Regrettably, Keystone Dry Dock experienced financial difficulties, entered bankruptcy, and there was reason to believe that the "repairs" mostly consisted of painting over rust and corrosion. A large portion of the port engine disappeared during this period also. Later, the shipyard's creditors sued the owners of the *Olympia*, until a sympathetic judge forced settlement by declaring that he would throw the ship into bankruptcy when he did the same for Independence Hall. Eventually, by 1964 a new Cruiser Olympia Association would be at the helm with greater resolve and dedication.[27]

On 6 October 1958, the "unveiling" of a "new" buff and white restored *Olympia* attracted three hundred fifty boisterous, paying guests as the ship was conveyed to a Race Street berth for public viewing. The strains of "There'll Be a Hot Time in the Old Town Tonight," so reminiscent of

Manila Bay sixty years earlier, belted out from a band aboard the vessel. "It's almost unbelievable—the work that's been accomplished to make the Olympia ship-shape for her new career as a museum," cooed Ruth Seltzer, The Philadelphia Scene columnist in the *Sunday Bulletin*. Dewey's mirrored sideboard and dining room chairs were waxed, a barber's chair was in place, and a gift shop made ready to operate near the old bakery, proclaimed the newswoman. Brass beds were polished (not that the ship ever had such things), while hammocks had been hung and the engine room and machine shop had been "cleaned up miraculously." And "Captain Charles V. Gridley's old bathtub is to be seen." Naval guns had been restored to the ship, but the large black tubes projecting from the 8-inch turrets were just that— replica iron pipes. Neither the guests nor the public would ever realize that only a fraction of the ship had been truly restored, as much still lay untouched on decks farther down.[28]

Despite her listing two degrees and initially getting stuck in river mud, tugs pulled the *Olympia* free as air force jets screamed overhead, coast guard cutters and fire boats leaned on their whistles, and a navy helicopter throbbed a hundred feet or so off the bow for the hour-and-one-half trip. An artillery battery fired off seventeen guns as she nudged to the municipal pier. Rear Adm. Ephraim R. McLean Jr., commandant of the Fourth Naval District, with his wife and son even returned a flag officer presence to her bridge. Pastorius and the guests were ecstatic, as 8,000 curiosity seekers toured the ship during her first two weeks at Race Street. No matter that the association remained $200,000 in debt. A "saved," "restored," and "visitable" *Olympia* had been returned to public appreciation. The faith and hard work of Learned, Pastorius, Charles J. Fish Jr., Judge Leo S. Weinrott, Dr. Bruce Baldwin, Francis J. Lederer, Chief Boatswain's Mate Charles L. Conner, and various veterans groups—among many others— had paid off.[29]

The city soon needed the space for commercial shipping, so within the year the *Olympia* shifted (ignominiously bumping the Benjamin Franklin Bridge, whose construction efforts she had helped initiate in 1922, in the process) from pier 9 to pier 4 at Chestnut Street. Here she was closer to the Independence Hall tourist area. Then the question of money arose once again—who would pay for the move and new berthing—until the city agreed to underwrite half the costs. Only two of the ship's Manila Bay crew were still living and, while free buses to the ship were offered in the interest of drumming up tourist interest, initial charges had to be altered when parents protested at paying for infant children. Still, by fall, she had her original hand steering wheels back in place and visitation for the first year of operation totaled over 100,000 visitors. The *Olympia* had been redeemed. As professor Dudden had phrased it back in 1955, "The USS Olympia has the same educational purposes to fulfill as restored battlefields, historical museums and descriptive monuments." The American public at the height of the Cold War era seemed to appreciate his words.[30]

Visitation began to trail off after the 1958 high point; 88,680 visitors in 1959 fell to 72,574 two years later. Revenues for the heavy cost of maintenance and development of visitor programs suffered. The navy hounded the association each year about the ship's restoration, seaworthiness, and current effectiveness as a memorial. Relics periodically arrived for her museum, either from her past (a six-inch decorative "O" from her name, removed by a Boston yard pipefitter in 1899, was returned to the ship in 1967) or the Spanish War and World War I periods. Her engine room served as a model for the movie "The Sand Pebbles" in 1967, simply because it was the only one still existent anywhere. Her hull remained as sound as when she was built despite substitution of fresh water and rust for salt water barnacles. But her weather decks were a different story.

The original Oregon pine decking was long gone and successive attempts at preservation added cement and other compositions to a mess that, in rainstorms, sent streams of water leaking onto museum displays and the decks below, making preservation of artifacts and interpretive programs non-productive. Location was everything, and three changes of berthing (including one almost directly under the Benjamin Franklin Bridge that covered the ship with a heavy splattering of blue paint when the bridge was given a bicentennial coat in 1976) were far from satisfactory. Finally, early the following summer, the *Olympia* was moved to the long-promised marina styled Penn's Landing, billed by one northern New Jersey writer as "a recreation paradise for boating enthusiasts, history buffs, children, lovers and people of all ages." Unfortunately, the association had taken on added financial burdens with acquisition of a World War II submarine, the *Becuna*, which diluted monies available for the bottomless restoration pit of the *Olympia*.[31]

A refurbished *Olympia* moving to berth near Benjamin
Franklin Bridge in Philadelphia on 4 October 1958.

Through the years the *Olympia* and the *Becuna* served the naval and veterans communities as much as the public. An amateur radio club used the
ship as its headquarters. Occasional trade promotions and a documentary
done in the 1980s on the life of Theodore Roosevelt added minor revenue.
Still, a visitor's self-guided tour and a gift shop in addition to the shipboard
memorabilia displays attracted the lay visitor. Historic ship preservation
was glamorously tied to an international organization for such warships as
the *Olympia*. Yet, day-to-day maintenance problems of painting, cleaning,
replacing decayed wood, and preventing pipes from winter freeze (and
springtime thaws) often took precedence over the efforts to find sinks for
officers' staterooms and restoring the appearance as well as the substance
of the ship to 1890s standards. Too many of the vital items of furniture,
hardware, and equipment were simply long gone. Operating funds from

donations and small tourist fees were never adequate. Deferred maintenance often took a side-seat to insurance, utilities, salaries and, in April 1985, when an employee's death brought a major lawsuit.[32]

On 1 January 1996, after several years of negotiation with the Cruiser Olympia Association, the Independence Seaport Museum agreed to assume "full responsibility for the ship's operation." The *Olympia*'s "bedraggled look," peeling paint, and rivulets of rust running down the ship's hull detracted from the rich collection of artifacts and shipboard exhibits awaiting the visitor. Maintaining historic ships—like any historic property, such as buildings, vehicles, and aircraft—is a costly, never-ending undertaking that largely escapes visitor understanding. Spokesmen for the Independence Seaport Museum understood better that a surprising amount of "historical fabric" remained on the century-old warship. A fresh paint job was a start, but the major initial stabilization programs include replacement of the weather deck, providing deck support welding, and evaluating hull plates (requiring costly dry-docking).[33]

Extensive research of ship's plans and structure currently commands attention beyond inaugurating new visitor services and opening new visitation areas aboard ship much less complete restoration to "the way she looked in 1898." At the end of the twentieth century, the price of restoration has been estimated at nearly $20,000,000 to bring her back to prime. Yet, the confidence and enthusiasm for this unique national treasure remains as high among the new stewards of naval heritage at the museum as it did among the founding directors of the old Cruiser Olympia Association. The venerable *Olympia,* well beyond her centenary mark, "is also an extraordinary bit of maritime and naval history worth saving," observes Seaport Museum official Paul DeOrsay.[34]

Writing about the USS *Olympia* in 1976, veteran historian of America's New Steel Navy, professor John D. Alden, observed that better days hopefully beckoned for the aging ship. If sufficient funds were obtained, he observed, "future generations will be able to stand in Commodore Dewey's footprints on the flying bridge of his flagship, look down over her bristling guns and massive ground tackle, and relive the stirring events of naval history created by the cruiser *Olympia* and her gallant crew." Nearly a quarter century later, that hope continues into the next millennium. Declared a National Historic Landmark in 1976, and her engines blessed as a National

Historic Engineering Landmark by the American Society of Mechanical Engineers eleven years later, she was accorded Official Project status by the Save America's Treasures program of the National Trust for Historic Preservation in 1999. Yet she still lacks appropriate government funding for her restoration.[35]

The *Olympia* remains the oldest steel warship afloat today. In fact, all other steam-and-steel-era warships are gone from around the world except the Russian cruiser *Aurora* and Japan's battleship *Mikasa,* both dating from 1900. True, the American cruiser's name has been passed to a warship of more recent vintage. Following destroyers and frigates honoring heroes like Dewey and Gridley, a 1980s capital ship of its time returned the name *Olympia* to navy lists. On 30 April 1983, this new *Olympia* hit the water at Newport News Shipbuilding in Virginia. SSN 717 *Olympia* was the twelfth 668-class submarine built at that yard. It honored—as did the 1890s cruiser (C-6)—Olympia, capital of Washington state, as well as the "American pioneer spirit that inspired its founding and enabled the city to flourish as an industrial, cultural and spiritual center of the Pacific Northwest." Somehow, despite its sophisticated design, this Los Angeles–class fast attack submarine lacked the glamour that marked her namesake. Yet, businesslike in shape and battle dress, she seemed a worthy successor to Dewey's flagship, which had certainly gotten the job done.[36]

The original *Olympia* spent nearly three decades serving the United States Navy and the American nation. Historical circumstances vaulted her from obscure squadron flagship to arguably the most famous warship of her class and era. Time dimmed both her role and luster, perhaps, but her tie with the indomitable George Dewey and his famous battle cry, "You May Fire When You Are Ready, Gridley," ensured *Olympia*'s survival. She floats today on the Delaware River tide as the sole survivor of the Spanish-American War and New Steel Navy that vaulted the United States to world power status at the turn of the twentieth century. This *Olympia* stands as a tribute to American industry and enterprise, to young men who went off to carve careers out of respect for flag and country, and to a nation ready and willing to embrace her place in the sun.

America's colonies are long gone. The Philippines, for example, gained independence in 1947, and even the Panama Canal has passed to Panamanian national control. Imperial pretensions remain, captured in global commitments and entangling alliances. Still, there are few monuments to the American empire other than the spread of democracy and the golden arches of McDonald's. On the road to Arlington National Cemetery stands a solitary statue to the "Hikers of '98." In that cemetery remains a mast from the battleship *Maine*. Across the river in Washington's West Potomac Park sits a forlorn, urn-like monument to victims of that disaster. There is, of course, a far more imposing memorial in "the City of Brotherly Love." This memorial was even part of the experience it honors. The uss *Olympia* reminds us of America's swaggering walk in the imperial sun. She was the herald of empire.

Notes

CHAPTER 1. A NEW NAVY FOR AN EXPANSIVE NATION

1. The Battle of Manila Bay has been well documented and analyzed in Ivan Musicant, *Empire by Default: The Spanish-American War and the Dawn of the American Century*, chapter 5; David F. Trask, *The War with Spain in 1898*, chapter 5; and Jack Sweetman, *Great American Naval Battles*, chapter 9.

2. Frederick Drake, *Empire of the Seas: A Biography of Rear Admiral Robert N. Shufeldt*, xi.

3. George Dewey, *Autobiography*, 150, 154, 162–63. For recent analyses see Walter R. Herrick Jr., *The American Naval Revolution*, chapter 1; and Kenneth J. Hagen, *In Peace and War: Interpretations of American Naval History, 1775–1978*, chapter 8.

4. For the contemporary interrelationship between trade and diplomacy see Walter LaFeber, *The American Search for Opportunity: 1865–1913*, chapters 1–5.

5. For Seward expansionism see Walter LaFeber, *The American Age: U.S. Foreign Policy at Home and Abroad, 1750 to the Present*, 138–40, 181–82.

6. LaFeber, *Search for Opportunity*, chapter 5; Dewey, *Autobiography*, 145.

7. Shulman, *Navalism and the Emergence of American Sea Power, 1882–1943*, 4, 64, 104, 113, 117, 118. Page 138 discusses the two naval strategies.

8. Ibid., 110–12, 114, 118, 125–26, 135; Herrick, *Naval Revolution*, 29, 30, 35–36, 64, 84.

9. Shulman, *Navalism*, chapters 1 and 3.

10. Donald Birkholz Jr., *Cruiser Olympia Historical Structure Report,* 5; Shulman, *Navalism,* 112, 126; Pittman Pulsifer, *Navy Yearbook, 1908,* 81.

11. Benjamin F. Cooling, *Gray Steel and Blue Water Navy: The Formative Years of America's Military-Industrial Complex, 1881–1917,* chapters 3 and 4.

12. United States Navy, Department of (henceforth abbreviated DN), *Annual Reports, 1888,* x; DN, *Annual Reports, 1889,* 521, 528; *Pittsburgh Dispatch,* 21 May 1890, Library of Congress, Manuscript Division, Mary Edith Powel Collection.

13. James L. George, *History of Warships from Ancient Times to the Twenty-First Century,* 111, 113.

14. Norman Friedman, *U.S. Cruisers: An Illustrated Design History,* 7; Shulman, *Navalism,* chapter 2; Robert G. Angevine, "The Rise and Fall of the Office of Naval Intelligence, 1882–1892: A Technological Perspective," *The Journal of Military History,* April 1998, 291–312; General Records of the United States Navy, Board on Construction, Minutes, National Archives and Records Administration, Record Group 80.

15. See for example DN, Bureau of Construction and Repair, *Specifications for Building Steel Twin-Screw Protected Cruiser No. 6, For The United States Navy;* Donald Birkholz Jr., *Physical History of the Cruiser Olympia.*

16. John D. Alden, "Growth of the New American Navy" in Randolph W. King, *Naval Engineering and American Sea Power,* 41; Vincent Littlebear, *The 8-Inch Guns of the USS Olympia,* 1, 2, back cover.

17. DN, *Annual Reports, 1890,* 9, plate 9; Board on Construction, Minutes, 10, and Proceedings, Book II, 9, 15–21, 24, 27, RG 80.

18. DN, *Annual Reports, 1890,* 9.

19. Ibid.; Board on Construction, Proceedings, Book III, 3, 5, and 17 July 1890, 11 November 1890, RG 80.

20. DN, *Annual Reports, 1890,* 9; Robert Gardiner, *Steam, Steel and Shellfire: The Steam Warship, 1815–1905,* 109–10.

21. DN, *Annual Reports, 1890,* 9; Robert C. Stewart, *Historical American Engineering Record—U.S.S. Olympia, Final Draft Report,* 15; Memorandum, JAG to Chief, Navigation, 10 September 1890, Office of Naval Records and Library, National Archives and Records Administration, Record Group 45.

22. *Scientific American,* 12 September 1891, Powel Collection.

23. F. P. Gilmore, "Ship-Building and Its Interests on the Pacific Coast," *Proceedings of the United States Naval Institute,* xv No. 3, 1889, 444; *New York Herald,* 7 April 1901, Powel Collection.

24. Gilmore, *Ship-Building,* 444; Bethlehem Steel Corporation, *San Francisco Yard: A Brief History;* Bethlehem Steel Corporation, *1849–1914: A Century of Progress,* 3–13.

25. Stewart, *Engineering Record,* 15; Bethlehem Steel, *San Francisco Yard,* 10; Gilmore, "Ship-Building," 446; Miscellaneous papers, San Francisco Maritime National Historical Park, David W. Dickie Collection.

26. Board on Steam Engineering, Statement, 2 September 1891, RG 80; and Board on Construction, Estimate, 25 September 1891, RG 80; Clipping, "The Cramps are Eager," c. December 1895, Powel Collection; "Bibliographic Notes—The Iron Age, No. 21, May 21," *Proceedings of the United States Naval Institute*, XVII No. 3, 1891, 357.

27. Board on Construction, Proceedings, Book III, RG 80. For various changes see Board on Construction, Regarding Cruiser Number 6, Olympia, Letters Sent, 22 March 1892–2 October 1893, 69, 143, 154, 174, 183, 186, 188, RG 80; as well as Board on Construction, Proceedings of the Board on Designs of Ships, Minutes, 9 June 1892–30 June 1893, RG 80.

28. James Dickie, "Launch of a Cruiser and a Battleship," Dickie Collection, 279–93; Telegram, Irwin to Irving M. Scot, 1 November 1892, National Archives and Records Administration–Pacific/Sierra Region (San Mateo, California), Naval Districts and Ship Establishments, Mare Island Naval Shipyard, Record Group 181.

29. On these important details see various communiqués between the Board on Construction President and the Secretary of the Navy. Board on Construction, Letterbook 2, 1892–1893, 218, 262, 349, 351, 357, 369, 378, 390, 398, 408, 451, 473, 481, 489, RG 80; Board on Construction, Minutes, 9 June 1892–30 June 1893, RG 80; Board on Construction, Minutes, 2, 23, and 29 December 1892, RG 80; Board on Construction, Minutes, 4 June 1893–30 June 1894, RG 80; Board on Construction, Minutes, 26 June 1893, RG 80.

30. Letter, Scot to Benjamin Franklin Tracy, 25 February 1893, RG 45; Letters received from Bureau of Equipment, 31 August 1892–24 April 1893, RG 181; Letters, endorsements, and memoranda from Bureau of Equipment to Commandant and Others, Mare Island, 15 April–19 December 1893, RG 181.

31. DN, *Annual Reports, 1893*, 391–94; Letter, Bureau of Steam Engineering Chief to Secretary of the Navy, 2 May 1893, RG 80; Letter, Bureau of Ordnance Chief to Secretary of the Navy, 18 May 1893, RG 80; Letter, Board on Construction and Repair Chief to Secretary of the Navy, 22 May 1893, RG 80.

32. For the *Olympia*'s armor story see the report of the Bureau of Ordnance Chief in DN, *Annual Reports, 1893*, 233; Statement, Bureau of Construction and Repair, 2 October 1893, RG 80; For Carnegie's fabrication details see Ledger Book, Record of Armor Plates, Carnegie Steel Ltd., Homestead Works, Independence Seaport Museum Library, Carnegie-Phipps Company Collection; For the early military-industrial story, see Cooling, *Gray Steel*.

33. American Society of Mechanical Engineers, *National Historic Mechanical Engineering Landmark: Vertical Reciprocating Steam Engines—U.S.S. Olympia, Program*, 30 March 1977, 6.

34. Ibid.; John J. Read, *Hand Book of the U.S.S. "Olympia," Flagship, Asiatic Station*, 2, 4, 5, 6, 26, 35, 36, 45, 48–57.

35. Read, *Hand Book*, 21–23, 25–26.

36. Ibid., 25–26.
37. Clipping, "Olympia Soon to be Tested," 7 September 1893, Powel Collection; Also see other miscellaneous clippings, c. 8 November 1893, Powel Collection; Letters received, Bureau of Equipment, 2 May–December 1893, RG 181.
38. "The Olympia," Professional Notes, *Proceedings of the United States Naval Institute*, XIX No. 4, 1893, 494; Miscellaneous clippings, c. 1893, Powel Collection; Read, *Hand Book*, 57–60.
39. Marcus Wiggin, "The Cruiser Olympia," *Harpers Weekly*, 6 September 1894, 112; Miscellaneous clippings, c. 1893, Powel Collection; "Record of Proceedings of the Board For The Trial of Cruiser No. 6," Independence Seaport Museum Library, Cruiser Olympia Collection; "The New American Ship, Olympia," *Scientific American*, 23 December 1898, cover, 405.
40. See various correspondence in letterbooks such as, letters received, Bureau of Equipment, 3 January–12 May 1894, 26 May–4 September 1894, 6 September 1894–25 February 1895, RG 181; Letters received, Bureau of Equipment, 17 May 1893–31 December 1895, RG 181; Letters and telegrams received, Bureau of Ordnance, February 1893–January 1907, RG 181; Telegrams received, Bureau of Ordnance 1894–1907, RG 181; Letters received, Bureau of Equipment and Recruiting, 1889–1898, June 1891–March 1895, RG 181; Unidentified clipping, c. 14 December 1894, Powel Collection.
41. Communiqués to and from Equipment and Ordnance bureaus, 1894, RG 181; Telegram, Secretary of the Navy to Henry L. Howison, 8 January 1895, RG 181; Telegram, Howison to Secretary of the Navy, 5 February 1895, RG 181; *Congressional Record*, Fifty-seventh Congress, First Session and Special Session, Senate Volume XXXV, Number 50, 5452.

CHAPTER 2. THE QUEEN OF THE PACIFIC

1. Hamersley Callahan, *Records of Living Officers*, 61; Miscellaneous clippings, John J. Read file, Cruiser Olympia Collection.
2. Various communiqués, Equipment and Ordnance bureaus, 1893–95, RG 181; Various communiqués, bureaus and Commandant's Office, 1893–95, RG 181; *Olympia* Ship's Log, January–April 1895 and 24 April 1895, National Archives and Records Administration, Record Group 24, Bureau of Navigation and Bureau of Personnel; Clipping, "To Investigate Affairs on the Olympia," 12 May 1895, Powel Collection.
3. Letter, Mare Island Commandant to Secretary of the Navy, 25 April 1895, RG 181; Letters and telegrams, Commandant, 1893–95, RG 181; Telegram, Assistant Secretary of the Navy to Commandant, 1 June 1895, RG 181; Letters from Secretary of the Navy, 15 April 1895–18 March 1896, RG 181; Young, L. S., *The Cruise of the U.S. Flagship "Olympia" from 1895 to 1899 from San Francisco to Manila Bay*, Part I, 1–2.

4. Herbert statement, Court Martial, 3 June 1895, Folder, Court Martial of Lt. E. J. Dorn, Huntington Library (San Marino, CA), William Henry Hoes (USS *Olympia*) Collection; Letters, Commandant to Secretary of the Navy, 4 and 11 June 1895, RG 181; Clipping, "Olympia Court Martial," Powel Collection.

5. Miscellaneous clippings, New York *Herald*, no dates, Powel Collection; Young, *Cruise* Part I, 2–3.

6. Clipping, 29 June 1895, Powel Collection; Young, *Cruise* Part I, 3–4.

7. Clippings, "Final Tests of the Cruiser Olympia," "Testing the Cruiser Olympia at Sea," "The Cruiser Olympia First-Class," "The New Cruiser Olympia All Right," 28, 29, and 30 June 1895, Powel Collection.

8. Clippings, "The Olympia Going to Asia," 15 June 1895, and "Departure of Olympia for China," 26 August 1895, Powel Collection; Commandant to Secretary of the Navy, 26 June 1895, RG 181; Letters and telegrams sent, 2 June 1894–1 July 1896, RG 181; Young, *Cruise* Part I, 5.

9. Clippings, "Can Olympia Beat Columbia: Her Officers Think She Can and She May Try," 12 August 1895, and "Olympia Out For A Record," 26 August 1895, Powel Collection.

10. General Order Number 4, 31 August 1895, Hoes Olympia Collection.

11. Olympia Ship's Log, 25 August–2 September and 10 September 1895, RG 24; Commanding Officer, Olympia, to Secretary of the Navy, 3 February 1896, RG 45; Young, *Cruise* Part I, 5–6.

12. Young, *Cruise* Part I, 6. For the onerous coaling duty see Strauss, Elliott B., "The Days of the 'Black Diamonds'," *Pull Together* 29, spring/summer, 1990, 5–6.

13. Clippings, "Olympia Takes Fire at Sea," 16 November 1895, and "A Rumor of Trouble," 1 December 1895, Powel Collection; Young, *Cruise* Part I, 6.

14. Clippings, "Olympia Weathers Heavy Sea," and "How the Olympia Rode the Seas," 29 November 1895, Powel Collection; Young, *Cruise* Part I, 7.

15. Clipping, "Olympia Takes Fire at Sea," 16 November 1895, Powel Collection; Young, *Cruise* Part I, 7.

16. Olympia Ship's Log, 23 October–15 November 1895, RG 24; Young, *Cruise* Part I, 8.

17. "Our Interests in New Japan," *New York Herald,* 27 September 1895.

18. Young, *Cruise* Part I, 9.

19. Olympia Ship's Log, 21 December 1895, RG 24; Young, *Cruise* Part I, 10.

20. Young, *Cruise* Part I, 11.

21. Ibid., 11–12.

22. Clipping, "Olympia Did Not Race," 11 March 1896, Powel Collection; Young, *Cruise* Part I, 13.

23. Young, *Cruise* Part I, 12–13.

24. Letters, Read to Secretary of the Navy, 3 February 1896, RG 45; General Order Number 6, 20 February 1896, Hoes Olympia Collection; Longenecher to parents, 26 January 1896, United States Army Military History Institute (Carlisle Bar-

racks, Pennsylvania), USS Olympia (Wayne L. Longenecher) Collection; Young, *Cruise* Part I, 13.

25. Young, *Cruise* Part I, 13–14.

26. General Orders, Number 7, 23 February 1896, Hoes Olympia Collection; General Orders, Number 8, 7 March 1896, Hoes Olympia Collection; General Orders, Number 10, 2 May 1896, Hoes Olympia Collection; General Orders, Number 11, 15 May 1896, Hoes Olympia Collection; General Orders, Number 12, 8 June 1896, Hoes Olympia Collection; General Orders, Number 13, 7 July 1896, Hoes Olympia Collection; "Memorandum for Flagship," no date, Hoes Olympia Collection.

27. Young, *Cruise* Part I, 15.

28. Ibid.

29. Ibid., 15–16.

30. Ibid., 16–17.

31. Ibid., 17–19; Olympia Ship's Log, 26 September 1896, RG 24.

32. Young, *Cruise* Part I, 19.

33. Ibid., 19–20.

34. Ibid., 20–21; Olympia Ship's Log, 23 May 1896, RG 24.

35. Young, *Cruise* Part I, 21.

36. Ibid.

37. Typescripts, 2–5 and 6–8, Library of Congress, Manuscripts Division, William H. Standley Collection.

38. Ibid., 6–8.

39. Young, *Cruise* Part I, 21.

40. Ibid.

41. Ibid., 22; Olympia Ship's Log, 28 June 1896, RG 24.

42. Young, *Cruise* Part I, 23–25.

43. Ibid., 25.

44. Ibid., 25–26.

45. Letter, Longenecher to brother, 27 December 1897, Longenecher Collection; Young, *Cruise* Part I, 26–27.

46. Young, *Cruise* Part I, 27–28.

47. Ibid., 28–29.

48. Ibid.

49. Ibid., 29–30.

50. Read, *Hand Book*, inter alia.

51. Young, *Cruise* Part I, 30; Letter Order, Secretary of the Navy to Gridley, 10 June 1897, Olympia Collection; Olympia Ship's Log, 28 July 1897, RG 24.

52. Clipping, "Gridley Dead," St. Louis *Globe Democrat*, 6 June 1898; Miscellaneous clippings, 1897–98, Olympia Collection. For a longer study of Gridley see Maxwell P. Schoenfeld, *Charles Vernon Gridley: A Naval Career*, chapters 1–8, 104.

53. "The Bounding Billow," 31 January 1898, in Young, *Cruise* Part II, 57–58.

54. Report, Read to McNair, 16 July 1897, RG 45.

55. General Orders, Number 16, 20 May 1897, Hoes Olympia Collection; Young, *Cruise* Part I, 30–32; Letter, Longenecher to brother, 27 December 1897, Longenecher Collection.

56. Young, *Cruise* Part I, 32–33; Invitation, Garrison Commander to Regular Army and Navy Union of the United States of America, 23 October 1897, Olympia Collection; Clipping, "Nobleman in Olympia's Crew," 23 September 1897, Powel Collection.

57. Questionnaire, United States Army Military History Institute (Carlisle Barracks, Pennsylvania), Spanish-American War/Philippine Insurrection/Boxer Rebellion Survey Collection.

58. "The United States Protected Cruiser Olympia," *Scientific American*, 21 March 1896, 177.

59. John M. Ellicott, "The Composition of the Fleet," *Proceedings of the United States Naval Institute*, XXII No. 3, 1896, 541, 557–58; Birkholz, "Physical History."

CHAPTER 3. THE HEROES OF MANILA BAY

1. Adelbert M. Dewey, *The Life and Letters of Admiral Dewey*, 193, 411; Margaret Leech, *In the Days of McKinley*, 159.

2. Letter, F. V. McNair to Dewey, no date, RG 45; Robert E. Johnson, *Far China Station: The U.S. Navy in Asian Waters, 1800–1898*, 256–57.

3. Dewey, *Life and Letters*, 193–94; Johnson, *Far China Station*, 256, 257, 259.

4. Scott R. Mraz, "Recognition Long Overdue," *Naval History*, 12 May/June 1998, 25; Ronald Spector, "Who Planned the Attack on Manila Bay?" in *Mid-America: An Historical Review*, volume 53, April 1971, 94–102; Ronald Spector, *Professors of War: The Naval War College and the Development of the Naval Profession*, chapter 7; Johnson, *Far China Station*, 256–59.

5. Dewey, *Autobiography*, 170–72.

6. DN, *Annual Reports, 1898*, 22; "The Bounding Billow," 31 January 1898, in Young, *Cruise* Part II, 53–59.

7. Dewey, *Life and Letters*, 194–95.

8. Dewey, *Autobiography*, 178.

9. Birkholz, *Historic Structure Report*, Figure 4; "The Bounding Billow," 31 March 1898, in Young, *Cruise* Part II, 63.

10. Mraz, "Recognition Overdue," 26; DN, *Annual Reports, 1898*, 23.

11. "The Bounding Billow," 31 March 1898, in Young, *Cruise* Part II, 68–69; DN, *Annual Reports, 1898*, 65.

12. Dewey, *Autobiography*, 181–85.

13. DN, *Annual Reports, 1898*, 65–66; Young, *Cruise* Part II, 68–69.

14. Young, *Cruise* Part II, 68–69.

15. Dewey, *Life and Letters*, 197–98; Young, *Cruise* Part II, 69.

16. Dewey, *Autobiography*, 192; DN, *Annual Reports, 1898*, 66, 67.

17. John Barrett, *Admiral George Dewey*, 59, also 57, 61–63.

18. Clipping, "Gridley's Last Letters on the Way to Manila," *Boston Globe*, 4 June 1933, Cruiser Olympia Collection; Letter, Longenecher to brother, 31 July 1898, Longenecher Collection; DN, *Annual Reports*, 1898, 67.

19. Clipping, "War with Spain," 2 March 1896, Cruiser Olympia Collection.

20. Clipping, "The Fleet and the Philippines," *New York Sun*, 6 March 1898, Olympia Collection.

21. Laurin Hall Healy and Luis Kutner, *The Admiral*, 171; Letter, D. A. Carpenter to mother, 3 May 1898, Library of Congress, Manuscript Division, D. A. Carpenter Collection; Charles O. Paullin, "The American Navy in the Orient in Recent Years, III: The Spanish-American War in the Philippine Islands, 1898"; *Proceedings of the United States Naval Institute*, xxxvIII, March 1912, 91; Dewey, *Autobiography*, 195–96; Letter, Longenecher to brother, 31 July 1898, Longenecher Collection.

22. L. G. T. Tisdale ("Lieu"), *Three Years Behind the Guns*, 212–13; Barrett, *Admiral Dewey*, 56–57; Dewey, *Life and Letters*, 206.

23. Tisdale, *Behind the Guns*, 212–13; Carlos Gilman Calkins, "Historical and Professional Notes on the Naval Campaign of Manila Bay in 1898," *Proceedings of the United States Naval Institute*, xxv, June 1899, 268.

24. Letter, Longenecher to brother, 31 July 1898, Longenecher Collection.

25. "The Bounding Billow," June 1898, in Young, *Cruise* Part II, 74–75.

26. Ibid.

27. Ibid.; Letter, Longenecher to brother, 31 July 1898, Longenecher Collection.

28. Tisdale, *Behind the Guns*, 214–15.

29. Letter, Longenecher to brother, 31 July 1898, Longenecher Collection; Paullin, "American Navy," 92.

30. Tisdale, *Behind the Guns*, 215–16.

31. Letter, Carpenter to mother, 3 May 1898, Carpenter Collection.

32. Trask, *War with Spain*, 95.

33. See Montojo's report in DN, *Annual Reports*, 1898, 89; Letter, Carpenter to mother, 3 May 1898, Carpenter Collection; Letter, Longenecher to brother, 31 July 1898, Longenecher Collection; "The Bounding Billow," June 1898 in Young, *Cruise* Part II, 75–76; Paullin, "American Navy," 92.

34. DN, *Annual Reports*, 1898, 89.

35. Ibid., 89–90, 93.

36. Healy and Kutner, *The Admiral*, 175; "The Bounding Billow," June 1898, in Young, *Cruise* Part II, 75; Letter, Carpenter to mother, 3 May 1898, Carpenter Collection; Letter, Longenecher to brother, 31 July 1898, Longenecher Collection.

37. Letter, Longenecher to brother, 31 July 1898, Longenecher Collection.

38. Memorandum, Rear Adm. H. V. Butler to Chief, Bureau of Navigation, 1 May 1898, DN, Naval Historical Center (Washington, D.C.), Operational Archives; Paullin, "American Navy," 92–93.

39. Trask, *War with Spain*, 98–99; Ronald Spector, *Admiral of the New Empire: The Life and Career of George Dewey*, 56–57; Young, *Cruise* Part II, 76.

40. Musicant, *Empire*, 218–19.

41. Walker, "The Battle of Manila Bay," 374–75, Naval War Collection (Newport, Rhode Island), Naval Historical Collection; "The Bounding Billow," June 1898, in Young, *Cruise* Part II, 76.

42. DN, *Annual Reports, 1898*, 70, 91; Letter, Longenecher to brother, 31 July 1898, Longenecher Collection.

43. Calkins, "Naval Campaign," 274; DN, *Annual Reports, 1898*, 90.

44. Musicant, *Empire*, 221–22.

45. Schoenfeld, *Gridley*, 92.

46. Tisdale, *Behind the Guns*, 222, 225.

47. Olympia Ship's Log, 1 May 1898, RG 24; Healy and Kutner, *The Admiral*, 181. Healey and Kutner claim that Dewey adamantly insisted the phrase as quoted was the correct one.

48. Trask, *War with Spain*, 102; "Gridley's Last Letter on the Way to Manila," *Boston Globe*, 4 June 1933, Gridley Collection; Letter, Longenecher to brother, 31 July 1898, Longenecher Collection.

49. Tisdale, *Behind the Guns*, 228; DN, *Annual Reports, 1898*, 73, 91–92; Letter, Longenecher to brother, 31 July 1898, Longenecher Collection; Letter, Carpenter to mother, 3 May 1898, Carpenter Collection.

50. Dewey, *Autobiography*, 219; "The Bounding Billow," June 1898, in Young, *Cruise* Part II, 78; Letter, Carpenter to mother, 3 May 1898, Carpenter Collection.

51. Clipping, "Gridley's Last Letters on the Way to Manila," 4 June 1933, Cruiser Olympia Collection; Dewey, *Autobiography*, 217–20; DN, *Annual Reports, 1898*, 70, 92.

52. Olympia Ship's Log, 1 May 1898, RG 24; DN, *Annual Reports, 1898*, 70, 71, 92; Letter, Longenecher to brother, 31 July 1898, Longenecher Collection.

53. "The Bounding Billow," June 1898, in Young, *Cruise* Part II, 78, 80; Letter, Longenecher to brother, 31 July 1898, Longenecher Collection.

54. Young, *Cruise* Part II, 78, 80.

55. John M. Ellicott, "Effect of Gun-Fire, Battle of Manila Bay, May 1, 1898," *Proceedings of the United States Naval Institute*, xxv, June 1899, 324–34; Paolo E. Colletta, *Admiral Bradley A. Fiske and the American Navy*, 55–56; Clipping, "Shows Where Spanish Shot Hit," Powel Collection; Letter, Office of Naval Records and Library to W. S. Green, 27 May 1910, RG 45; Clipping, "Gridley's Last Letters," Cruiser Olympia Collection.

56. Dewey, *Autobiography*, 234.

57. R. Daveluy, "Naval Strategy," *Proceedings of the United States Naval Institute*, xxxvi, 419–21.

CHAPTER 4. HERALD OF EMPIRE

1. "The Bounding Billow," June 1898, in Young, *Cruise* Part II, 83.

2. Murray S. Holloway, "Autobiography," 13, 23, Olympia Collection.

3. Healy and Kutner, *The Admiral*, 187; Frank H. Fayant, "Letters to the Editors," *Life Magazine*, 16 March 1953, 5, 6.

4. DN, "Appendix to the Report of the Chief of the Bureau of Navigation" in *Annual Reports*, 1898, 68.

5. Musicant, *Empire*, 229–31; Hugh Rodman, *Yarns of a Kentucky Admiral*, 251.

6. DN, *Annual Reports*, 1898, 73–75.

7. Ibid., 74.

8. Ibid., 74, 82.

9. Schoenfeld, *Gridley*, 100–101; DN, *Annual Reports*, 1898, 103.

10. Tisdale, *Behind the Guns*, 266; Schoenfeld, *Gridley*, 101.

11. *Congressional Record*, Fifty-fifth Congress, Third Session, Volume 32, Part III, 2156, 2157; Letter, Harry Kay to Ruth Waldron Gridley, 9 December 1898, Olympia Collection; "The Bounding Billow," June 1898, in Young, *Cruise* Part II, 84; Schoenfeld, *Gridley*, 101–6, 108; DN, *Annual Reports*, 1898, 103.

12. *Congressional Record*, Fifty-fifth Congress, Third Session, Volume 32, Part III, 2156, 2157; Dewey, *Life and Letters*, 427–28.

13. Trask, *War with Spain*, 271–72.

14. Gardiner, Robert (editorial director), *Conway's All the World's Fighting Ships 1860–1905*, 146; John D. Alden, *American Steel Navy*, 366, 367.

15. Trask, *War with Spain*, 274–77; Gardiner, *Conway's Fighting Ships*, 151; Alden, *American Steel Navy*, 371.

16. Gardiner, *Conway's Fighting Ships*, 65, 110, 227, 253, 304.

17. Trask, *War with Spain*, 378–79; Gardiner, *Conway's Fighting Ships*, 245, 253, 254.

18. Trask, *War with Spain*, 379–80.

19. Ibid., 381, 384.

20. Harden, "Dewey at Manila," 383, Olympia Collection.

21. Trask, *War with Spain*, 391–402.

22. Healy and Kutner, *The Admiral*, 222–25; Richard E. Welch Jr., *Response to Imperialism: The United States and the Philippine-American War, 1899–1902*, 3, 13.

23. DN, *Annual Reports*, 1898, 125–26; Rodman, *Yarns*, 259.

24. Healy and Kutner, *The Admiral*, 232–34; Barbara B. Tomblin, "The United States Navy and the Philippines Insurrection" in *The American Neptune*, xxxv, July 1975, 184.

25. Rodman, *Yarns*, 260.

26. Healy and Kutner, *The Admiral*, 235; DN, *Annual Reports*, 1898, 122–25.

27. Tisdale, *Behind the Guns*, 274–83; Dewey, *Life and Letters*, 212.

28. Asiatic Squadron Roster of Officers, 6 October 1898, Carpenter Collection; Tis-

dale, *Behind the Guns*, 283, 287; "The Bounding Billow," August–September 1898, in Young, *Cruise* Part II, 94–95, 99–100.

29. Healy and Kutner, *The Admiral*, 235, 237–38; Tisdale, *Behind the Guns*, 287.

30. Tisdale, *Behind the Guns*, 271–72; Rodman, *Yarns*, 257–58; Reports, Officers to Commanding Officer, May–December 1898, Library of Congress, Manuscript Division (Washington, D.C.), USS Olympia Ship Collection.

31. Tisdale, *Behind the Guns*, 271–72; Rodman, *Yarns*, 257–58.

32. Holloway autobiography, 24, Olympia Collection; Tisdale, *Behind the Guns*, 269. On Spanish warship salvage, see letter, E. A. Patt to Naval History Division, 7 May 1957 and reply 3 July 1957, Operational Archives; Typescript, Rear Adm. A. Farenholt, "Some Notes Concerning the Spanish Wrecks Captured in Manila Bay," April 1959, Operational Archives.

33. Spector, *New Empire*, 67, 97–98.

34. Kutner and Healy, *The Admiral*, 239–44; Dewey, *Life and Letters*, 383–90; Vernon L. Williams, "George Dewey, Admiral of the Navy" in James Bradford (editor), *Quarterdeck and Bridge: Two Centuries of American Naval Leaders*, 262–63; J. S. Ruhlman, "Dewey Did March Two Step," 1898, Olympia Collection.

35. Sanford Sternlicht, *McKinley's Bulldog: The Battleship Oregon*, 117–18; "The Bounding Billow," November–December 1898, in Young, *Cruise* Part II, 101–3, 107.

36. "The Bounding Billow," November–December 1898, in Young, *Cruise* Part II, 101–3, 107; Clipping, "Vet Claims to Be First to Know of Dewey Promotion," *National Tribune/The Stars and Stripes*, 1958, Olympia Collection.

37. "The Bounding Billow," November–December 1898, in Young, *Cruise* Part II, 102, 103, 104, 105; Letter, William Ammand to Secretary of the Navy, 6 January 1899, Hoes Olympia Collection.

38. Spector, *New Empire*, 98–99; DN, *Annual Report*, 1899, 942–45. For further discussion of the insurrection and its implications see Welch, *Response to Imperialism*, chapter 2, as well as Bonificacio Salamanca, *The Filipino Reaction To American Rule*, *1901–1913*, 26–29; On crew restiveness see Letter, Longenecher to brother, 13 February 1899, Longenecher Collection.

39. Spector, *New Empire*, 100; Frederick Palmer, *George Dewey, Admiral: Impressions of Dewey and the Olympia on their Progress from Manila*, 15, 23; Barrett, *Admiral Dewey*, 180–81; DN, *Annual Reports*, 1899, 890–91; Dispatch, Dewey to Commanding Officer USS *Solace*, April 1899, RG 45; Squadron Order 14, 4 March 1899, Carpenter Collection.

40. DN, *Annual Report*, 1898, 614, 650, 705, 806, 812; Invoice of Provisions issued by Daniel A. Smith, Pay Master, USS *Olympia*, Third Quarter 1899, Hoes Olympia Collection; Quarterly Survey, Pay Department, 1 April 1899, Fourth Quarter ending 30 June 1898, Hoes Olympia Collection.

41. DN, *Annual Report*, 1898, 701–4.

42. Dinwiddie's photograph may be found in Barrett, *Admiral Dewey*, 247, as well as in Robert L. Blagg, *Career and Triumphs of Admiral Dewey*, 151–52. Watson relieved Dewey of command on 15 January 1899 according to the "List of Officers Serving as Commanders in Chief of United States Squadrons in Asiatic Waters," 16 April 1937, Operational Archives.

43. Kutner and Healy, *The Admiral*, 244–45; Gardiner, *Conway's Fighting Ships*, 67. On the salute see Assistant Director for Naval History to Maj. W. B. Williams, 30 Dec 1953, Operational Archives.

CHAPTER 5. FLAGSHIP IN A GREAT WHITE FLEET

1. Letter, Capt. Samuel G. Kelly to Maj. W. B. Williams, 23 December 1953, Operational Archives; Blagg, *Career and Triumphs*, 155.

2. Spector, *New Empire*, 101–2; Healy and Kutner, *The Admiral*, 246; "Services of the USS *Olympia*," 2, Operational Archives; "Itinerary of the USS *Olympia*" 20 May 1899, RG 45; Letter, Longenecher to brother, 13 February 1899, Longenecher Collection; Birkholz, "Physical History," Figure 6.

3. Letter, Longenecher to brother, 13 February 1899, Longenecher Collection.

4. Report, B. K. Lamberton to *Olympia* Commander in Chief, 30 June 1899, RG 45; "Itinerary of the USS *Olympia*," 20 May 1899, RG 45; "Services of the USS *Olympia*," 2, Operational Archives.

5. "Itinerary of the USS *Olympia*," 20 May 1899, RG 45; "Services of the USS *Olympia*," Operational Archives; Philip Y. Nicholson, "Admiral George Dewey after Manila Bay: Years of Ambition, Accomplishment, and Public Obscurity," *The American Neptune*, XXXVII, January 1977, 26–27; Healy and Kutner, *The Admiral*, 247; Spector, *New Empire*, 103; Blagg, *Career and Triumphs*, 172–73.

6. "Visit to Trieste Grave Recalls A Note from History," *All Hands*, September 1968, 20–22.

7. Blagg, *Career and Triumphs*, 172–73.

8. Ibid., 174–75; "Itinerary of the USS *Olympia*," 20 May 1899, RG 45; "Services of the USS *Olympia*," 2, Operational Archives.

9. Letter, F. H. Bailey to *Olympia* Commanding Officer, 20 July 1899, Hoes Olympia Collection; Birkholz, *Olympia Physical History*.

10. Blagg, *Career and Triumphs*, 266–67; Cruising Report, quarter ending 30 September 1899, Hoes Olympia Collection; Memorandum, F. H. Bailey to *Olympia* Commanding Officer, 20 July 1899, Hoes Olympia Collection.

11. Blagg, *Career and Triumphs*, 267–68; Spector, *New Empire*, 104.

12. Blagg, *Career and Triumphs*, 268–69; Fred T. Alder and Harry C. Green (compilers), *The Official Dewey Souvenir Programme*, 20–39.

13. Blagg, *Career and Triumphs*, 270–71.

14. Ibid., 271–73.

15. Ibid., 273.

16. Ibid., 274–75; Letter, James A. Haight to Secretary of the Navy, 19 August 1899, Operational Archives; Second Endorsement, Bureau of Navigation, 28 August 1899, Operational Archives; William S. Dewey, "From 'Olympia' to 'Olympia,'" *The Numismatist,* January 1940, 6–7.

17. Blagg, *Career and Triumphs,* 277–80; Spector, *New Empire,* 105; Alder and Green, *Souvenir Programme,* 29 September 1899, program page.

18. Blagg, *Career and Triumphs,* 280.

19. Ibid., 278–80; Alder and Green, *Souvenir Programme,* 30 September 1899, program page.

20. Fifth Avenue Bank of New York, *Fifth Avenue Events,* 37; Blagg, *Career and Triumphs,* 289, 291.

21. "The Dewey Arch" in P. D. Leger (compiler), *Admiral George Dewey,* unpublished study, 1953, United States Naval Academy (Annapolis, Maryland), Chester Nimitz Library, Academy Archives, Special Collections, Dewey Vertical File.

22. Spector, *New Empire,* 105–6; "Smoker and Concert Announcement," 30 September 1899, Olympia Collection.

23. Spector, *New Empire,* chapter 5; Healy and Kutner, *The Admiral,* chapters 25, 26.

24. Leger, *Admiral Dewey,* 15. For other examples of this kind of memorabilia see shipboard displays and study collections on the *Olympia* at the Independence Seaport Museum Library in Philadelphia, Pennsylvania.

25. Alden, *American Steel Navy,* 57; "Services of the USS *Olympia,*" 2, Operational Archives; Blagg, *Career and Triumphs,* 291–319; For Dewey's post–New York celebrations see Spector, *New Empire,* 108–21; Nicholson, "Admiral George Dewey," 28–30; Vernon L. Williams, "George Dewey" in James Bradford (editor), *Quarterdeck and Bridge: Two American Naval Leaders,* 263–64.

26. Miscellaneous notes, Boston Navy Yard, Operational Archives.

27. Birkholz, "Physical History"; Bureau of Construction and Repair Chief, *Annual Report, Fiscal Year Ending 30 June 1903.*

28. DN, *Annual Report, 1899,* 482, 818; DN, *Annual Report, 1900,* 977.

29. Endorsement, Bureau of Navigation, 19 April 1901, RG 45; Clippings, *New York Herald,* 22, 24, 25 December 1899, Powel Collection.

30. DN, *Annual Report, 1900,* 725.

31. DN, *Annual Report, 1902,* 298, 306, 365, 606; Birkholz, *Historic Structure Report,* 19; Alden, *American Steel Navy,* 58.

32. DN, *Annual Report, 1902,* 802, 805; DN, *Annual Report, 1901,* 318, 324, 379, 569; First endorsement, letter to Frank L. Vanmess, 21 December 1901, DN, Naval Historical Center (Washington, D.C.), Early Records Collection; Memorandum for Bureau of Equipment, 22 January 1902, RG 45; Birkholz, "Physical History," Figure 8.

33. C. M. Fahs, "Report of Target Practice, 31 March 1902," RG 45.

34. Memorandum, Charles W. Stewart to Lt. Cdr. James Gilmer, 10 March 1913,

Operational Archives; William V. Pratt, "Autobiography," DN, Naval Historical Center (Washington, D.C.), William V. Pratt Collection.

35. DN, *Annual Report, 1903,* 19; DN, *Annual Report, 1902,* 463.

36. DN, *Annual Report, 1903,* 19, 480.

37. Birkholz, "Physical History."

38. DN, *Annual Report, 1902,* 394, 463, 994–95; DN, *Annual Report, 1903,* 466–67; United States Navy Record of William F. Kasterer, log for 1902–1903, Olympia Collection; Report of Lt. Cdr. A. P. Niblack, 18 August 1902, RG 45.

39. DN, *Annual Report, 1902,* 392–93; DN, *Annual Report, 1903,* 15–16, 468, 958.

40. Report, H. W. Lyon to Commander in Chief, 8 September 1902, RG 45.

41. DN, *Annual Report, 1903,* 478–79.

42. Spector, *New Empire,* chapter 7.

43. Letter, H. C. Taylor to Secretary of the Navy, 14 December 1902, 763–66, Library of Congress, Manuscript Division (Washington, D.C.), W. H. Moody Collection; Sargent's comments are quoted in Spector, *New Empire,* 144; Kasterer, "Naval Record," 8 September–29 December 1902, Olympia Collection; DN, *Annual Report, 1903,* 631–34, 646–50.

44. Letter, H. C. Taylor to Secretary of the Navy, 14 December 1902, 765, Moody Collection.

45. Spector, *New Empire,* 144–45; "Greetings from U.S.F.S. "Olympia," unidentified printed itinerary, no date, Olympia Collection.

46. Letter, Secretary of the Navy to Rear Admiral Coghlan, 4 March 1903, RG 45; Clipping, *New York Herald,* May 1903, Library of Congress, Manuscript Division (Washington, D.C.), Charles Stanhope Cotton Collection; Kasterer, "Naval Record," 1903, Olympia Collection; DN, *Annual Report, 1903,* 24, 25, 299, 484–85, 633–34.

47. Letter, Captain, U.S.F.S. Olympia to Commander in Chief, North Atlantic Fleet, 1 July 1903, RG 45; Logbook, 5 March 1903, The Mariners Museum Library (Newport News, Virginia), Francis Cunningham Lowry Collection.

48. Logbook, 5 March 1903, Lowry Collection; Alden, *American Steel Navy,* 206. Alden describes "Gunnery training devices such as the 'dotter,' in which a minia-ture target suspended just beyond the gun barrel was maneuvered by guy wires while a solenoid-operated pencil marked the printer's 'fall of shot,' and the related 'Morris tube,' which used a shooting gallery rifle instead of the pencil enabled gun pointers to practice without actually firing the big guns."

49. DN, *Annual Report, 1903,* 468, 478, 631, 729, 1060; DN, *Annual Report, 1904,* 532–33.

50. Alden, *American Steel Navy,* 234; DN, *Annual Report, 1904,* 524.

51. DN, *Annual Report, 1904,* 524–25, 532.

52. Ibid., 532, 535–36.

53. DN, *Annual Report, 1903,* 468, 478.

54. DN, *Annual Report, 1904,* 724, 727, 975.

55. Ibid., 373, 377, 379, 483–84, 544.

56. Ibid., 853, also 545–46, 987; Letter, Director of Office in Charge of Naval Records and Library to Elizabeth Bayley Rogers, 6 November 1946, Operational Archives; For the Raisuli/Perdicaris episode see William J. Hourihan, "Marlinspike Diplomacy," *Proceedings of the United States Naval Institute*, cv, January 1979, 41–51, 105.

57. DN, *Annual Report, 1904,* 117.

58. Letter, Frank McDonnell to sister, 26 October 1904, Olympia Collection; "Greetings from U.S.F.S. "Olympia," Olympia Collection; L. Lowe, "An Inquirer of Harvard University," no date, Operational Archives; DN, *Annual Report, 1905,* 429, 455–57, 470.

59. DN, *Annual Report, 1905,* 455–57, 458–59, 465, 470–72; Lowe, " Inquirer," no date, Operational Archives.

60. DN, *Annual Report, 1905,* 463, 472, 474, 790, 802.

61. Letter, Secretary of the Navy to Commander in Chief North Atlantic Station, 5 April 1906, RG 45; Letter, J. D. Adams to Commander in Chief North Atlantic Fleet, 31 December 1905, RG 45; Letter, Charles W. Stewart to Lt. Cdr. James Gilmer, 10 March 1913, Operational Archives; Lowe, "Inquirer," no date, Operational Archives.

CHAPTER 6. IN RESERVE

1. Drawings from Norfolk Navy Yard, 14 May 1907, in Birkholz, "Physical History."

2. DN, *Annual Report, 1906,* 373, 376, 380, 382, 510, 766, 776; *The Book of the United States Navy,* 7, 33, 144, 166.

3. William G. Groesbeck, "Considerations Affecting The Determination of a Naval Programme," *Proceedings of the United States Naval Institute,* xxxii, March 1906, 35, 203–4; W. H. Beehler, "The Navy and Coast Defence," *Proceedings of the United States Naval Institute,* xxxv, June 1909, 356–60.

4. Letter, Secretary of the Navy to President, 6 July 1906, Library of Congress, Manuscript Division (Washington, D.C.), Charles J. Bonaparte Collection. For American naval development during the Theodore Roosevelt era see Gordon Carpenter O'Gara, *Theodore Roosevelt and the Rise of the Modern Navy,* especially chapter 5, and Kenneth Wimmel, *Theodore Roosevelt and the Great White Fleet: American Sea Power Comes of Age.*

5. DN, *Annual Report, 1906,* 403–4; DN, *Annual Report, 1907,* 7–11, 15, 497, 561, 729, 805. For Progressive Era naval developments see Alden, *American Steel Navy,* especially the lavishly illustrated "Ships of the American Steel Navy" section.

6. Letter, Secretary of the Navy to President, 6 July 1906, Bonaparte Collection.

7. Letter, Naval Academy Superintendent to Bureau of Navigation Chief, 17 June 1907, United States Naval Academy, Chester Nimitz Library (Annapolis, Maryland), Academy Archives, Special Collections, Record Group 405.

8. Various memoranda, letters, instructions, and lists such as Academy Board Secretary to Commandant of Midshipmen, 9 May 1907, and Naval Academy Superintendent to Howard, no date, RG 405; *The Arkansas Traveler, 1907 Summer Cruise*, Volume I Number 1, 12, United States Naval Academy, Chester Nimitz Library (Annapolis, Maryland), Special Collections, T. E. Howard Collection.

9. Correspondence concerning "Hornet" damage, with endorsements, 5–15 June 1907, Howard Collection; Letter, Secretary of the Navy to Olympia Commanding Officer, 16 May 1907, RG 405.

10. United States Naval Academy, *Lucky Bag*, 1908, 283; Order, 3 May 1907, RG 405; Memorandum, to Olympia Commanding Officer, 6 June 1907, RG 405.

11. Letter, Surgeon to Commanding Officer, 12 June 1907, RG 405; Letter, Executive Officer to Commanding Officer, 12 June 1907, RG 405.

12. *The Arkansas Traveler*, Volume I Number 1, 12, Howard Collection; *Lucky Bag*, 1908, 282; Letter, Superintendent to Bureau of Navigation Chief, 14 June 1907, RG 405; Letter, Howard to Superintendent, 14 June 1907, RG 405; Telegrams, Howard to Sands and Sands to Howard, 15–17 June 1907, RG 405; Telegram, Howard to Superintendent, 26 June 1907, RG 405.

13. *The Arkansas Traveler*, Volume I Number 1, 12, Howard Collection.

14. *The Arkansas Traveler*, Volume I Number 1, 12–13, Howard Collection; *Lucky Bag*, 1908, 282–85.

15. *The Arkansas Traveler*, Volume I Number 1, 13–14, 22, Howard Collection; Report, Howard to Superintendent, 8 July 1907, RG 405.

16. Reports, Howard to Superintendent, 26 June and 8 July 1907, RG 405; *The Arkansas Traveler*, Volume I Number 1, 14, 15; *Lucky Bag*, 1908, 283.

17. Letter, Howard to Superintendent, 5 July 1907, RG 405; Letter, Secretary of the Navy to Superintendent, 13 June 1907, RG 405; Report, Howard to Superintendent, 17 June 1907, RG 405; Reports, Howard to Superintendent, 26 June and 5 July 1907, RG 405.

18. *Lucky Bag*, 1908, 286, 287; *The Arkansas Traveler*, Volume I Number 1, 26, Howard Collection.

19. Letter, Superintendent to Howard, 14 August 1907, RG 405; Report, H. S. Crosby to Secretary of the Navy, 10 August 1907, RG 405.

20. *The Arkansas Traveler*, Volume I Number 1, 21, 22, 34, Howard Collection.

21. *Lucky Bag*, 1908, 283, 286–87; Report, Howard to Superintendent, 22 July 1907, RG 405; Report, Howard to Secretary of the Navy, 2 August 1907, RG 405.

22. *The Arkansas Traveler*, Volume I Number 1, 22, 34, Howard Collection; *Lucky Bag*, 1908, 288; Itinerary, Midshipmen's Summer Cruise, 1907, RG 405.

23. Letter, Superintendent to Howard, 14 August 1907, RG 405; Letter, Superintendent to Secretary of Navy, 31 July 1907, RG 405; Letter, Acting Secretary of the Navy to Superintendent, 12 August 1907, RG 405; Memorandum, Aid to Superintendent, 15 August 1907, RG 405.

24. Letter, Howard to Superintendent, 12 August 1907, RG 405.

25. Letter, Executive Officer to Olympia Commanding Officer, 17 August 1907, RG 405.

26. Letter, Executive Officer to Olympia Commanding Officer, 17 August 1907, RG 405; Estimate, Olympia Reserve Complement, 17 August 1907, RG 405; Letter, Superintendent to Howard, 22 August 1907, RG 405; Telegram, Superintendent to Olympia Commanding Officer, 23 August 1907, RG 405; Letter, Bureau of Medicine and Surgery Chief to Superintendent, 24 August 1907, RG 405; Letter, Superintendent to Naval Academy Practice Squadron Commanding Officers, 26 August 1907, RG 405; Telegram, Superintendent to USS Hartford Commanding Officer, 28 August 1907, RG 405; Telegram, Olympia Wireless Office to Naval Academy Station, 29 August 1907, RG 405; Telegram, Commanding Officer to Superintendent, 30 August 1907, RG 405; Report, Olympia Reserve Complement, 30 August 1907, RG 405; Various lists of men granted leaves of absence, 30 August 1907, RG 405; Telegram, Olympia Commanding Officer to Superintendent, 30 August 1907, RG 405; Miscellaneous lists, Olympia Reserve Complement, 6 September 1907, RG 405; Memorandum, Department of Ordnance and Gunnery Chairman to Superintendent (includes latter's comments), 21 December 1907, RG 405.

27. DN, *Annual Report, 1908*, 106, 357, 396–97, 420, 824–25; Correspondence, Lt. Cdr. D. E. Dismukes, 1907, RG 405.

28. Itinerary, Summer Cruise, 1908, RG 405; Memorandum, Commandant of Midshipmen to Superintendent, 20 January 1908, RG 405; Letter, Bureau of Navigation Chief to Superintendent, 30 March 1908, RG 405; Memorandum, Olympia Commanding Officer to Commandant of Midshipmen, 17 March 1908, RG 405; Letter, Superintendent to Bureau of Navigation Chief, 12 May 1908, RG 405; Letter, Gardner to Superintendent, 13 May 1908, RG 405; List, Complement of USS Olympia, 13 May 1908, RG 405; Order, Number 18, 15 May 1908, RG 405; DN, *Annual Report, 1908*, 106, 357, 396–97, 410, 824–25.

29. Mary Klachko and David Trask, *Admiral William Shepherd Benson: First Chief of Naval Operations*, 16–17; *Lucky Bag, 1909*, 274–86.

30. *Lucky Bag, 1909*, 274–86; "The Reminiscences of Vice Admiral Olaf M. Hustvedt, U.S. Navy (Retired)," 24, United States Naval Academy, Chester Nimitz Library (Annapolis, Maryland), Olaf M. Hustvedt Collection.

31. Letter, Kraus to Olympia Commanding Officer, 26 August 1908, RG 405; Letter, Bureau of Navigation Chief to Superintendent, 25 September 1908, RG 405; Letter, Superintendent to Norfolk Navy Yard Commandant, 11 November 1908, RG 405.

32. DN, *Annual Report, 1908*, 5–18, 664; DN, *Annual Report, 1909*, 29, 300–301; For the cruise of the "Great White Fleet" see Alden, *American Steel Navy*, 333–47 and Wimmel, *Great White Fleet*, chapter 10.

33. DN, *Annual Report, 1909*, 367–68, 401, 405, 409; Also see 21–24, 328, 448, 507, 593, 669, 786, 819, 830–31, 1003.

34. *Lucky Bag, 1910,* 382; *Lucky Bag, 1912,* 298–99; Telegram, Taussig to Superintendent, 6 March 1909, RG 405; Telegram, Badger to Norfolk Navy Yard Commandant, 7 March 1909, RG 405; Letter, Secretary of the Navy to Superintendent, 11 March 1909, RG 405; Letter, Superintendent to unidentified recipient, 7 April 1909, RG 405; Order, Commandant of Midshipmen, 2 May 1909, RG 405; Memorandum, Commandant of Midshipmen to Superintendent, 3 May 1909, RG 405; Commandant of Midshipmen and Naval Academy Practice Squadron Commander to Olympia Commanding Officer, 29 May 1909, RG 405.

35. *Lucky Bag, 1910,* 328–40; *Lucky Bag, 1911,* 326; *Lucky Bag, 1912,* 298–99.

36. Paul Foley, "The Naval Academy Practice Cruise: Its Organization Along Modern Lines," *Proceedings of the United States Naval Institute,* xxxvi, March 1910, 242, 248.

37. DN, *Annual Report, 1910,* 94, 287; Letter, Olympia Commanding Officer to Secretary of the Navy (through Superintendent), 11 January 1910, RG 405; Letter, Paymaster General to Superintendent, 13 February 1910, RG 405; Thirteenth endorsement, Olympia construction and repairs, 28 August 1910, RG 405; Miscellaneous comments, Olympia Commanding Officer and Bureau of Construction and Repair, no date, RG 405; Memorandum, Olympia Commanding Officer to Superintendent, 20 November 1910, RG 405.

38. DN, *Annual Report, 1910,* 722–33; Also see 36, 606–7, 749.

39. Letter, Acting Secretary of the Navy to Superintendent, 27 August 1909, RG 405; Letter, Paymaster General E. B. Rogers to Superintendent, 18 February 1910, RG 405; Correspondence, Cdr. J. H. Hood to Secretary of the Navy, 11 January 1910 and subsequent, RG 405; Correspondence, Cdr. A. H. Scales to Superintendent, 20 November 1910, RG 405; Shipment orders, October 1910, RG 405.

40. Alden, *The American Steel Navy,* 349.

41. Memorandum, Secretary of the Navy (Division of Material) to Bureau of Navigation, 21 February 1912, Operational Archives.

42. Roosevelt's enjoinder to Taft can be found in Wimmel, *Great White Fleet,* 244; Also see U.S. Navy Department, Bureau of Navigation, *Movements of Vessels,* 1 July–30 June for years 1911–16; DN, *Annual Report, 1911,* 42, 109; George R. Clark, "Protecting American Interests," *Proceedings of the United States Naval Institute,* xxxv, June 1909, 393.

43. DN, *Annual Report, 1911,* 40, 239, 401; *U.S. Navy List and Directory, January 1, 1911,* 53.

44. *U.S. Navy List and Directory,* 1 January 1911, 31, 35–36, 39, 40.

45. DN, *Annual Report, 1912,* 18–19.

46. DN, *Annual Report, 1911,* 35–36; DN, *Annual Report, 1912,* 21.

47. DN, *Annual Report, 1912,* 21–22.

48. Ibid., 39, 142, 414–15; Also see 15, 18–19.

49. DN, *Annual Report, 1913,* 37; Also see 9–14, 295, 338.

50. DN, *Annual Report, 1914,* 9, 13, 14–15, 17–18, 21–26, 43, 64, 71, 160, 298.

51. Navy Department, *Movements of Vessels 1915*; Letter, Frank P. Lederer to Cruiser Olympia Association, no date, Olympia Collection; DN, *Annual Report, 1915,* 12, 15–17, 214.
52. DN, *Annual Report, 1915,* 1–8, 73–76, 79–93, 604, 633; DN, *Annual Report, 1916,* 118, 369. Also see David F. Trask, "The American Navy in a World at War, 1914–1919" in Hagen, *Peace and War,* 208–9; George W. Baer, *One Hundred Years of Sea Power: The U.S. Navy, 1890–1990,* 59–61.
53. Birkholz, "Physical History"; John Alden, "Growth of the New American Navy" in Randolph W. King (editor), *Naval Engineering and American Sea Power,* 41.
54. Baer, *One Hundred Years,* 61.
55. DN, *Annual Report, 1916,* 5–6, 67–70; William Sims, "What Should be the Relations Between the Battle Fleet and the Reserve Fleet," *Proceedings of the United States Naval Institute,* XL, May/June 1914, 727–39; "General Board's Report of July 30, 1915" in "Professional Notes," *Proceedings of the United States Naval Institute,* XLII, March/April 1916, 588–89.

CHAPTER 7. INTERVENTIONISM AND THE
FIRST WORLD WAR

1. DN, *Annual Report, 1917,* 77–78; Vernon L. Williams, "George Dewey: Admiral of the Navy" in Bradford, *Quarterdeck and Bridge,* 265, 267–68, 269; Nicholson, "Admiral George Dewey," 33–35.
2. Healy and Kutner, *The Admiral,* 308–13.
3. Paul G. Halpern, *A Naval History of World War I,* 314–28, 335–36, 340–41, 356. Also see Baer, *One Hundred Years,* chapter 4, and Trask, "World at War," 205–20.
4. Baer, *One Hundred Years,* 61, 64–74; Halpern, *World War I,* 358.
5. Klachko and Trask, *Benson,* 69; Holger H. Herwig and David Trask, "The Failure of Imperial Germany's Undersea Offensive Against World Shipping, February 1917–October 1918," *The Historian,* volume 33, August 1971, 626–28.
6. Stewart, *Engineering Record,* 85; "Grounding of the 'Olympia'" in "Naval War Notes," *Proceedings of the United States Naval Institute,* XLIII, July–December 1917, 1865.
7. Birkholz, "Physical History"; "Historic Plan Notes," Olympia Collection.
8. Lloyd Thomas O'Kelly, "My Life," 28–29, Independence Seaport Museum Library (Philadelphia, Pennsylvania), Olympia Collection; Stewart, *Engineering Record,* 86; Chester V. Jackson, "Recollections," DN, Naval Historical Center (Washington, D.C.), Operational Archives, Chester V. Jackson Collection.
9. O'Kelly, "My Life," 39–40; Stewart, *Engineering Record,* 86.
10. Stewart, *Engineering Record,* 86, 87; Jackson, "Recollections," 1–2, Jackson Collection.
11. Charles J. Weeks, *An American Naval Diplomat in Revolutionary Russia: The Life and Times of Vice Admiral Newton A. McCully,* 135. For relevant background on

this episode see David S. Foglesong, *America's Secret War Against Bolshevism: U.S. Intervention in the Russian Civil War, 1917–1920*, chapter 7; E. M. Halliday, *The Ignorant Armies*, chapter 2; Benjamin D. Rhodes, *The Anglo-American Winter War with Russia, 1918–1919: A Diplomatic and Military Tragicomedy*, chapter 1; Leonid I. Strakhovsky, *The Origins of American Intervention in North Russia, 1918*; Ilya Somin, *Stillborn Crusade: The Tragic Failure of Western Intervention in the Russian Civil War, 1918–1920*, chapters 2 and 3; and Richard H. Ullman, *Intervention and the War: Anglo-Soviet Relations, 1917–1921*, Volume I.

12. Weeks, *Naval Diplomat*, 134; Arthur Link (editor), *The Papers of Woodrow Wilson*, volume 47, 290.

13. O'Kelly, "My Life," 30–31; Lloyd Thomas O'Kelly, "Shipboard Diary," Book I, 3–9, Olympia Collection.

14. O'Kelly, "Shipboard Diary," Book I, 3–9; Jackson, "Recollections," 2, Jackson Collection.

15. Jackson, "Recollections," 2, Jackson Collection; O'Kelly, "Shipboard Diary," 10, Olympia Collection.

16. O'Kelly, "My Life," 31; O'Kelly "Shipboard Diary," Book I, 9–19; Jackson, "Recollections," 2.

17. O'Kelly, "Shipboard Diary," Book I, 20–23, Olympia Collection; Jackson, "Recollections," 3, Jackson Collection.

18. George F. Kennan, *The Decision to Intervene in Soviet-American Relations, 1917–1920*, Volume II, 58–59; Link, *Wilson Papers*, volume 47, 61, 226–27, 246, 263, 290, 355–57, 503–5.

19. Kemp Tolley, "Our Russian War of 1918–1919," *Proceedings of the United States Naval Institute*, xcv, February 1969, 62.

20. Kennan, *Decision to Intervene*, 56–59.

21. Kelly, "Shipboard Diary," 22–23, Olympia Collection; Jackson, "Recollections," 4, Jackson Collection.

22. O'Kelly, "Shipboard Diary," Book I, 23–24, Olympia Collection.

23. Ibid., 24–31, 35–36, 40.

24. Tolley, "Our Russian War," 62; O'Kelly, "Shipboard Diary," 24, 27, 43, Olympia Collection; Jackson, "Recollections," 3, Jackson Collection.

25. David R. Francis, *Russia from the American Embassy*, 265. On the U.S. Marines comment see Jackson, "Recollections," 12, Jackson Collection; and Chester V. Jackson, "Mission to Murmansk," *Proceedings of the United States Naval Institute*, xcv, February 1969, 87.

26. Jackson, "Mission to Murmansk," 87; O'Kelly, "Shipboard Diary," Book I, 44–45, Olympia Collection.

27. O'Kelly, "Shipboard Diary," Book I, 40–49, Olympia Collection.

28. Ibid., 34.

29. Jackson, "Mission to Murmansk," 85.

30. Jackson, "Mission to Murmansk," 85–86.

31. O'Kelly, "Shipboard Diary," Book I, 50, 52, Olympia Collection.

32. Somin, *Stillborn Crusade*, 94–95.

33. Tolley, "Our Russian War," 64–65; Halliday, *Ignorant Armies*, 28–29.

34. Tolley, "Our Russian War," 65–66.

35. Tolley, "Our Russian War," 66–67; Halliday, *Ignorant Armies*, chapter 2.

36. Jackson, "Mission to Murmansk," 88–89; O'Kelly, "Shipboard Diary," Book I, 53, 59, Olympia Collection.

37. Tolley, "Our Russian War," 65, 66, 68; Jackson, "Recollections," 10–12, Jackson Recollection; O'Kelly, "Shipboard Diary," Book I, 55, Olympia Collection.

38. Weeks, *Naval Diplomat*, 140–42.

39. O'Kelly, "Shipboard Diary," Book I, 60, Olympia Collection; Weeks, *Naval Diplomat*, 140–42; Tolley, "Our Russian War," 67; Jackson, "Mission to Murmansk," 89.

40. O'Kelly, "Shipboard Diary," Book I, 64–65, Olympia Collection; Tolley, "Our Russian War," 68–69; Rhodes, *Winter War*, 44–45; Halliday, *Ignorant Armies*, 88–89; Weeks, *Naval Diplomat*, 145; Henry P. Beers, *U.S. Naval Forces in Northern Russia (Archangel and Murmansk), 1918–1919*, 36–37.

41. O'Kelly, "Shipboard Diary," Book I, 65–68, Olympia Collection; O'Kelly, "My Life," 37; Beers, *Naval Forces*, 20–21; Jackson, "Mission to Murmansk," 89; Stewart, *Engineering Record*, 88.

42. O'Kelly, "Shipboard Diary," Book II, 71–75, Olympia Collection; Beers, *Naval Forces*, 21a.

43. O'Kelly, "Shipboard Diary," Book II, 1–21, Olympia Collection.

44. Ibid., 21–33; Stewart, *Engineering Record*, 88.

45. DN, *Annual Report, 1920*, 800–802, 2509, 2510; DN, *Annual Report, 1921*, 93; Wagner A. Album, Olympia Collection.

46. O'Kelly, "Shipboard Diary," Book II, 33–46, 52, 56, 57, 66, Olympia Collection; O'Kelly, "My Life," 42–43; Stewart, *Engineering Record*, 88–89; Letter, Josen W. Chaud to sister, 1 March 1919, Olympia Collection; "Reminiscences of Vice Admiral Gerald F. Bogan," United States Naval Academy, Chester Nimitz Library (Annapolis, Maryland), Gerald F. Bogan Collection.

47. Stewart, *Engineering Record*, 89; O'Kelly, "Shipboard Diary," Book II, 67–79, 80–81, Olympia Collection.

48. Letter, Chaud to mother, 4 May 1919, Olympia Collection; O'Kelly, "Shipboard Diary," Book II, 82–102; Birkholz, "Physical History," Figure 11.

49. Unidentified poem found by Jack Steelman, May 1983, Cruiser Olympia Collection; O'Kelly, "Shipboard Diary," Book II, 103–17, Olympia Collection; Stewart, *Engineering Record*, 89.

50. DN, *Annual Report, 1919*, 56–57.

51. Stewart, *Engineering Record*, 89–90; Birkholz, "Physical History," Figure 12.

52. Stewart, *Engineering Record*, 90–92; DN, *Annual Report, 1921*, 93.

53. Clipping, "Christmas in the Adriatic" in W. Kunz, notebook, Olympia Collection.

54. Stewart, *Engineering Record*, 90–93; DN, *Annual Report, 1921*, 2–3.
55. DN, *Annual Report, 1917*, 284; DN, *Annual Report, 1918*, 737; DN, *Annual Report, 1919*, 845; DN, *Annual Report, 1921*, 312.
56. DN, *Annual Report, 1920*, 4–5; DN, *Annual Report, 1921*, 6.
57. DN, *Annual Report, 1919*, 59; DN, *Annual Report, 1920*, 36; DN, *Annual Report, 1921*, 6.
58. Rhodes, *Winter War*, chapter 10; Foglesong, *Secret War*, conclusion.

CHAPTER 8. FINAL HONORS AND A LAST HURRAH

1. See Philip T. Rosen, "The Treaty Navy, 1919–1937" in Hagan, *Peace and War*, 221–28.
2. DN, *Annual Reports, 1922*, Report of the Secretary, 1–3.
3. B. C. Mossman and M. W. Stark, *The Last Salute: Civil and Military Funerals, 1921–1969*, 8.
4. Ibid., 3–9.
5. Ibid., 9; Birkholz, "Physical History," Figure 13; Memorandum, Commander United States Atlantic Fleet, 24 October 1921, Olympia Collection.
6. Stewart, *Engineering Record*, 35; Mossman and Stark, *Final Salute*, 9.
7. Mossman and Stark, *Final Salute*, 10–18; Birkholz, "Physical History," Return of the Unknown Soldier; Miscellaneous clippings, W. Kunz notebook, Olympia Collection; Washington *Star*, 9 November 1921, Olympia Collection.
8. Clipping, "First Unknown Inspired Epic," c. 1958, Olympia Collection.
9. Stewart, *Engineering Record*, 94.
10. Miscellaneous clippings, Kunz notebook, Olympia Collection; Letter, Henry O. Meisel to Cruiser Olympia Association, 5 March 1966, Olympia Collection; Stewart, *Engineering Record*, 94.
11. "Reminiscences of Rear Admiral Schuyler Nelson Pyne," 1972, United States Naval Academy, Chester Nimitz Library (Annapolis, Maryland), Special Collections, Schuyler Nelson Pyne Collection; United States Naval Academy, *Annual Register, 1922–1923*, 31; DN, *Register of Commissioned and Warrant Officers of the United States Navy and Marine Corps, 1922*, 14.
12. Stewart, *Engineering Record*, 95; *Lucky Bag, 1925*, "Youngster Cruise"; Clipping, T. R. Dotzler, "The Olympia Floats," 8 November 1922, Olympia Collection.
13. DN, *Annual Report, 1923*, 138.
14. DN, *Annual Report, 1921*, 312, 385, 594, 713, 1134; DN, *Annual Report, 1922*, 8, 10.
15. Dotzler, "The Olympia Floats," Olympia Collection.
16. Stewart, *Engineering Record*, 43, 95; Miscellaneous clippings, *Our Navy*, mid-October 1925–mid-September 1929, Olympia Collection; Clipping, *Boston Globe*, 11 February 1941, Olympia Collection; *The Bounding Billow*, Thirty-Fifth Anniversary edition, 14 May 1933, Olympia Collection; Letter, Charles W. Mixer

to Andrew F. Demshaw, 8 December 1941, United States Naval Academy, Chester Nimitz Library (Annapolis, Maryland), Special Collections, Olympia Vertical File.

17. Healy and Kutner, *The Admiral*, 289, 314, 315; Harry Edward Neal, "History of the Auction Block," *Colliers*, 11 December 1948, RG 405.

18. Washington *Star*, 17 March 1928, Olympia Collection; United States House of Representatives, Document 343, *A Hearing on (H.R. 1204) To Provide for the Use of the U.S.S. Olympia as a Memorial to the Men Who Served the United States in the War With Spain*, 26 February 1930, 1231–39, Operational Archives.

19. United States House of Representatives, House Document 343, February 1930, 1232, Operational Archives.

20. Ibid., 1234–36. Also see Seventy-First Congress, Second Session, House of Representatives, Report No. 900, *To Provide For The Use Of The USS "Olympia" As A Memorial To The Men And Women Who Served The United States In The War With Spain*, 13 March 1930, Operational Archives.

21. United States House of Representatives, House Document 378, *Hearing on H.R. 4206, Authorizing The Secretary Of The Navy In His Discretion To Deliver To The Custody Of The City Of Olympia, State Of Washington, The Silver Service Set Formerly In Use On The U.S. Cruiser "Olympia,"* 13 March 1930, Operational Archives.

22. Letter, Mixer to Demshaw, 8 December 1941, Olympia Vertical File; Letter, D. W. Knox to F. W. Mathias, 9 August 1944, Operational Archives; House Document No. 389, *To Provide For The Use Of The U.S.S. "Olympia" As A Memorial To The Men And Women Who Served The United States In The War With Spain (H.R. 95). Mr. Cochran Of Missouri*, 25 February 1932, Operational Archives.

23. Stewart, *Engineering Record*, 43.

24. Miscellaneous clippings, Philadelphia *Evening Bulletin* and *New York Times*, 25 March 1947, Olympia Collection; Clipping, Philadelphia *Daily News*, 20 May 1957, Olympia Collection; Clipping, *Commercial America*, February 1958, 6–7, Olympia Collection; Stewart, *Engineering Record*, 44; *The Washington Post*, 7 November 1954, Olympia Collection; Letter, Director of Naval History to Allan McElwain, 20 June 1955, Operational Archives; Birkholz, "Physical History," Figure 15.

25. Clipping, Philadelphia *Daily News*, 20 September 1957, Olympia Collection; Clipping, Philadelphia *Evening Bulletin*, 11 September 1957, Olympia Collection; Clipping, *The National Tribune—The Stars and Stripes*, 15 August 1957, Olympia Collection; Clipping, *The National Tribune—The Stars and Stripes*, 19 September 1957, Olympia Collection; Clipping, *The North America Fieldman*, November 1957, Olympia Collection; Clipping, *Junior American*, February 1958, Olympia Collection; Clipping, *The Flying Eglet Numismatic Magazine*, 3 April 1958, Olympia Collection; Clipping, Miami Beach *Times*, 23 May 1958, Olympia Collection; Clipping, Philadelphia *Sunday Bulletin*, 1 June 1958, Olympia Col-

lection; Letter Edward H. Wiswesser to Francis Pastorius, 17 October 1957, Olympia Collection. On controversial propeller medals, see Letters, William Dewey to William S. Gordon, 23 December 1983 and 20 January 1984, Olympia Collection; Letter, Dewey to Andrew Chernak, 28 December 1983, Olympia Collection; Gordon to Dewey, 25 January 1984, Olympia Collection; Personal communication, Gary Patterson to author, 23 April 1984; Letter, William Dewey to Bridgeport Brass Company, 11 May 1984, Olympia Collection; Dewey to William H. Cavistan, 25 July 1984, Olympia Collection.

26. Blanche Day, "Historic 'Olympia,'" *Today* (*Philadelphia Inquirer* magazine), 27 April 1958, Olympia Collection; E. Reynolds, "Relics of Spanish War Sought Here," San Francisco *Examiner*, 26 May 1958, Olympia Collection; Clipping, Philadelphia *Inquirer*, 13 June 1958, Olympia Collection; Clipping, *Evening Bulletin*, 30 June 1958, Olympia Collection; Clipping, *Temple Terrace* (Florida) *News*, 19 June 1958, Olympia Collection; Clippings, Philadelphia *Daily News*, 18 and 21 July 1958, Olympia Collection; Clipping, *The National Tribune—The Stars and Stripes*, 24 July 1958, Olympia Collection; Clipping, Philadelphia *Daily News*, 25 July 1958, Olympia Collection; Clipping, *Evening Bulletin*, 25 July 1958, Olympia Collection; Clipping, Philadelphia *Evening Bulletin*, 1 May 1959, Olympia Collection.

27. Program, American Society of Mechanical Engineers Dedication of Vertical Reciprocating Steam Engines—U.S.S. Olympia as National Historic Mechanical Engineering Landmark, 30 March 1977.

28. Clipping, "The Philadelphia Scene," Philadelphia *Sunday Bulletin*, 28 September 1958, Olympia Collection; Clipping, Philadelphia *Inquirer*, 5 October 1958, Olympia Collection.

29. Clipping, Philadelphia *Daily News*, 29 September 1958, Olympia Collection; Clipping, Philadelphia *Bulletin*, 7 October 1958, Olympia Collection; Clipping, *Sunday Bulletin*, 19 October 1958, Olympia Collection; Clippings, Philadelphia *Inquirer*, 5 and 19 October 1958, Olympia Collection; Clipping, Ridgewood (New Jersey) *Sunday News*, 12 October 1958, Olympia Collection.

30. Clipping, Philadelphia *Inquirer*, 22 March 1955, Olympia Collection; Clippings, Philadelphia *Inquirer*, 24 and 28 June 1959, 21 and 23 September 1959, 3 and 25 October 1959, Olympia Collection; Clippings, Philadelphia *Bulletin*, 14 and 28 May 1959, 5, 16, and 29 June 1959, 1, 6, 12, and 14 July 1959, 21 and 23 September 1959, 8 November 1959, Olympia Collection; Clipping, *Christian Science Monitor*, 21 July 1959, Olympia Collection.

31. Letter, Edward Crenshaw to Director of Naval History, 31 July 1962, Olympia Collection; Letter, Assistant to Chief of Bureau for Legislative and Special Matters, Navy Department, to Edward Crenshaw, 5 July 1962, Olympia Collection; Miscellaneous statements, 1962, Olympia Collection; Clipping, *Sunday Herald News*, 17 April 1977, Olympia Collection; United States Navy Press release, "Scotland Man Donates Relic to U.S. Museum," United States Navy, Olympia

Collection; Clipping, Philadelphia *Inquirer*, 2 May 1967, Olympia Collection. On filming of the movie *The Sand Pebbles* see Jerry Gaghan's column in Philadelphia *Daily News*, 24 January 1967.

32. John Hummel, "Penn's Landing: Olympia and Becuna," *Naval History*, volume 3. Winter 1989, 77–78; Blaine Taylor, "'Fire When Ready, Gridley!'" *Sea Classics*, volume 21, December 1988, 33.

33. Birkholz, *Historic Structure Report*, 18–22.

34. Edward Collimore, "Give up the Ship? Not the Olympia," Philadelphia *Inquirer*, 26 May 1996; Interview, author with Director and Restoration Director, Independence Seaport Museum, 17 April 1999.

35. John Alden, "Olympian Legacy," *Proceedings of the United States Naval Institute*, cv, September 1976, 67.

36. Brochure, "Launching OLYMPIA SSN 717," Newport News Shipbuilding, 30 April 1983, Olympia Collection.

Bibliography

MANUSCRIPT COLLECTIONS

Chester Nimitz Library, United States Naval Academy (Annapolis, Maryland)
    Academy Archives, Office of the Superintendent (RG 405)
    Special Collections
    Gerald F. Bogan Reminiscences (Bogan Collection)
    George Dewey Vertical File (Dewey Vertical File)
    Thomas Benton Howard Papers (Howard Papers)
    T. E. Howard Collection (Howard Collection)
    Olaf M. Hustvedt Reminiscences (Hustvedt Collection)
    Olympia Vertical File (Olympia Vertical File)
    Schuyler Neilson Pyne Reminiscences (Pyne Collection)
Huntington Library (San Marino, California)
    William Henry Hoes (USS *Olympia*) Collection (Hoes Olympia Collection)
Independence Seaport Museum Library (Philadelphia, Pennsylvania)
    Carnegie-Phipps Company Collection (Carnegie-Phipps Collection)
    Cruiser Olympia Collection (Cruiser Olympia Collection)
Library of Congress, Manuscript Division (Washington, D.C.)
    Charles J. Bonaparte Papers (Bonaparte Collection)
    D. A. Carpenter Papers (Carpenter Collection)
    Charles Stanhope Cotton Papers (Cotton Collection)
    W. H. Moody Papers (Moody Collection)

Naval Historical Foundation Collection
Olympia, USS (ship) Collection (Olympia Collection)
Mary Edith Powel Papers (Powel Collection)
William H. Standley Papers (Standley Collection)
The Mariners Museum Library (Newport News, Virginia)
Francis Cunningham Lowry Collection (Lowry Collection)
National Archives and Records Administration—Pacific/Sierra Region (San Mateo, California)
Record Group 181, Naval Districts and Ship Establishments, Mare Island Naval Shipyard (RG 181)
National Archives and Records Administration (Washington, D.C.)
Record Group 24, Bureau of Navigation and Bureau of Personnel (RG 24)
Record Group 45, Office of Naval Records and Library (RG 45)
Record Group 80, General Records of the Navy (RG 80)
San Francisco Maritime National Historical Park (San Francisco, California)
David W. Dickie Collection (Dickie Collection)
United States Army Military History Institute (Carlisle Barracks, Pennsylvania)
Spanish-American War/Philippine Insurrection/Boxer Rebellion Survey Collection (Survey Collection)
USS Olympia (Wayne L. Longenecher) Collection (Longenecher Collection)
United States Department of the Navy, Naval Historical Center, Operational Archives (Washington, D.C.)
Early Records Collection, Z files (Early Records Collection)
Chester V. Jackson Collection (Jackson Collection)
William V. Pratt Papers (Pratt Collection)
United States Department of the Navy, Naval War College (Newport, Rhode Island)
Naval Historical Collection (RG 14)

UNITED STATES GOVERNMENT DOCUMENTS

United States Congress, Fifty-seventh, First Session and Special Session, Senate. *Congressional Record*, xxxv. Washington, D.C.: U.S. Government Printing Office, 1902.
———. Fifty-seventh, Second Session. House Document 290. *Register of the Commissioned and Warrant Officers of the Navy of the United States and of the Marine Corps To January 1, 1903*. Washington, D.C.: U.S. Government Printing Office, 1903.
———. Seventy-first, Second Session. House Report 900. *Provide For the Use of the USS "Olympia": as A Memorial To the Men and Women Who Served The United States in the War with Spain*. Washington, D.C.: U.S. Government Printing Office, 13 March 1930.
United States Naval Academy, *Annual Register, 1922–1923*. Annapolis, Md.: United States Naval Academy, 1923.
———. *The Lucky Bag*. 1908–12, 1925.

United States Navy, Department of. *Annual Reports, 1882–1923*. Washington, D.C.: U.S. Government Printing Office, 1893–1924.

United States Navy, Department of. *Dictionary of American Naval Fighting Ships*. Volume v, L–Q. Appendices. Washington, D.C.: U.S. Government Printing Office, 1970.

———. *Register of Commissioned and Warrant Officers of the United States Navy and Marines Corp—1922*. Washington, D.C.: U.S. Government Printing Office, 1922.

United States Navy, Department of, Bureau of Construction and Repair. *Specifications for Building Steel Twin-Screw Protected Cruiser No. 6 for the United States Navy*. Washington, D.C.: U.S. Government Printing Office, 1890.

United States Navy, Department of, Bureau of Navigation. *Movements of Vessels: 1911–1916*. Washington, D.C.: U.S. Government Printing Office, 1912–16.

———. *The Making of a Man-o'-Warsman*. Washington, D.C.: Department of the United States Navy, January 1913.

United States War Department. *Correspondence Relating to the War With Spain*. Volume 2. Washington, D.C.: U.S. Government Printing Office, 1902.

BOOKS

Alden, John D. *American Steel Navy*. Annapolis and New York: Naval Institute Press and American Heritage Press, 1972.

Baer, George W. *One Hundred Years of Sea Power: The U.S. Navy, 1890–1990*. Stanford, Calif.: Stanford University Press, 1994.

Barrett, John. *Admiral George Dewey*. New York: Harper and Brothers, 1899.

Bennett, Frank M. *The Steam Navy of the United States*. New York: W. T. Nicholson, 1896.

Beyer, Thomas. *The American Battleship and Life in the Navy*. Chicago: Laird and Lee, 1908.

Birtle, Andrew J. *U.S. Army Counterinsurgency and Contingency Doctrine 1860–1941*. Washington, D.C.: Center of Military History, United States Army, 1998.

Blagg, Robert L. *Career and Triumphs of Admiral Dewey*. Springfield, Ohio: Crowell and Kirkpatrick, 1899.

The Book of the United States Navy. New York: A. B. Benson Company, 1905.

Bradford, James (editor). *Admirals of the New Steel Navy: Makers of the American Naval Tradition, 1880–1930*. Annapolis, Md.: Naval Institute Press, 1990.

——— (editor). *Quarterdeck and Bridge: Two Centuries of American Naval Leaders*. Annapolis, Md.: Naval Institute Press, 1997.

Callahan, Edward W. (editor). *List of Officers of the Navy of the United States and of the Marine Corps From 1775 to 1900*. New York: L. R. Hamersly and Company, 1901.

Coletta, Paolo E. *Admiral Bradley A. Fiske and the American Navy*. Lawrence: Regents Press of Kansas, 1979.

Cooling, Benjamin Franklin. *Gray Steel and Blue Water Navy: The Formative Years of America's Military-Industrial Complex, 1881–1917.* Hamden, Conn.: Archon, 1979.

Davis, George T. *A Navy Second to None: The Development of Modern American Naval Policy.* New York: Harcourt, Brace, 1940.

Dewey, Adelbert M. *The Life and Letters of Admiral Dewey.* New York: Woolfall Company, 1899.

Dewey, George. *Autobiography.* New York: Charles Scribner's Sons, 1913.

Drake, Frederick. *Empire of the Seas: A Biography of Rear Admiral Robert N. Shufeldt.* Honolulu: University of Hawaii Press, 1984.

Evans, Stephen H. *The United States Coast Guard 1790–1915.* Annapolis, Md.: Naval Institute Press, 1949.

Fic, Victor M. *The Collapse of American Policy in Russia and Siberia, 1918: Wilson's Decision Not to Intervene (March–October, 1918).* Boulder, Colo.: East European Monographs, 1995.

Foglesong, David S. *America's Secret War Against Bolshevism: U.S. Intervention in the Russian Civil War, 1917–1920.* Chapel Hill: University of North Carolina Press, 1995.

Francis, David R. *Russia from the American Embassy.* New York: Scribner's Sons, 1928.

Friedman, Norman. *U.S. Cruisers: An Illustrated Design History.* Annapolis, Md.: Naval Institute Press, 1984.

Gardiner, Robert (editorial director). *Conway's All the World's Fighting Ships, 1860–1905.* London: Conway Maritime Press, Ltd., 1979.

_____ (editor). *Steam, Steel and Shellfire: The Steam Warship, 1815–1905.* London: Conway Maritime Press, Ltd., 1992.

George, James L. *History of Warships From Ancient Times to the Twenty-First Century.* London: Constable, 1999.

Hagan, Kenneth J. (editor). *In Peace and War: Interpretations of American Naval History, 1775–1978.* Westport, Conn.: Greenwood Press, 1978.

Halliday, E. M. *The Ignorant Armies.* New York: Harper and Brothers, 1958.

Halpern, Paul G. *A Naval History of World War I.* Annapolis. Md.: Naval Institute Press, 1994.

Healy, Laurin Hall and Luis Kutner. *The Admiral.* Chicago: Ziff Davis, 1944.

Herrick, Walter R. Jr. *The American Naval Revolution.* Baton Rouge: Louisiana State University Press, 1966.

Johnson, Robert E. *Far China Station: The U.S. Navy in Asian Waters, 1800–1898.* Annapolis, Md.: Naval Institute Press, 1979.

Kennan, George F. *The Decision to Intervene in Soviet-American Relations, 1917–1920.* Volume II. Princeton, N.J.: Princeton University Press, 1958.

King, Randolph W. (editor). *Naval Engineering and American Sea Power.* Baltimore, Md.: Nautical and Aviation, 1989.

Klachko, Mary and David Trask. *Admiral William Shepherd Benson: First Chief of Naval Operations.* Annapolis, Md.: Naval Institute Press, 1987.

LaFeber, Walter. *The American Age: U.S. Foreign Policy at Home and Abroad, 1750 to the Present*. New York: W. W. Norton, 1989.

_____. *The Cambridge History of American Foreign Relations: The American Search for Opportunity, 1865–1913*. Volume II. Cambridge: Cambridge University Press, 1993.

Leech, Margaret. *In the Days of McKinley*. New York: Harper, 1959.

Link, Arthur (editor). *The Papers of Woodrow Wilson*. Princeton, N. J.: Princeton University Press, 1966–94.

Littlebear, Vincent. *The 8-Inch Guns of the USS Olympia*. Philadelphia: Rutter Publishing, 1988.

Mossman, B. C. and M. W. Stark. *The Last Salute: Civil and Military Funerals, 1921–1969*. Washington, D.C.: Department of the Army, 1971.

Musicant, Ivan. *Empire by Default: The Spanish-American War and the Dawn of the American Century*. New York: Henry Holt, 1998.

Nofi, Albert A. *The Spanish-American War 1898*. Conshohocken, Pa.: Combined Books, 1996.

O'Gara, Gordon Carpenter. *Theodore Roosevelt and the Rise of the Modern Navy*. Princeton, N.J.: Princeton University Press, 1943.

Packard, Wyman H. *A Century of U.S. Naval Intelligence*. Washington, D.C.: Department of the Navy, 1996.

Padfield, Peter. *Guns at Sea*. New York: St. Martin's, 1974.

Palmer, Frederick. *George Dewey, Admiral: Impressions of Dewey and the Olympia on their Progress from Manila*. New York: Doubleday and McLure, Co., 1899.

Peck, Taylor. *Round-Shot to Rockets: A History of the Washington Navy Yard and U.S. Naval Gun Factory*. Annapolis, Md.: Naval Institute Press, 1949.

Pulsifer, Pittman (compiler). *Navy Yearbook, 1908*. Washington, D.C.: U.S. Government Printing Office, 1908.

Read, John J. (compiler). *Hand Book of the U.S.S. "Olympia," Flagship, Asiatic Station*. Hong Kong: Kelly and Walsh, Ltd., 1897.

Rhodes, Benjamin D. *The Anglo-American Winter War with Russia, 1918–1919: A Diplomatic and Military Tragicomedy*. New York: Greenwood Press, 1988.

Rodman, Hugh. *Yarns of a Kentucky Admiral*. Indianapolis, Ind.: Bobbs Merrill, 1928.

Salamanca, Bonificacio. *The Filipino Reaction To American Rule, 1901–1913*. Hamden, Conn.: The Shoe String Press, 1968.

Schoenfeld, Maxwell P. *Charles Vernon Gridley: A Naval Career*. Erie, Pa.: Erie County Historical Society, 1983.

Shulman, Mark Russell. *Navalism and the Emergence of American Sea Power, 1882–1893*. Annapolis, Md.: Naval Institute Press, 1995.

Society of Naval Architects and Marine Engineers. *Historical Transactions, 1893–1943*. New York: The Society of Naval Architects and Marine Engineers, 1945.

Somin, Ilya. *Stillborn Crusade: The Tragic Failure of Western Intervention in the Russian Civil War, 1918–1920*. New Brunswick: Transaction Publishers, 1996.

Spector, Ronald. *Admiral of the New Empire: The Life and Career of George Dewey.* Baton Rouge: Louisiana State University Press, 1974.

_____. *Professors of War: The Naval War College and the Development of the Naval Profession.* Newport, R.I.: Naval War College Press, 1988.

Sprout, Harold and Margaret Sprout. *The Rise of American Naval Power, 1776–1918.* Princeton: Princeton University Press, 1939.

Sternlicht, Sanford. *McKinley's Bulldog: The Battleship Oregon.* Chicago: Nelson-Hall, 1977.

Stickney, Joseph L. *Life and Glorious Deeds of Admiral Dewey.* Chicago: Charles B. Ayer Company, 1898.

Strakhovsky, Leonid I. *The Origins of American Intervention in North Russia, 1918.* Princeton, N.J.: Princeton University Press, 1937.

Sweetman, Jack (editor). *Great American Naval Battles.* Annapolis, Md.: Naval Institute Press, 1998.

Tisdale, L. G. T. ["Lieu"], *Three Years Behind the Guns.* New York: Grosset and Dunlap, 1907.

Todd, Daniel and Michael Lindberg. *Navies and Shipbuilding Industries.* Westport, Conn.: Praeger, 1996.

Trask, David F. *The War with Spain in 1898.* New York: The Free Press, 1981.

Ullman, Richard H. *Intervention and the War: Anglo-Soviet Relations, 1917–1921.* Volume I. Princeton, N.J.: Princeton University Press, 1961.

Vivian, Thomas J. (editor). *With Dewey at Manila.* New York: R. F. Fenno, 1898.

Weeks, Charles J. *An American Naval Diplomat in Revolutionary Russia: The Life and Times of Vice Admiral Newton A. McCully.* Annapolis, Md.: Naval Institute Press, 1993.

Welch, Richard E. Jr. *Response to Imperialism: The United States and the Philippine-American War, 1899–1902.* Chapel Hill: University of North Carolina Press, 1979.

Wheeler, Gerald E. *Admiral William Vezey Pratt, U.S. Navy: A Sailor's Life.* Washington, D.C.: Naval History Center, 1974.

Wilden, Robert N. *Statistical and Chronological History of the United States Navy 1775–1907.* New York: Burt Franklin, 1907.

Wimmel, Kenneth. *Theodore Roosevelt and the Great White Fleet: American Sea Power Comes of Age.* Washington, D.C.: Brassey's, 1998.

ARTICLES

Alden, Carroll Storrs. "The Santee: An Appreciation." *Proceedings of the United States Naval Institute*, XLVIX, June 1913: 763–74.

Alden, John D. "Olympian Legacy." *Proceedings of the United States Naval Institute*, CII, September 1976: 61–67.

"The American War Ship Olympia." *Scientific American*, volume 69, 23 December 1893: cover, 405.

Angevine, Robert G. "The Rise and Fall of the Office of Naval Intelligence,

1882–1892: A Technological Perspective." *The Journal of Military History*, volume 62, April 1998: 291–312.

Apt, Benjamin L. "Mahan's Forebears: The Debate over Maritime Strategy, 1868–1883." *Naval War College Review*, Summer 1997: 86–111.

Beach, Edward L. "Manila Bay in 1898." *Proceedings of the United States Naval Institute*, XLVI, April 1920: 587–602.

Beehler, W. H. "The Navy and Coast Defence." *Proceedings of the United States Naval Institute*, XXXV, June 1909: 343–84.

"Bibliographic Notes—The Iron Age, No. 21, May 21." *Proceedings of the United States Naval Institute*, XVII No. 3, 1891: 557.

Bullard, W. H. G. "United States Naval Radio Service." *Proceedings of the United States Naval Institute*, XL, March/April 1914: 431–71.

Calkins, Carlos Gilman. "Historical and Professional Notes on the Naval Campaign of Manila Bay in 1898." *Proceedings of the United States Naval Institute*, XXV, June 1899: 267–321.

Clark, George R. "Protecting American Interests." *Proceedings of the United States Naval Institute*, XXXV, June 1909: 393–403.

"Comments of Rear Admiral Pluddemann, Germany Navy, On the Main Features of the War with Spain." *Proceedings of the United States Naval Institute*, XXIV No. 4, 1898: 771–78.

"Contraband of War." *Proceedings of the United States Naval Institute*, XXIV No. 3, 1898: 534.

Cooling, Benjamin Franklin. "Olympia—Last Survivor of the New Steel Navy." *Military Collector and Historian*, volume 26, Spring 1974: 42–43.

"The Cruiser Olympia." *Harpers*, volume 38, 1894: 112.

Daveluy, R. "A Study of Naval Strategy [fifth part]." *Proceedings of the United States Naval Institute*, XXXVI No. 2, June 1910: 393–428.

Dewey, William S. "From 'Olympia' to 'Olympia.'" *The Numismatist*, January 1940: 6–7.

Dickie, James. "Launch of A Cruiser and A Battleship." *Transactions of the Society of Naval Architects and Marine Engineers*, 1900: 279–91.

Earle, Ralph. "Battleships." *Proceedings of the United States Naval Institute*, XLII, September/October 1916: 1413–42.

Ellicott, John M. "The Composition of the Fleet." *Proceedings of the United States Naval Institute*, XX No. 3, 1896: 537–60.

_____. "The Defenses of Manila Bay." *Proceedings of the United States Naval Institute*, XXVI, June 1900: 279–87.

_____. "Effect of Gun-Fire, Battle of Manila Bay, May 1, 1898." *Proceedings of the United States Naval Institute*, XXV, June 1899: 325–34.

_____. "The Naval Battle of Manila." *Proceedings of the United States Naval Institute*, XXVI, September 1900: 489–514.

Fiske, Bradley A. "Why We Won At Manila." *Century Magazine*, volume 57, November 1898: 128–35.

Foley, Paul. "The Naval Academy Practice Cruise." *Proceedings of the United States Naval Institute*, xxxvi, March 1910: 240–48.

Gilmore, F. P. "Ship-Building and Its Interests on the Pacific Coast." *Proceedings of the United States Naval Institute*, xv No. 3, 1889: 443–49.

Groesbeck, William G. "Considerations Affecting The Determination of a Naval Programme." *Proceedings of the United States Naval Institute*, xxxii, March 1906: 173–208.

"Grounding of the 'Olympia'—Naval War Notes." *Proceedings of the United States Naval Institute*, xliii, July/December 1917: 1865.

Hackemer, Kurt. "The U.S. Navy and the Late Nineteenth-Century Steel Industry." *The Historian*, volume 57, Summer 1995: 703–12.

Herwig, Holger H. and David Trask. "The Failure of Imperial Germany's Undersea Offensive Against World Shipping, February 1917–October 1918," *The Historian*, volume 33, August 1971: 626–28.

Hourihan, William J. "Marlinspike Diplomacy: The Navy in the Mediterranean, 1904." *Proceedings of the United States Naval Institute*, cv, January 1979: 42–51.

Hummel, John. "Penn's Landing: Olympia and Becuna." *Naval History*, volume 3, Winter 1989: 76–78.

Hunt, Michael H. "1898: The Onset of America's Troubled Asian Century." *Organization of American Historians Magazine of History*, volume 12, Spring 1998: 30–36.

Johnson, Paul H. "Queen of the Revenue Marine." *Alumni Bulletin*, volume 33, March/April 1971 (United States Coast Guard Academy): 2–9.

Johnson, Thomas Lee. "Large Versus a Greater Number of Smaller Battleships." *Proceedings of the United States Naval Institute*, xlii, July/August 1916: 1079–116.

Long, John W. "American Intervention in Russia: The North Russian Expedition, 1918–19." *Diplomatic History*, volume 6, Winter 1982: 45–67.

Mraz, Scott R. "Recognition Long Overdue." *Naval History*, volume 12, May/June 1998: 24–26.

Nicholson, Philip Y. "Admiral George Dewey after Manila Bay: Years of Ambition, Accomplishment, and Public Obscurity." *The American Neptune*, volume 37, January 1977: 26–39.

Normand, M. J. A. "The Size of Battleships as a Function of Their Speed." *Proceedings of the United States Naval Institute*, xxxiii, March 1907: 125–36.

Olsson, Lars O. "'To See How Things Were Done in a Big Way': Swedish Naval Architects in the United States, 1890–1915." *Technology and Culture*, volume 39, July 1998: 436–56.

"The Olympia—Professional Notes." *Proceedings of the United States Naval Institute*, xxviiii No. 4, 1893: 494.

Paullin, Charles Oscar. "The American Navy in the Orient in Recent Years, III. The Spanish-American War in the Philippine Islands, 1898." *Proceedings of the United States Naval Institute*, xxviii, March 1912: 87–116.

Pickett, Charles. "Long Live Olympia!: The Pride of Philadelphia," *Sea Classics*, volume 28, January 1995: 4–46.

"Ships of War in Action—Professional Notes." *Proceedings of the United States Naval Institute*, xxiv No. 3, 1898: 501–9.

Sims, William. "The Inherent Tactical Qualities of All-Big-Gun, One-Caliber Battleships of High Speed, Large Displacement and Gunpower." *Proceedings of the United States Naval Institute*, xxii, December 1906: 1337–66.

_____. "What Should Be The Relations Between the Battle Fleet and the Reserve Fleet?" *Proceedings of the United States Naval Institute*, xl, May/June 1914: 727–39.

"The Spanish-American War—Professional Notes." *Proceedings of the United States Naval Institute*, xxv, June 1899: 421–25.

Spector, Ronald. "Who Planned the Attack on Manila Bay?" *Mid-America: An Historical Review*, volume 53, April 1971: 94–102.

Sterling, Yates. "Another Argument for Speed in Battleship Design." *Proceedings of the United States Naval Institute*, xxxiv, March 1908: 247–52.

Stockton, C. H. "Submarine Telegraph Cables in Time of War." *Proceedings of the United States Naval Institute*, xxv No. 3, 1893: 451–56.

Stokesbury, James L. "Manila Bay: Battle or Execution?" *American History Illustrated*, volume 14, August 1979: 4–7.

Strauss, Elliott B. "The Days of the 'Black Diamonds.'" *Pull Together*, volume 29, Spring/Summer 1990: 5–6.

Taylor, Blaine. "Fire When Ready, Gridley!" *Sea Classics*, volume 21, December 1988: 26–33.

Tolley, Kemp. "Our Russian War of 1918–1919." *Proceedings of the United States Naval Institute*, xcv, February 1969: 58–72.

Tomblin, Barbara B. "The United States Navy and the Philippines Insurrection." *The American Neptune*, volume 35, July 1975: 183–96.

"The United States Protected Cruiser Olympia." *Scientific American*, volume 74, 21 March 1896: 177.

"Views of Admiral Cervera Regarding The Spanish Navy in the Late War." *Proceedings of the United States Naval Institute*, xxiv No. 4, 1898: 747–70.

"Visit to Trieste Graveyard Recalls A Note From History." *All Hands*, September 1968: 20–22.

Wainwright, Richard. "A Further Argument for the Big Ship." *Proceedings of the United States Naval Institute*, xxiii, September 1906: 1057–64.

Yarnell, Harry E. "The Greatest Need of the Atlantic Fleet." *Proceedings of the United States Naval Institute*, xlix, March 1913: 1–40.

UNPUBLISHED AND PRINTED MATERIALS

Alder, Fred T. and Harry C. Green (compilers). *The Official Dewey Souvenir Programme*. New York: Alder and Green, 1899.

American Society of Mechanical Engineers. *National Historic Mechanical Engineering Landmark: Vertical Reciprocating Steam Engines—U.S.S. Olympia, Program*, 30 March 1977. Philadelphia, 1977.

Beers, Henry P. *U.S. Naval Forces in Northern Russia (Archangel and Murmansk)*, *1918–1919*. Washington, D. C.: Navy Department, Office of Records Administration, Administrative Office, November 1943.

Bethlehem Steel Corporation. *1849–1914: A Century of Progress*. San Francisco: Bethlehem Steel Company Shipbuilding Division, 1949.

———. *San Francisco Yard: A Brief History*. San Francisco: Bethlehem Steel Company Shipbuilding Division, 1979.

Birkholz, Donald Jr. *Cruiser Olympia Historical Structure Report*. Philadelphia: Independence Seaport Museum, 2000.

———. *Physical History of the Cruiser Olympia*. Philadelphia: Independence Seaport Museum, 2000.

Fifth Avenue Events. New York: The Fifth Avenue Bank, 1916.

Newport News Shipbuilding. *Launching Olympia SSN 717*. 30 April 1983.

Patriotic Order of the Sons of America. *U.S.S. Olympia: Admiral Dewey's Flagship*. Philadelphia: The Patriotic Order Sons of American, no date.

Stewart, Robert C. *Historic American Engineering Record—U.S.S. Olympia [HAER No. PA-428]. Final Draft Report*. Philadelphia, 1998.

Young, L. S. *The Cruise of the U.S. Flagship "Olympia" from 1895 to 1899 from San Francisco to Manila Bay*. Parts I and II.

Index

About the Author

Benjamin Franklin Cooling is a professor of grand strategy and mobilization at the Industrial College of the Armed Forces (National Defense University) in Washington, D.C. A graduate in history from Rutgers University, he earned his Ph.D from the University of Pennsylvania. Dr. Cooling previously served as chief historian and research director with the Department of Energy and as a historian with the army, air force, and National Park Service historical programs, as well as with the Cruiser Olympia Association.

Dr. Cooling's most recent publications include *Monocacy: The Battle that Saved Washington* and *Fort Donelson's Legacy: War and Society in Tennessee and Kentucky, 1862–1863*. A recipient of various awards for his writings, including the Victor Gondos Memorial Service Award from the Society for Military History, he is now completing his trilogy on war and society in Kentucky and Tennessee during the Civil War and early Reconstruction.